Monks, Money, and Morality

ALSO AVAILABLE FROM BLOOMSBURY:

Buddhism in the Global Eye, edited by John S. Harding,
Victor Sogen Hori and Alexander Soucy
A Critique of Western Buddhism, Glenn Wallis
The Culture of Giving in Myanmar, Hiroko Kawanami

Monks, Money, and Morality

The Balancing Act of Contemporary Buddhism

EDITED BY
CHRISTOPH BRUMANN, SASKIA
ABRAHMS-KAVUNENKO,
AND BEATA ŚWITEK

BLOOMSBURY ACADEMIC
LONDON • NEW YORK • OXFORD • NEW DELHI • SYDNEY

BLOOMSBURY ACADEMIC
Bloomsbury Publishing Plc
50 Bedford Square, London, WC1B 3DP, UK
1385 Broadway, New York, NY 10018, USA
29 Earlsfort Terrace, Dublin 2, Ireland

BLOOMSBURY, BLOOMSBURY ACADEMIC and the Diana logo
are trademarks of Bloomsbury Publishing Plc

First published in Great Britain 2021

Cover design: Toby Way
Cover image © Hannah Rosa Klepeis

A catalogue record for this book is available from the British Library.

Library of Congress Cataloging-in-Publication Data
Names: Brumann, Christoph, editor. | Abrahms-Kavunenko, Saskia,
editor. | Switek, Beata, editor.
Title: Monks, money, and morality : the balancing act of contemporary
Buddhism / edited by Christoph Brumann, Saskia Abrahms-Kavunenko, and Beata Świtek.
Description: 1. | New York : Bloomsbury Academic, 2021. |
Includes bibliographical references and index.
Identifiers: LCCN 2020055189 (print) | LCCN 2020055190 (ebook) |
ISBN 9781350213760 (paperback) | ISBN 9781350213753 (hardback) |
ISBN 9781350213777 (ebook) | ISBN 9781350213784 (pdf)
Subjects: LCSH: Buddhism–Economic aspects. | Economics–Religious aspects–
Buddhism. | Buddhist monks–Conduct of life. | Values–Religious aspects–
Buddhism. | Buddhism–Social aspects. | Religion and ethics.
Classification: LCC BQ4570.E25 M66 2021 (print) | LCC BQ4570.E25 (ebook) |
DDC 294.3/373–dc23
LC record available at https://lccn.loc.gov/2020055189
LC ebook record available at https://lccn.loc.gov/2020055190

ISBN: HB: 978-1-3502-1375-3
         PB: 978-1-3502-1376-0
         ePDF: 978-1-3502-1378-4
         eBook: 978-1-3502-1377-7

Typeset by Integra Software Services Pvt. Ltd.

To find out more about our authors and books visit www.bloomsbury.com
and sign up for our newsletters

CONTENTS

PART THREE Managing Temples and Monasteries

PART FOUR Capitalism, Decline, and Rebirth

ILLUSTRATIONS

Introduction: Sangha Economies

Saskia Abrahms-Kavunenko,
Christoph Brumann, and Beata Świtek

A hot and muggy August day in Kyoto, 2016. The neighborhood in which Brumann earlier observed participation in the famous Gion matsuri festival (2009; 2012, 156–208) has assembled for the traditional summer festival Jizōbon. Before the children's entertainment central to this day begins, there is a ritual propitiating the bodhisattva Jizō (Skt. Kṣitigarbha), guardian of small children, and the neighborhood has entrusted the priest of a nearby Jōdo shinshū temple—part of the largest sect of Pure Land Buddhism in Japan—with conducting a ritual. While the priest, dressed in formal robes and with his head cleanly shaven, recites a sutra in front of a small shrine (hokora) housing the Jizō image, the neighbors take turns in placing incense into a small box with glowing charcoal before bowing in reverence toward Jizō. On a traditional lacquer tray next to the incense box, several envelopes are piling up. When the priest is finished, he turns to the assembled neighbors for a short sermon. As his key point, he emphasizes the fundamental distinction between donations to Buddhist priests (o-fuse) and everyday payments. He says he has no idea what the envelopes contain and continues to be surprised in his ritual practice how what he receives deviates from what the donor's economic station might let one expect. The feelings (kimochi) behind the donation are key, and it is futile to fix money amounts and attach price tags to everything. When he is finished, he pockets the unopened envelopes and is seen off, mounting his scooter to his next ritual appointment on this busy day. The neighbors, however, are unimpressed by his message: what they give, they tell me, is set by custom, not by feelings, and if unsure, more experienced people can tell one the appropriate amounts.

The vignette illustrates conflicting tendencies in Buddhism and the ways it is commonly viewed: more so even than the followers of other "world religions," devout Buddhists are believed to pay scant attention to economic considerations. They give and receive selflessly, with their virtuosos—the monastic renunciates—owning only a minimum of possessions. Disconnected from the economies within which they operate, they rely instead on the laity's alms, donations, and general goodwill. A spirit of calculation is absent when believers give what they can spare while monks and nuns make do with what they receive, unbound by any sense of obligation. Economic matters are a secondary concern in a religion dedicated to the pursuit of enlightenment and compassion.

Nevertheless, the neighbors in Kyoto see their envelopes with bank notes as clear payments for a delivered service, whatever the priest claims in his sermon. The priest, in turn, while never discussing amounts with those who call him, knows from similar engagements what he can expect and factors the likely sums into his calculations for managing his temple. He is not obsessed with pecuniary gain and instead spreads his religious message through unconventional means, such as hosting concerts or debating circles in the temple. Yet he is also aware that sustaining the institution and his family who—instead of a celibate monastic community as in other Buddhist countries—lives there with him depends on the followers' regular demand for memorial rites and other ritual services, which these reward with the customary remunerations. Buddhist laypeople and specialists alike have everyday concerns.

These different perspectives on "sangha economies" (the way the community of Buddhist monks, priests, nuns, and priestesses, the sangha, deals with money, goods, and services) and how these perspectives interrelate are the topics of this book. It demonstrates how the entanglements that come with sustaining Buddhist institutions, rather than being a peripheral concern, are actually a central part of the lives of Buddhist specialists and their interactions with the lay public. The volume assembles eleven chapters by anthropologists and religious studies scholars who have conducted long-term ethnographic field studies of Buddhist religious practitioners and followers. They spread out over the entire geographical range of Buddhism in Asia: six chapters concern themselves with the Vajrayāna Buddhist sphere (in China, Mongolia, and Russia), one looks at Mahāyāna Buddhism in Japan, and four address the Theravāda tradition in Sri Lanka, Thailand, and China. Buddhism is a global religion today, with followers in probably every country, but for this volume, we chose to focus on societies where Buddhism has been an accustomed presence for centuries or even millennia, not a new arrival in a diaspora situation where it is forced to react to moralities and value orientations on which other religions have left a much larger imprint. The chapters demonstrate that the two images evoked above form a dialectical relationship in which one feeds on the other: we see Buddhists dealing with cash and resources in a rather matter-of-fact fashion, but we also see them striving to distinguish themselves from the laity's ordinary economic concerns and practices in various ways. Taken together, the chapters show that in a (mostly) capitalist framework, religious specialists' relationships with money have become a key moral issue, provoking a lively debate where the boundaries of the acceptable are to be drawn.

Images and Realities

The idealized view of sangha economies owes a lot to the textual bias of much initial Buddhist studies. Scholars noted that the Vinaya—the monastic rules by one of whose versions most branches of Buddhism abide—limits monastic possessions to a very small number of necessities and prohibits both productive activities and the handling of money. Early textual studies nurtured the idea that Buddhist religious specialists must have led a disciplined and ascetic life with negligible economic entanglements. Within many doctrinal sources, *dāna*—giving to religious specialists—is believed to be most meritorious when it is truly altruistic and there is no expectation of a return, be it in form of the recipient's gratitude or karmic merit. In Buddhism and other South Asian religions, only the gift given with pure intention creates merit (Heim 2004). This might lead to a better future rebirth, so by giving generously to the sangha, the laity receives cosmological benefits. Eventually after countless lifetimes, the lay donors will be reborn as monks and can spend their lives in the solitary practice of meditation and devoted to the pursuit of enlightenment.

As foreign scholars became interested in Buddhist societies, anthropologists and historians were bemused by how what appeared to them as a world-renouncing religion could be the dominant one of entire nations. What seemed particularly strange was that laypeople supported temples when these seemed to be defined by their disengagement from lay lives. Unlike Christian churches, Buddhist temples did not appear to be involved in charitable activities or in educating the public about religious doctrine—or so foreign scholars thought. For authors such as Strenski (1983), Buddhist economies are defined by material flows in one key direction—from the laity to the sangha. In the other direction, the sangha, by receiving these donations, enables the laity to obtain merit. The view of Buddhism as "uneconomic" is brought to extremes in Max Weber's writings: largely relying on others' analyses of textual sources, not on observations of lived practice, he argued that Buddhism lacked the foundations for capitalist development: there was no "methodical lay morality," and while the monks were prohibited from owning money, lay riches remained essentially unaddressed in Buddhist doctrine (1958, 216–18). "A rational economic ethic could hardly develop in this sort of religious order," he concluded (1958, 216–17).

Popular Western understandings of Buddhism tend to emphasize the image of the lone renunciate monk, divorced from social relationships and other worldly concerns. When one looks at recent textual, historical, and anthropological studies, however, one finds that Buddhist specialists as well as institutions have always needed to sustain themselves with tangible resources. As the chapters in this book demonstrate, the challenge of maintaining Buddhist institutions is not trivial. In monasteries such as Ganden Sumtsenling (introduced in Hannah Rosa Klepeis's chapter), maintaining the dozens of ceremonial and residential buildings, providing tantric iconography, ritual implements, and decorations, as well as clothing and feeding the hundreds of monks require careful stewardship. Even where the Vinaya is strictly enforced, daily alms rounds (as in Prabhath Sirisena's chapter) can fall short of sustaining large institutions, requiring additional sources of income.

Historical and textual studies have shown that Buddhist societies did not have wholly negative attitudes toward wealth. In the sutras, money is not seen as detrimental. Rather, an excessive clinging or an aversion to wealth is problematic (Findly 2003, 11). Although the Vinaya has explicitly stated that monastics should not touch money, specifically coins, from early times, religious specialists needed resources to practice and Buddhist commentators were very much aware of the fact that without support from the laity, it would be difficult for any form of collective (or even individual) renunciation to occur. Many early sutras and commentaries point out that in order to keep up Buddhist practice, the broader population should have a healthy amount of wealth.

Capitalist development certainly contributes to changing mores: in Thailand where the Vinaya's injunctions against cash were still universally heeded a couple of decades ago (cf. Bunnag 1973), contemporary monks in Bangkok (in Thomas Borchert's chapter) use purses, bank accounts, and credit cards similarly to laypeople, and the charismatic *khruba* monk-saints on the northern border (in Alexander Horstmann's chapter) can be seen handing out bank notes to the huge numbers of followers congregating for their rituals, rather than having lay assistants handle them.

Buddhist prosperity and entrepreneurialism predate the arrival of capitalism. By the turn of the twentieth century, temples and Buddhist institutions in Inner Asia and the Himalayan region had amassed substantial wealth, in land, buildings, livestock, objects, and often also bonded labor. Premodern Tibetan monasteries likewise were not only dependent on the laity for support. Many monks and nuns in the Himalayan region were, and still are, supported by family and kin, sometimes making temples rather unequal places (Gutschow 2004; Mills 2001). In some Tibetan monasteries, there was a separate class of administrative and managerial monks (Jansen 2018; Silk 2008). Others supported themselves by engaging in business activities and giving out loans against interest to the populace (Caple 2010; Jansen 2018, 106–13; see also Klepeis's chapter). From very early on,

Buddhist monastics have owned private wealth and engaged in a wide range of economic activities including money-lending not just for their own but also for the monastery's benefit (Schopen 2004), a sideline that kept being cultivated in the following millennia (Benavides 2005, 85–6; Ornatowski 1996). "Buddhists—including monastics and including even the earliest generations of the Buddha's followers—have hardly been reluctant to engage in, or be formed by, their economic activity," writes Matthew King (2016, 3). Too much success in accumulating wealth has even motivated persecution at times, such as in the famous crackdown on Buddhism in ninth-century Tang China (Ch'en 1956), and it was significant also in more recent cases of state oppression (for instance in Mongolia and Tibet).

Despite the long history of engagement in economic activities, clerical as well as popular assessments of Buddhist specialists are often informed by highly idealized images of a Buddhist past purportedly disconnected from material concerns. Against such representations the present is seen as in decline, even when Buddhism has just been revitalized (in Saskia Abrahms-Kavunenko's chapter). Japanese Buddhism, for instance, has been cultivating a self-image as "corrupt," not really the match of what it once was, for well over a century now (Covell 2005, 14). The actual disruptions that the socialist persecution of religion caused in many Buddhist societies and the increased distance of Japanese laypeople from temple priests allow for these images of an idealized past to persist. This raises the standards for Buddhist specialists, in a time when their support base is often less stable than it used to be, and encourages the critical debates reported in our chapters.

Just as historical studies have been working to correct the idea that Buddhist religious specialists have stood aloof from monetary affairs (Gernet 1995; Schopen 2004; Silk 2008; Walsh 2010), this volume compiles contemporary challenges to this story, building on what others have already started (e.g., Covell 2005; Rowe 2011). In our detailed ethnographies, the narrative of donation to renunciates in return for cosmological rewards rarely features. Building on a more nuanced understanding of their economic entanglements, we can see how enmeshed Buddhist religious specialists are in their societies, in not only economic but also social and political terms. We focus on the lived reality of Buddhist practitioners, at a time when commercialization and financialization are reaching unprecedented heights and the challenges to noncapitalist value orientations are mounting. We understand this book as a call to give the everyday economies of contemporary Buddhist specialists and institutions the attention they deserve.

Reciprocity, Money, and Trust

Ohnuma claims that "the very existence of Buddhism as such has been dependent on the gift" (Ohnuma 2005, 104), and the one economic topic that has provoked most scholarly reflection—although most often on a general level than through the close-up study of real-life cases—are acts of giving between the sangha and the laity. These have caught attention for the way they diverge from standard anthropological ideas about the gift: within the discipline, generations have followed Marcel Mauss's lead (2016 [1925]) in expecting it to beckon returns, thus creating social ties that bind giver and receiver and force them into an ongoing relationship. Laidlaw, however, states that *dan* (i.e., *dāna*) given to Jain renunciates (comparable to Buddhist specialists) "makes no friends," with neither party to the transaction seeing it as establishing a social tie and mutual obligations (2000). In his comprehensive overview of giving in Buddhism, Sihlé also concludes that quite a bit of the laity's prestations to the sangha cannot be seen as an instance of reciprocity in the strict sense (2015, 358–64). Mauss's hunch—he entertained the possibility of Hindu forms of *dāna* constituting an exception to the usual logic of gifts in a footnote (2016 [1925], 161–2)— thus finds support.

Yet while alms rounds or the annual lay donations of new robes to Southeast Asian monks may indeed be one-sided, Sihlé emphasizes that reciprocity does occur in a broad and neglected field of Buddhist practice, the remunerations laypeople give to religious specialists that provide them with ritual services on demand, such as funerary rites or household rituals (2015, 369–76). In these encounters, there may be reticence to acknowledge that an exchange is taking place, such as by framing the ritual and the remuneration as unrelated expressions of piety and goodwill, by avoiding contractual agreements of a written or oral nature, or by using terms such as *dāna* or *o-fuse*, just like in the introductory vignette. To make sense of such restraint, Sihlé draws on Alain Testart's observations (Testart 2001) of the illusory side of "hiding the reality of exchange behind the fiction of the gift" (Testart, as cited in Sihlé 2015, 356) and on Bourdieu's reflections about the "misrecognition" of the economic side of the gift that is tantamount to its social efficacy, "such that the outward forms of the act present a practical denial of the content of the act, symbolically transmuting an interested exchange or a simple power relation into a relationship set up in due form for form's sake" (Bourdieu 1977, 194).

In contrast to Bourdieu, who appears to assume a general lack of awareness of such social pageantry among those involved, privileging the interested aspect as the "truth" of the transaction (Smart 1993, 395), others have emphasized the latter's coexistence with the formal "front side" of the gift. On that side, proper performance requires the negation of calculative and obligatory aspects; on the informal "rear side," however, these aspects are carefully considered and discussed, even if only with one's intimates (Brumann 2000; Smart 1993). This may help to explain why, for example, a lay sponsor suspecting careless performance complains to the inquisitive ethnographer but does not confront the monks conducting the ritual (in Klepeis's chapter). The great variety across Buddhist contexts where practices range from strong verbal euphemism to the unadorned use of terms such as "prices" and "trade" concerning rituals in Tibet (Sihlé 2015, 358) may therefore depend on the specific social circumstances and registers in which these matters are being discussed—"front" or "rear"—not just on general tendencies. Yet the price lists for rituals to be paid for at cash registers in the temple halls of Ulaanbaatar (in Saskia Abrahms-Kavunenko's chapter) or the online sale of funerary rites through Amazon Japan (in Beata Świtek's chapter) clearly show that Bourdieusian denial is by no means universal in Buddhism. What is interesting, then, is how distinctions to common market exchange are being made, which vocabulary is employed in which social contexts, and to which lengths open commercialization is allowed to go.

This volume demonstrates how looking at donative relationships out of context does not help to explain the multifaceted dynamics between Buddhist religious specialists and the societies in which they find themselves. In most of the chapters, money does not only flow in one direction. There is instead a wide variety of economic practices. In some instances, temples give to the laity (Jonutytė). In others, they are involved in alternative economic activities in order to obtain independence from lay donations (Caple, Casas, Klepeis). While for some communities, merit-making is an important incentive to donate to temples (Borchert, Horstmann, Jonutytė, Sirisena), in others donations are motivated by desires for individual (Abrahms-Kavunenko) or collective ritual purification (Mills).

Returning us to Japan, one of the most commercialized contexts for contemporary Buddhism, the first chapter by Beata Świtek inquires into Buddhist business in Tokyo. Since the Second World War, the provision of mortuary rites and cemeteries has been the economic mainstay of the usually small temples that are most often run by single priests and their families. This provokes the kind of confusion that, in the introduction, makes a laywoman wonder whether she is really a "believer" or rather a "customer" of the temple to which her family is attached as parishioners (*danka*). There are moments when the line between religion and business cannot remain blurred, however, such as when clergy and laity debate the suitability of advertising Buddhist ritual packages on Amazon or when a tax office meticulously divides temple premises into religious (i.e., tax-exempt) and secular (i.e., taxable) space. Priests reflect about these aspects intensely and one solution can be the abdication of personal agency: Świtek reports the examples of a temple event for which the head priest encourages participation fees but does not enforce them, defying control at the cost of a net loss, and of a priest running a Buddhist-themed bar who bases his investment decisions on coincidental events rather than his own planning, interpreting them as signs of buddha Amida's providence.

Taking us to another huge Asian city, Thomas Borchert's chapter on Buddhism in Bangkok starts off with a monk who, against all conventions, asks him for a higher donation than the one he offers during a temple visit. Juxtaposing this with the tax evasion charges levied against a prominent Buddhist leader, Borchert reviews the gifts, donations, payments, and other transfers subsumed under *dāna*, perusing also the personal budgets of a number of monks. While the Thai sangha has become mired in high-profile corruption scandals, most monks dismiss the charges of embezzlement in recent years as unfounded, seeing these deeds as reflecting ignorance or improper paperwork, not bad intentions. The current military government's signature campaign against corruption and broader concerns about greed in the larger economy seem to play a large role in brandishing these cases as corruption. Increasingly, however, monks internalize the layperson's gaze, such as by avoiding the use of ATMs close to their temples where adherents might spot them. Economic conditions are highly diverse, however: many monks and temples see themselves as more precarious than the laity imagines, though not all are overly concerned with it.

Nicolas Sihlé stretches our notions of the sangha by taking up non-monastic tantrists (*ngakpa*). They live ordinary family lives but are nonetheless committed religious specialists, mastering religious practices and ritual powers that are often complementary to those of the monks. Repkong County in the Tibetan Amdo region (Qinghai Province, China) is renowned for its large numbers of powerful practitioners, and with road and communication networks expanding, the tantrists often travel hundreds of kilometers to conduct rituals in their patrons' homes. After taking us on one such expedition, Sihlé delves into the ambivalences. The home rituals are suitably compassionate uses of beneficial ritual power and bring reputation, prestige, and remunerations, but they also pull the tantrists away from their own personal and collective ritual practice which they value more highly in religious terms. Too much attention to ritual services and income is frowned upon, but then, demands such as for funerary rituals cannot be rejected. In Sihlé's terms, a whole "bundle of values" is at play here, calling for judicious choices on the tantrists' side.

Further south in Yunnan Province, China, Hannah Rosa Klepeis looks at the borderlands of the Tibetan cultural region, to "Shangri-La" (former Zhongdian) and the monumental Ganden Sumtsenling Monastery with its 700 monks. That institution and the scenic town have become major tourist attractions visited by large numbers of Han Chinese tourists and both Tibetan and Han immigrants. The new wealth flowing in has not stopped donations to the monastery and remunerations to monks performing rituals but provokes doubts, mistrust, and a lively debate. Concerns about money corrupting both givers and recipients are widespread, such as when monks are criticized for investing in businesses rather than responding to the laity's needs for house rituals; when donations by rich Han businessmen are rejected for fear that the improper initial acquisition of these monies might taint the monk; or when monks soliciting donations provoke suspicions of their being "fake." Within long-term cycles of reciprocity between sangha and laity who trust each other, the use of cash is not problematic, but the current abundance of money threatens to break up these ties, with bureaucratic countermeasures—such as demanding receipts for donations—providing only limited protection.

Lamentably, none of our chapters deals with female ritual specialists, as other commitments prevented the colleagues approached for this purpose from contributing.[1] In most historical and contemporary Buddhist contexts, male Buddhist monks, priests, and other specialists are numerically, hierarchically, and ritually dominant. In Japan, for example, nuns and priestesses but also the priests' wives (who play an indispensable role in the large non-celibate, family-run temples) keep struggling for full recognition (Arai and Robinson 1999; Covell 2005, 109–39; Niwa 2019; Rowe 2017; Starling 2019). For Vajrayāna nuns in Zangskar, northern India, Gutschow (2004) has described the economic consequences of male bias: believed to be less ritually efficacious, nuns are remunerated for household rituals at reduced rates. This increases their dependency on natal households, which then feel justified to call on the nuns' agricultural labor power in return, pulling them even further away from religious pursuits—a vicious circle. Cook (2008) finds that the *mae chee* in Thailand—who live as nuns but are withheld formal ordination—play an important mediating role in the generalized reciprocity between sangha and laity. By giving to monks, they seem to confirm their subordinate status, but as they receive alms from the laity both in their own name and that of the monastery, they are reaffirmed as monastics (see also Cook 2009; Falk 2007). Female religious specialists and their economic entanglements invite further study. Laywomen's perspectives do feature in a number of our chapters, however, and where there is no specification, what our (seven male and five female) authors say about the laity applies to all genders.

Beyond Reciprocity

Reciprocity has also been claimed for contexts where money, remunerations, and commercialization play a much smaller role than in the preceding cases. In the Burma of more than half a century ago, for example, Melford Spiro found "a perfectly symmetrical system, exemplifying the general pattern of reciprocity and exchange which, as Mauss ... has shown, characterizes all gifts" (Spiro 1970, 412). If this reasoning does not rest on conceiving of merit as being conferred by the monk or nun or of those specialists' passive provision of a "field of merit" to the pious layperson as a return in its own right, reciprocity must refer to the general complementarity of clergy and laity in Buddhist societies: the laity takes care of the sangha's material needs and provides them with novices; the sangha attends to the laity's ritual and spiritual needs. To acknowledge this as "collective, diffuse, weak reciprocity" (Sihlé 2015, 365) requires a shift of perspective, from the relationship between individuals implicit in Laidlaw's (2000) and others' analyses to the one between sangha and laity as collective entities, including the benefits that the continued existence of the sangha may have for the giver's future self, their offspring, and so on. The most elaborate formulation of this idea is Strenski's article (1983) on the "generalized exchange" connecting

Buddhist clergy and laity. Making itself available to lay generosity was the very impetus for the wandering sangha to "domesticate" and settle down in permanent monasteries, he argues, which gave rise to Buddhist society.

"Weak reciprocity," however, is still built on the tacit premise of an essentially bilateral relationship, which can hamper the understanding of certain aspects of Buddhist practice, as the next two chapters on Vajrayāna Buddhism demonstrate. Kristina Jonutytė makes new theoretical headway by arguing that relations between sangha and laity are best understood in a non-dichotomous framework. In her contribution on Buryatia, she focuses on donations from sangha to laity, rather than the other way round. Buddhism has experienced a revival in the postsocialist period and in Ulan-Ude, the capital of this Siberian republic, more than a dozen temples have been built since the 1980s. Through her ethnographic analysis of two case studies—a "model" temple planned by a maverick lama and a sheep donation project with which the main organization of the Buryat sangha motivates families in need to start their own flocks—Jonutytė shows that sangha and laity supersede their boundary and "pool" their resources in the pursuit of a common cause. Following Marshall Sahlins, she argues that the sangha-laity nexus is transformed from a "between" to a "within" relationship where sangha and laity unite for rebuilding Buddhism, its public presence, and its infrastructure with which Buryat ethnic identity is intimately intertwined.

Buryat Buddhists also see their more clearly bilateral transfers—such as remunerations to monks for ritual services—as indirectly contributing to this goal, an aspect of which they approve. In the language of economics, we might speak of "externalities" here, effects on parties beyond those directly involved in a given economic transaction. This we also see in other chapters: Jane Caple describes how customers of monastic shops derive satisfaction from knowing that the proceeds sustain a monastery even when this is, first of all, a commercial transaction, not a donation. Providing model temples or start-up flocks to Buryat laypeople can also be seen as an instance of the larger phenomenon of Socially Engaged Buddhism (e.g., S. King 2009) in which the sangha turns from beneficiary of the laity to their benefactor. For example, Elizabeth Williams-Oerberg reported in our preparatory workshop how charismatic monks and reincarnates (*tulku*) in Ladakh, North India, engage in charity projects, using the funds provided by their international supporters. And when the *khruba* saints (in Horstmann's chapter) prepare brochures that celebrate their religious and welfare projects, they must also count on the effect this has on those who shower them with donations. All this is owed at least in part to the presence of other religious and nonreligious value systems: socialism has not tired of brandishing organized religion as parasitic and feudalistic, meaning that Tibetan monks now themselves believe that the former reliance on lay support was problematic (Caple 2010). A Christian presence can likewise create pressure to engage in charity, as it clearly does in Ulaanbaatar, Mongolia, where Buddhist temples and dharma centers feel now urged to follow suit (see Abrahms-Kavunenko's chapter).

As the second chapter intent on transcending the sangha-laity binary, Martin Mills strives to "exorcise Mauss's ghost," as he has it. He focuses on the Leh Dosmoché, an annual exorcist rite held in the capital of Ladakh. Here, monks lead a procession parading large votive cakes and a contraption in which they have ritually caged demons. On the supporting trays, believers heap dough balls thought to carry away afflictions and cash offerings when they pass them by in the streets, with the two kinds of offerings signaling a larger transition from subsistence to cash-based economy. Outside the central city, all this is burnt, and young laymen scramble to get their share of the auspicious ashes. According to Mills, rather than an exchange between monks and believers, this is an instance of "collective work": the clergy becomes an extension of the laity, acting in the latter's name instead of pursuing an independent agenda. There is no more of an economic transaction here than there is between a parent and a child when the former has the latter put a coin in a donation box. If anything is transferred, then between different lay generations, since the only participants to appropriate anything in the rite are the youngsters rushing toward the ashes. Both Jonutyte's and Mills's arguments invite a rereading of other Buddhist cases: lay support for and co-ownership of community temples has been duly captured in the literature (see also Casas's and Caple's chapters), but these two chapters point to novel aspects.

Managing Temples and Monasteries

Moving beyond the interaction between sangha and laity, the ethnographic literature has also cast some light on the organizational framework of temples and monasteries. Arrangements are often surprisingly complex; in large Vajrayāna monasteries, for example, the institution as a whole is a property-owning unit, but so are the college-like subdivisions, and residential buildings often belong to outside families whose children turned monastics then occupy them over the generations. Resources flow both among these different units and between them and the individual renunciates, and general accounts exist alongside dedicated ones, such as those set up for holding a particular major ritual (Gutschow 2004, 77–122; Mills 2001, 53–81). Japanese temples such as that of the Kyoto priest are often registered as "religious corporations," as this gives their religious activities tax exemption; the priest and sometimes also his family are then employees of the corporation and receive an income which, however, is duly taxed in its turn (cf. also Covell 2005, 140–64).

Three of our chapters take a closer look on similar intricacies of economic temple management. Bringing us to Yunnan Province again, Roger Casas considers the Theravāda Buddhism of the Tai Lue minority in multiethnic Sipsong Panna (Xishuangbanna), a part of Yunnan Province which borders Laos and Myanmar. A son's (most often temporary) ordination can bring status to the household but removes him from the highly competitive Chinese education system. In this situation, state-led development largely based on resource extraction and commerce, coming with increasing Han Chinese immigration, offers alternative pathways to success. In his portrayal of one village temple, Casas depicts the resulting economic challenges to the temple's abbot. Although respected and widely consulted, that monk is sensitive to rumors and speculation surrounding his use of villagers' donations and offerings. The impression that these benefit the lives of the ordained, rather than the temple which is very much perceived as a community resource, must be avoided. In an attempt to distinguish his own support from temple finances, the abbot starts a side business of making decorative items and religious paraphernalia. The venture takes off but when he feels that it distracts him from his religious duties, he ends up abandoning it.

In another Theravāda context, Prabhath Sirisena demonstrates the value of auto-ethnography for gaining insight into Buddhist economies. Based on several years of living as a forest monk in Sri Lanka, he describes a relatively recent Buddhist reform movement which itself is responding to perceptions of moral decline. It champions a strict interpretation of the Buddhist monastic rules, far more so than that of ordinary village monasteries—or, for that matter, any other Buddhist context addressed in this volume. Forest monks live a secluded life dedicated to meditation and study. Their frugality brings them much admiration from merit-seeking laity, which paradoxically encourages a steady stream of donations, requiring what Sirisena calls a "balancing act" from the monastery's stewards. The monks refuse to handle cash and leave economic matters to a lay council and a couple of assistants who, as a kind of "embedded" laity, live in the monastery with the monks. Yet here again, the abbot is a key figure, as he communicates with donors and makes important economic decisions. Ironically, ascetic rigorism makes the storerooms overflow, and this calls for creative solutions: while the strict interpretation of the rules prohibits redistributing the material excess to impoverished laypeople, passing it on to other sangha—ordinary monasteries known to practice charity—is acceptable.

Jane Caple returns us to Tibetan Buddhism in the Amdo region, this time to monastics rather than tantrist householder. She explores the moral evaluation of monastic shops that have become an increasingly popular way of boosting temple finances over the last ten to fifteen years. Found both within and outside monastic compounds, these businesses stock the same merchandise as their secular competitors, with the exception of religiously problematic products (such as meat, alcohol, or tobacco) and the occasional addition of Buddhist items. While lay donations and remunerations still play a dominant role in financing monasteries and individual monks, the shops contribute a growing share. In the broader context of distrust and fear that food scandals and other incidents have created around Chinese products, the shops offer a more trustworthy source of goods. For the lay buyers, purchases are ordinary business transactions, but they appreciate the added benefit of sustaining the monastery and its monks. In contrast, many monks feel ambivalent: generating an income reduces the need for donations (a burden on the laity) and the performance of household rituals for remunerations (a religious activity regarded as problematic). Yet the need to make a profit and its association with deception places the businesses and the monks who manage them uncomfortably close to secular practices.

Capitalism, Decline, and Rebirth

The two final chapters reflect on the question how the prospects of Buddhism are connected with the larger capitalist economy, general perceptions of decline or growth, and the hopes and fantasies that these engender. Urbanization, commercialization, and monetization were already crucial background conditions for the rise of Buddhism (Benavides 2005, 77–102); after all, "a degree of abundance is the prerequisite for asceticism" (2005, 82). The chapters by Klepeis, Caple, and Casas illustrate how alongside new possibilities, the Chinese economic boom also puts strains on ethnic minority Buddhisms, offering alternative possibilities to potential novices and undermining both clerical and lay moralities. Only Sihlé's tantrists seem to be relatively undisturbed, using improved infrastructures to make their networks of clients even more far-flung. A pervasive sense of economic crisis in Russian Buryatia, by contrast, seems to pull together sangha and laity in joint projects, as Jonutytė reports. The situation is still more complex and contradictory in Ulaanbaatar, Mongolia, as described in Saskia Abrahms-Kavunenko's chapter. She looks at the dynamic tension between metaphors of rebirth and decline, from the regenerating pilgrimages to the Energy Centre to perceptions of a moral crisis among the Mongolian sangha. Temples lost their lands, livestock, and labor entitlements during the socialist period so that in contemporary times, temples and lamas find it difficult to support themselves from irregular donations and remunerations for ritual services. The optimism of the early 1990s brought transnational Buddhist organizations and modern-style dharma centers to the country, with contradictory effects. Here, as in Sihlé's chapter, the lines that demark the laity from religious specialist are somewhat porous, with many lamas having families. Again, we see expected remuneration for ritual services, but also ambivalence about the set prices and perceived commodification that comes with them. Buddhist institutions are perceived by some lamas and laypeople to be in both a state of decline and a site of the future flourishing of Buddhism, complete with prospects of the Dalai Lama being reborn in Mongolia.

Abundance rather than decline characterizes Alexander Horstmann's case of the *khruba*, charismatic monks and living saints attracting large followings in the Mekong river region of Northern Thailand and the adjacent, Thai-speaking areas of Myanmar, Laos, and China. The *khruba* are "wealthy ascetics," believed to command miraculous powers and attracting a lively flow of donations in cash, kind, and services, both from marginalized and impoverished highland communities and from political and economic elites near and far, all the way up to business tycoons and the Thai royal family. This prosperity is invested into temples, stupas, schools, and hospitals the *khruba* set up but also redistributed in spontaneous potlatch-style displays of generosity, such as when these saints hand out bank notes to the large numbers of believers congregating for their rituals or birthday celebrations. While the vast class differences among the followers remain unaddressed, the *khruba*'s charisma and spiritual power and the capital flows they engender appear to feed on each other, calling to mind downright Buddhist prosperity cults such as Dhammakāya (Scott 2009). Ultimately, Buddhist doctrine is less concerned with riches than with an attachment to them, and the *khruba* monk-saints as nodes of economic flows that pass through, rather than stay with, them bring this tendency to extremes.

The Balancing Act

Across our cases and independent of geographical location, the Theravāda/Mahāyāna/Vajrayāna divide, and the vast gulf between the temple cash registers of Ulaanbaatar and the Sri Lankan forest monks, it becomes clear that sangha economies are prone to ambivalence, uncertainty, and debate. Even where money and prosperity are everyday parts of the Buddhist experience, the idealized image of sangha economies is still being deployed by both laypeople and clerics in order to reflect on, justify, or else challenge their own and each other's practices. We do see concerns, such as about Buddhist practitioners becoming corrupt and obsessed with money (Sihlé, Klepeis, Borchert, Świtek, Abrahms-Kavunenko); online sale of rituals transforming these into commercial services (Świtek); a solitarily funded Buddhist project denying supporters the opportunity for merit-making donations (Jonutytė); cash being an unsuitable substitute for in-kind offerings (Mills); ordinary businesses becoming too absorbing for the monks tasked with them (Caple, Casas); or lay donations piling up with those monks who least need them (Sirisena). We sense potential concerns when the *khruba* publish booklets about their charitable projects, feeling the need to demonstrate that their wealth of donations is put to good effect (Horstmann).

Sirisena speaks of a "balancing act" that is required of the forest monks, and we think that this metaphor can be generalized to the entirety of our cases. Our examples ranging from Southeast Asia to Russia show that sangha economies are a central part of the lives of Buddhist religious specialists and their interactions with the lay public. But despite the diversity of situations, practices, and surrounding economic conditions, they are never simple and straightforward. Money operates within Buddhist communities in complex ways. Through the analysis of these economic relationships, we can see how deeply enmeshed in their societies Buddhist religious specialists are. The economy emerges as a central arena for reflecting upon and debating contemporary Buddhist practice, not just a marginal field, and for many Buddhists, it provides a touchstone for putting moral and doctrinal commitments to the test. We are sure that more attention to sangha economies—to stay in the discourse—will pay off.

*

The idea for this book stems from the discussions that the members of the research group "Buddhist Temple Economies in Urban Asia"—Abrahms-Kavunenko, Brumann, Jonutytė, Klepeis, and Świtek—had at the Max Planck Institute for Social Anthropology, Halle, from 2014 to 2018. We then were members of the department "Resilience and Transformation in Eurasia," headed by Chris Hann for whose support of the conference and of the ethnographic projects that flowed into the members' chapters we are grateful. Patrice Ladwig gave crucial intellectual input. For bringing together the chapters, we held a writing workshop at the institute on September 21–22, 2017, in which we discussed first drafts. Elisabetta Porcu had to cancel participation due to conditions beyond her control and Harrison B. Carter, Daniel Friedrich, Ariya Sasaki, and Elizabeth Williams-Oerberg, while presenting captivating papers and contributing greatly to our discussions, had to withdraw from the final volume. David Gellner acted as an engaged and lucid general discussant and session chairs Stephen Covell, Laura Hornig, Elzyata Kuberlinova, Patrice Ladwig, Shilla Lee, Dittmar Schorkowitz, and Nikolay Tsyrempilov also contributed stimulating ideas. At Bloomsbury, we profited from the dedicated work of Lalle Pursglove, Lily McMahon, Sophie Beardsworth, and Shanmathi Priya Sampath. We would like to express our gratitude to all of them.

PART ONE

Reciprocity, Money, and Trust

CHAPTER ONE

Economic Agency and the Spirit of Donation: The Commercialization of Buddhist Services in Japan

Beata Świtek

In a slip of the tongue Keiko referred to herself and others affiliated with the same Buddhist temple as "customers" (*o-kyaku*). According to the commonly used religious terminology, she was a *monto* (follower, adherent) of that temple.[1] Keiko began her affiliation when her mother passed away: the father chose this temple to officiate his wife's burial and rented a space for the family grave at the cemetery managed by the temple. From that point on, Keiko and her father began to actively participate and help in its various activities. When Keiko made her linguistic slip, we were discussing a priest working at the temple who would often fail to return greetings to Keiko's father. She found such an attitude incredulous, because she believed that as "customers," her father, herself, and other people similarly affiliated with the temple through burial of a family member, deserved at least a minimum of courtesy.[2] Keiko quickly noticed the faux pas, smiled at the recognition of the implication it had, and rephrased her comment, this time replacing "customer" with "follower." When doing so, she repeated *monto* a couple of times, indicating with the tone of her voice and a jovial expression on her face that she was putting the word in imaginary inverted commas. While that day we did not set off to discuss anything to do with the economy of the temple, at least not in my initial understanding, Keiko's slip of the tongue suggested that in her view, a contract based on an economic exchange was at the core of the relationship between her family and the temple. Priests as parties to that contract had particular obligations toward their paying customers.

Introduction

A recent book on consumption in Japan (Cwiertka and Machotka 2018) shows Japanese society to be one in which "veneration of material comfort and convenience" (ibid., 16) has persisted since Japan achieved economic affluence in the period of rapid post–Second World War development. In this "society of consumers" (ibid.), even the prolonged economic regression that has befallen Japan ever since the 1990s did not do away with the "all-encompassing nature of commodification and consumption" (ibid., 17). Keiko's take on her relationship with the temple where her mother is buried suggests that consumerist expectations apply also to religious institutions. However, Buddhist temples would rather be seen as responding to the spiritual needs of the laity than as businesses selling services for compensation. While involvement of Buddhist specialists in profit-making ventures is nothing new or limited to Japan (e.g., Goodwin 1994; Hur 2000; Schopen 2004), in the idealized form, a Buddhist priest is to remain detached from material and financial goods.[3] A practical manifestation of such disinterest is reliance for sustenance on—sometimes even unacknowledged (Bowie 1998; Parry 1986; Sihlé 2015)—donations. Even though in classical and medieval Japan the Buddhist *kanjin* fund-raising campaigns "had to be motivated by profit making economy thinking, which saw money primarily as a tool to meet the expenses of timber, tile, and labor [for temple and other construction projects] … the promise of salvation remained without a set value" (Goodwin 1994, 44). Also under the relatively restricting social conditions imposed by the Tokugawa regime of the Edo period (1603–1868), the amounts offered to temples varied depending on a range of factors such as the quality of services offered, local custom, social status of the donor, and so on, and "were determined through a 'mutual understanding and agreement'" between the offering laity and the temple (Hur 2007, 232). Because of such lack of popularly known historical precedents (which almost certainly took place, e.g., Hur 2007, 225) and for reasons outlined below, setting an absolute price on religious services today is seen to expose a "spirit of calculation" (Bourdieu 1998, 105–7) that does not fit the disinterested image, particularly when the sums involved are considerable.[4] However, as I will show below, that is exactly the direction in which Buddhist temples in Japan are heading. In this chapter I thus consider what happens to the "spirit of donation" as Buddhist specialists engage in economic transactions in a highly commercialized consumer society. To get a full picture we first take a look at the existing organization of the relations between the sangha and the laity;[5] and secondly, we consider the positioning of temples (and therefore priests) in relation to the broader economic field of funerary rites.

One relationship within which transfers going by the name of donations have been constitutive is that between a temple and a group of families affiliated with it, the *danka*. As of late, under this system with origins in the Edo period, *danka* families like Keiko's have maintained their relationship with temples mainly through the rites of ancestral veneration.[6] The temples could also call on the affiliated families to donate toward a particular cause, such as the restoration of temple buildings or the purchase of new chairs. However, modernization and its corollaries (higher education levels, urbanization, consumerism, rise of secular ideologies, population aging) have taken their toll on this tradition-sanctioned relationship.[7] Today, it is not uncommon to hear of people who do not know with which temple their family is affiliated, who decline to offer money to temple refurbishing projects, or who have lost touch with the family temple in the countryside after moving to a distant urban region and do not seek out new affiliation in a city.[8] In the Japanese countryside which is experiencing depopulation as a result of outflow of people to urban centers and the aging (and dying out) of those who remain, temples deprived of a support base offered by the *danka* have been known to close down (Ukai 2015).

Having already lost their social functions as educational sites, community hubs, and distributors of medicines to state institutions and private organizations during the late nineteenth and the early twentieth centuries (Nelson 2013, 44–5; also Hur 2000), deprived of income from land during post–Second World War reforms (Rowe 2011, 26), and now facing an increasingly shaky *danka* system, temples have become dependent on funerary income.[9] Coinciding with this shift has been the gradual commercialization and formalization of payment for the services offered by the temples. As urbanization and nuclearization of families brought about the loss of multigenerational knowledge about how to perform funeral and memorial rites and as small urban apartments did not allow for the wake to be held at home any longer, commercial companies entered the market. From offering the rental of funeral halls to instructing the mourners on their ritual duties and more recently finding out which Buddhist sect they might belong to, the funerary companies have come to offer full-service packages. As the prices have become fixed, so grew the pressure from the mourners to be offered a set price for the priest's services as well. Reflecting this trend is the fact that in recent years, some abbots decided to put up itemized price lists for rituals and other services they offer at their own temples (see also Rowe 2011).[10] Consequently, no study of contemporary temple Buddhism[11] in Japan can avoid accounting for its strong association with ancestral veneration, mortuary practices, and the vibrant commercial market of funerary services where Buddhist temples operate alongside and often in cooperation with commercial companies. In Tokyo, this marketization taps into the demand for resting places generated by people who have lost their relationships with their regional home temples. The city's still growing population, quite in contrast to a country predicted to shrink by sixteen million by year 2040 (NIPSSR 2017), and the forthcoming "mass dying" (*tashi* or *tairyōshi*; Ukai 2016, 2) of the postwar baby boomers between 2020 and 2040 promise an economically stable future for the capital temples and funerary companies able to cash in on the demographic transformations. The flip side of the story is the perception that temples operate as businesses (see also Covell 2005, 140).

This reality notwithstanding, much of the official discourse produced by the Japanese sangha (community of Buddhist specialists) promotes the idea (and ideal) of donations offered to priests out of the lay donor's willing conscience (*o-kimochi*). Studies of contemporary Japanese Buddhism have shown time and again how Buddhist priests are at pains to fight the explicitly commercial representations of their activities that imply remuneration for services (e.g., Covell 2005, 161, 184–5; Nelson 2013, 143; Rowe 2011, 29–30).[12] This continuing "misrecognition" of transactions (Borup 2008, 172–3; see also Bourdieu 1998, 121, as well as the introduction to this volume) and the overt reliance on donations allow the priests to disclaim any economic agency in their relationship with the laity.[13] In this way, they are able to distance themselves from criticisms of self-interest even as they rely on this income for their own salaries. However, for the reasons outlined above, stylizing transfers between the sangha and the laity as donations is becoming increasingly untenable in Japan.

The cases I present in this chapter situate mortuary rites and the associated financial transfers squarely in the realm of market transactions. One consequence of this explicit understanding of money offered to a priest or temple as a payment rather than a donation is that the priest becomes a party to an exchange, which unlike a donation, imbues him or her with economic agency. To compound this, the fragmentation of the Japanese sangha (discussed subsequently) renders each temple an individual economic unit and by extension individualizes the economic agency to particular priests rather than generalizing it to the whole sangha. Suggestive of self-interest rather than a religious commitment to the well-being of the masses, such individualization of economic agency gives rise to the negative image that the Japanese sangha faces today. However, as I show in the final part of this chapter, even if the ideal of donation is being unmasked as mere misrecognition of market transactions, the priests who openly receive payments from the laity modify the nature of the exchange by extracting themselves from it as active agents.

I base my considerations on four case studies. The first two of them (the Priest Delivery service offered on Amazon and the taxation of an affluent Tokyo temple) were on many priests' minds during my fourteen months of ethnographic fieldwork among Buddhist priests and laypeople primarily in and around Tokyo between 2015 and 2017. While people directly involved in these two cases were not included in my research on the ground to a great extent, their stories nevertheless resurfaced several times in conversations with other priests and the laity alike, sometimes serving as examples of the processes we were talking about. Hence, in this chapter they serve to paint the background for discussion of the two remaining cases I encountered directly during fieldwork: a temple that organizes chanting events and a priest running a bar. I also draw on information publicly available on websites run by the institutions to which I refer.

Recognition of Exchange

A Japanese company, Minrevi,[14] had been offering a Priest Delivery (*o-bōsan bin*) service since 2013, but in December 2015, they joined forces with Amazon to widen their reach. According to the company itself, this was in response to a significant number of inquiries from interested potential customers. The service allows people to order via the internet a Buddhist priest to perform funerals and commemorative services. In their statement of purpose, Minrevi refer to the weakening of religiosity (*shūkyōkan no kihakuka*), estrangement from temples (*o-tera-banare*), and people's difficulty in establishing good relationships with priests, particularly in cities. This is where the Priest Delivery aims to ease the situation by offering hassle-free service packages at set prices that on request (and sometimes incurring an additional, but always clearly specified, fee) may include a posthumous monk's or nun's name for the deceased, reading of sutras together with the families, and so on. In a lingo typical of the online platform, the customers are able to purchase tickets that entitle them to a particular "size" of the product (*shōhin*): 45,000 yen[15] for the simplest package; 55,000 yen when the priest travels between the house and the cemetery to chant sutras in both locations and give a sermon but does not confer a posthumous name; 65,000 yen when the priest does not travel but confers the posthumous name; and 75,000 yen when all is included. Regardless of the option chosen, the customer is not expected to offer additional money to the priest who will receive his or her share of the price via Minrevi. While the company does not disclose detailed information, after moving to Amazon, it reported that the sales of the service increased sevenfold in 2016 (Ukai 2016, 154). Most customer comments on the Amazon website praise the service for the transparency of charges and their reasonable rates (*yasuku sunde yokatta*).

Despite its popularity, the advertising of the Priest Delivery on Amazon elicited a critical response. One such critical voice came from the Japanese Buddhist Federation (*Zen Nihon Bukkyōkai*). On December 24, 2015, and later in March the following year, its chairman issued a press release and an open letter addressed to the president of the Japanese branch of Amazon, respectively. In these documents, the chairman protested against setting prices for what is essentially a "religious act of [giving] alms" (*shūkyō kōi toshite aru o-fuse*) and thus against turning the alms into remuneration and items such as posthumous names into commodities and urged Amazon to suspend the sales of the new product.[16]

Praise for the service as well as the comments expressing relief at the low cost suggest that while the presence of a religious specialist is still desirable (for some at least), this religious element in a final farewell is not perceived as delivered by a priest disinterested in a possible return, that is, in an exchange value of his or her actions. Neither is the amount transferred via the online retailer left to the "conscience" (*o-kimochi*) of a lay customer, as a donation would be. Rather whatever money gets transferred is weighed on the cheap-expensive scale—a consideration that befits an exchange embedded in a market where goods and services are expected to be duly remunerated. Despite the insistence of the Japanese Buddhist Federation that these transfers are donations freely offered by the laity, services such as those offered by Minrevi and their high visibility on a giant online platform make it impossible to maintain such claims. As my friend's slip of the tongue also indicates, the lay definition of the relationship with temples is already devoid of such misrecognition, even if the unmasking of the contractual nature of the exchanges is still mostly done "behind the scenes," in informal situations out of the priests' earshot. But abbots who put up price lists are also moving away from the claim to a donation economy. Such "recognition" of the nature of exchanges between the Japanese sangha and the laity is of course a part of wider transformations manifesting themselves not only in popular attitudes to religion and its institutions as noted above but also in the workings of the state vis-à-vis these institutions. Let us move to considering the latter.

Not for Public Benefit

One consequence of demographic changes affecting metropolitan areas in Japan is an increase in demand for space where people can put their remains to final rest. Thus, while temples might still have some empty lots to allocate or can, for example, transform parts of their premises into cemeteries, many temples in large cities such as Tokyo are now choosing to construct *nōkotsudō*, literally "bone storage chambers." These chambers take the form of multistory buildings where each floor is lined with rows of small lockers containing urns with ashes and a few personal items, sometimes also a photograph of the deceased placed there by family members. Alternatively, the chambers can be automated, with the urn delivered by a system of lifts to specially designed visitor booths, much like a vending machine. Such solutions not only allow the temples to accommodate large numbers of urns on less land (a temple I visited in 2016 had at the time 2,000 urns stored in two separate buildings and I have heard stories about a temple in central Tokyo storing 8,000) but also translate into lower costs of purchasing and later maintaining the graves for the families.[17] For temples too, the larger number of smaller and cheaper graves represents a more profitable solution than having more expensive and larger graves but less of them. While traveling on the Tokyo underground, one is likely to spot posters featuring funeral companies or temples advertising cemeteries and bone chambers. Some temples with larger budgets place such advertisements on television as well.

The emergence of this form of entombment and its profitability has triggered a discussion over whether it constitutes a religious practice. Kuno-san,[18] an abbot of a Pure Land (*Jōdo*) temple who operates it primarily on income generated from nonreligious sources such as real-estate rents, recognized the equivocal nature of such set-ups:

> Kuno-san: They [*nōkotsudō*] came to resemble multistory car parks ... people who don't want to have a relationship with a temple but are looking for a place to throw away the bones (*hone no sutebasho*) go for such an option.
> Beata: Do you still call these people "believers" (*shinja*)?
> Kuno-san: Well, you still call them believers, don't you? As a temple, if you didn't call them believers, then how would you explain the difference between them [*nōkotsudō*] and a regular parking business? If you don't say that this temple performs rituals for these people, that these are religious rituals, then naturally it becomes a storage business and gets taxed. That's why I think they frame it as a religious activity.

Despite such voices, the majority of *nōkotsudō* existing today are still formally recognized as constituting religious practice. Most Japanese Buddhist temples as well as other religious organizations hold the status of a religious juridical person (*shūkyō hōjin*). This status implies that temples are public benefit juridical persons (*kōeki hōjin*) that operate on a not-for-profit basis. When fulfilling these conditions, the temples are freed from property tax (*kotei shisan zei*) on such assets as temple buildings and grounds (including cemeteries) that are used for religious purposes. Similarly, income generated by the temple or its priest through religious practices as an employee of that juridical person is also exempt from corporate tax (*hōjin zei*).[19] The system that puts religious activities outside of the taxman's reach was introduced as one of the formal administrative means guarding against the mutual influence between the state apparatus and religious organizations. This meant that there has been a need to distinguish between what constitutes religious activity (*shūkyō katsudō; shūkyō kōi*) and what does not.

One of the more clear-cut cases where such a distinction is made relatively common is the classification of income generated from, for example, rents whereby temples transform parts of their premises either into communal parking lots or into apartment blocks rented to private or corporate entities. In such cases, this part of the temple's income is subject to taxation. Until recently, however, "bone storage chambers" have been uniformly deemed to fall within the parameters set for a religious legal person and thus have been operating free of taxes. However, a recent case has challenged this status quo and is widely seen as a harbinger of the changes to come.

In 2015, Dentōin, a Sōtō Zen temple that runs a *nōkotsudō* in the affluent Tokyo district Akasaka, was required to pay property tax on the premises. The decision by the local tax office was substantiated by the office's understanding that the activities taking place at the *nōkotsudō* were not of a religious nature. The abbot appealed twice, but with the tax office upholding the decision, the priest took the case to court. However, the court ruling supported the tax office decision with respect to specified areas of the chamber. Consequently, out of the total 845.58 square meters of floor space, 630.16 square meters were deemed subject to property tax. According to the excerpts from the court proceedings quoted in *Abbot Monthly* (*Gekkan Jūshoku*, a magazine devoted to various economic and administrative issues pertinent to running Buddhist temples), one reason for not recognizing the *nōkotsudō* activities as religious was that the temple accepted people regardless of their religious affiliation or lack thereof. It was pointed out that on occasions when a priest of a different denomination (or simply from a different temple) comes to perform rituals on site at the request of the bereaved, the chamber becomes nothing else but a rental space. As such, it does not "solely fulfil the intended/original function" (*moppara sono honrai no yō ni kyō sareru*). Similarly, the first-floor worship room (*sanpaishitsu*) where the urns with ashes are automatically delivered to specially designed booths operated by the touch of an electronic card was defined as "bone storage business" (*nōkotsudō jigyō*) and hence taxed. The same reasoning was applied to the underground space where all the urns are stored. As the third floor included the secondary temple hall with a reception room used not only as a waiting room before funeral ceremonies but also for different seminars not necessarily limited to Sōtō denominational teaching as well as for classes in flower arrangement, it too was deemed not to fulfil its original function and thus taxed. The taxable common areas of the building were calculated proportionally to the size of the areas classified as not conforming to the original function of the temple as a religious legal person (Gekkan Jūshoku 2016). Ultimately, the taxes imposed on the temple amounted to four million yen (roughly 37,500 US dollars), a sum that, according to the abbot's son running the *nōkotsudō* in question, could pay a yearly salary of one additional staff member (Gekkan Jūshoku 2016).

While the lack of denominational focus was given as a reason by the tax office and later by the court, the abbot of the temple managing the chamber argued that not only were the non-Sōtō Zen entombments a minority, but that the set-up offered a resting place to the many people in Tokyo who did not have any relationship with a temple up to the point of purchasing a chamber space. In this sense, the temple and the chamber it runs was to fulfil its original function as a religious person, that is, spreading the Sōtō Zen teaching.

Dentōin's case was closely followed by the wider Buddhist community and when the court ruling was finally made public, one of my priest friends brought me a newspaper clipping with an article covering the case. It was significant that through their meticulous partitioning of the temple into taxable and nontaxable spaces, it was the state officials who ultimately defined what counted and what did not as religious, what counted as a donation and what as payment. This active intervention by the state and the overturning of the temple's definitional attempts was an indication of what its abbot himself referred to as a "demarcation suited for the times" (*jidai ni atta senbiki*) when I talked to him while the trial was still ongoing. It officially confirmed what some priests already felt themselves, as suggested by Kuno-san's comments: despite the overt claims of a religious nature for *nōkotsudō* and the income they generate, they are in fact operating according to an economic calculus where a particular service (storage of the ashes and commemorative rituals) is met with remuneration rather than a donation based on the lay believer's conscience. A further symbolic meaning of the court decision lies in the negation of Dentōin's status as a not-for-profit organization that operates for public benefit. If the temple receives taxable remuneration for its services, then not only is it profiting from these exchanges, but more importantly for the argument in this chapter, the benefits are private, not public.

Economic Agency and Fragmentation of the Sangha

Despite the growing public openness of priests about the economic dealings that they need to engage in to sustain the temples and various religious undertakings, the sentiment that profiting and religious rituals are not comfortable bedfellows remains widespread (but see Rowe 2011).[20] A *manshon* priest (a priest who does not reside in a temple)[21] in his forties, who at the time of our conversation was helping at two temples, told me:

> That's why there is a part of a priest that thinks like a businessman, isn't there? How much will I get for a funeral, how many ceremonies this month, can I secure enough income … and so on … if you attach too much weight [to these issues], then, really, the essence gets lost, doesn't it? That's what I think. That's why I think it is more genuine (*junsui*) to earn your income from something else. In the countryside, having an additional job is more common.

While it has become something of a cliché that Buddhist priests are unduly profiteering from overpriced funerals in Japan, what upholds the unease about "businessing" religion as hinted on in this quote is not the engagement in a quid pro quo exchange of money per se but what it implies about the actors involved. Here, drawing personal income from the laity suggests that the priest is invested in the transactions as an individual rather than as a representative of the sangha. In other words, it reveals the priest as a willful agent acting on his or her own behalf and in his or her own (material) interest.[22] With the (mis)representation of the transfers as donations difficult to uphold, personal gain starts to dominate the picture. In Japan this is further abetted by the fragmentation of the Japanese sangha.

The multiple denominations within Japanese Buddhism all have their own organizational structure topped by the head temple (or temples) and denominational headquarters that attend to overall administrative and financial matters of the whole organization. But more than the split into several schools, it is the fragmentation into a multitude of local administratively independent temples that has the greatest impact on the priests' relationship with both economic dealings and the laity. The existence of temples and churches as outlets of religious organizations serving the needs of the wider population is, of course, not specific to Japan or Buddhism. The fragmentation of the Japanese sangha consists rather in the outsourcing of the temple management to typically one head priest and his or her closest family, and in the concomitant division of the laity into the multigenerational kin groups of the *danka*. Temples known as tourist sites aside, it is extremely unlikely that one would just walk into a temple in Tokyo, for example, unless there is a preexisting relationship that the person has with it. The only temple that a person would feel fairly free to step into and the only priest to call upon is the one with already preexisting ties, economic or otherwise.[23] With the visibility in "lay" mass media of high-profile cases such as Priest Delivery and the court battle of Dentōin, this fragmentation of the sangha and the related "privatization of temples" (Covell 2005, 124) have now colluded to individualize priests as agents in economic exchanges.[24]

Alongside, however, there are priests who engage in overt economic exchanges but who nevertheless withdraw their agency from the transactions to allow space for disinterested dealings with the laity in ways similar to those made possible by the institution of donations. One of them is the abbot of a Pure Land temple located not far away from one of Tokyo's landmarks, the Tokyo Tower.

In the Red

On one June evening in 2016, a group of us were sitting around low tables in a lounge just outside the main hall of the temple. One of the disciples of the abbot brought sandwiches and some sweets from a shop nearby, while another disciple started opening a 1.8 liter bottle of Japanese rice wine. Although it was only around 7 p.m., we were all quite tired having just finished a twenty-four-hour gathering during which every four hours, we

FIGURE 1.1 A Buddhist priest chanting *nenbutsu*, Tokyo, 2016 (Photo: Beata Świtek).

performed one hour of circumambulations of the central image of buddha Amida in the temple's main hall. With alcohol adding to the relaxation, a lively conversation was jumping from subject to subject. At one point, it focused on another twenty-four-hour event that took place about a month earlier, the Unceasing Chant—a flagship *nenbutsu* chanting event of the temple. Reminiscing about it, the abbot wondered out loud how to shape it in the future so as to attract more people and encourage long-term participation. Among the gathered in the lounge was a woman in her twenties, Uwamura-san. This was her second time to take part in an event organized by this temple, the first being the Unceasing Chant. The abbot was curious to know her impressions about the May event as a relative newcomer to the temple.

In her response, Uwamura-san commented on the pricing structure. At the time, the event was open to anyone. It was possible to pre-register for full participation for a fee of 5,000 yen or just drop by at any time for a one-coin donation. An additional stipulation on posters advertising the event stated that the one-coin participation was for those who planned to take part up to two hours, but this was not strictly policed, not least because those who only dropped in usually stayed for less than an hour anyway. In Uwamura-san's view it was quite difficult to decide to come as a full participant, that is, to pay 5,000 yen, because it was "either this or '*o-kimochi*' [one's conscience]," one coin. The gap between the two was too wide in her eyes:

a person could participate for as little as one yen while the largest coin of 500 was still far away from the full participation fee of 5,000 yen. She suggested that there should be more gradation and perhaps an *o-susume*, a recommendation package akin to a bundle of activities purchased at a set price in travel agencies. For example, if someone paid 2,000 yen, then in addition to joining in the chant in the main hall they could also try their hand at copying a sutra or an image of a buddha. As it was, regardless of what people paid, they were able to take part in exactly the same activities during the event, which, according to Uwamura-san, could cause grievances. She further speculated that with a greater variety in pricing, it could also be expected that more people would join in and that the event would therefore be more profitable.[25]

The abbot's logic was different. The 5,000-yen fee was to cover the costs incurred by the temple rather than bring profit. To run the event, the abbot rented premises from the sect's head temple that could accommodate more people than his own. This covered not just the space for the chant itself but also break rooms where participants could rest over a cup of tea, have a snack, engage in activities such as sutra copying, or take a nap.[26] Two meals were also included. Breakfast was served in the head temple's cafeteria, and the catering company operating it charged the organizers a slightly higher rate for having to provide services outside the usual operating time. Hand-made buckwheat noodles (*teuchi soba*) served in the evening were provided by a group of volunteers who have a close relationship with the abbot. Because they used high-quality ingredients, however, the cost per person was also on the high side. A large chunk of the outlay was spent on a hallmark of the event: its live-broadcasting over the internet and simultaneous streaming of groups participating in it in several countries around the globe back to the main venue in Tokyo. While I was asked not to reveal details of the event's balance sheet, it showed that only half of the costs incurred were covered by the participation fees and the one-coin donations. The remaining part came from the temple's resources. What was not reflected in the participation fee was any valuation of the time devoted by the abbot, his disciples, and a handful of lay volunteers (regular participants in monthly *nenbutsu* evenings) who led the chant, ran the reception, or offered hand-written seal stamps of the event (*go-shuin*). The 5,000-yen fee was thus not set based on the activities offered in order to make a profit, as Uwamura-san assumed, but to contribute to the overhead costs of each of the overnight attendees.

The year 2016 was not the first year when the event brought financial losses to the temple. This has been the case ever since the number of participants grew (from around ten people during the first edition twelve years ago to 250 people in 2016), calling for a bigger venue, and since live-streaming of the event over the internet began. Every year, the event is run with the assumption that the final figures will be in the red (*akaji*). While his disciples openly voiced concern over this practice, the abbot was, at least overtly, more focused on growing the event and attracting more participants who would stream their own chant into the main venue from outside Japan (something that does not require a registration fee). During our first interview, he did stress that the temple would be better off had there been no events, but at the same time he never missed the opportunity to highlight how unusual his temple was, precisely because he organized a range of *nenbutsu*-related events.[27]

By running the Unceasing Chant at a loss, by setting the participation price to cover the costs incurred, and by not imposing a price list on packages of activities as suggested by Uwamura-san, the abbot eschewed control over the pricing of the event and any possible income (and profit) that it might have generated. The *o-kimochi* donations of one coin as well as the full participation fee were both dependent on entities external to the abbot and his disciples: the one-coin donations on the participants and the participation fee on the hosting temple, the catering company, and the volunteers responsible for preparing wheat noodles.

The Power of the Other

Another priest who articulated the shift of agency away from oneself delivers funerary services as a *manshon* priest, but also runs a business: the main outlet where he interacts with the laity is a small Buddhist-themed bar where he holds daily sermons and sutra-chanting sessions with the customers. At the time of our conversations, the owner was self-employed (*jieigyō*). This meant that all the proceeds from the bar activities were entering his own account where he would earmark portions to become his private income and those to reinvest in operating the bar and related activities. When we met, he was thinking of turning the bar into a company with a proper board of directors. He envisaged that such a change could increase his leverage in negotiations with other businesses when it came to, for example, the development of new products. It would also take away some of his own decision-making powers and organizationally make the bar more similar to the way Buddhist temples operate. As of autumn 2016, he had been on the verge of changing the status three times, having had consulted lawyers (from among his bar's customers) and had the necessary documents drafted. Yet each time, events took place that made the change impossible financially or opened up new solutions. To the owner, this coincidence was a sign that he should not do it after all:

> It is good to allow things to happen, you know, *tariki*. Really, when you try to come up with something yourself, it turns into failure quite often. There are things you should decide by yourself, but there are things you should leave to happen by themselves, somehow there is a difference, you can learn how to discern these with time.

I do think that if you apply Buddhist law (*bukkyō no hōsoku*) to management you will definitely succeed. Well, maybe not definitely, but you are very likely to. I feel this way having done so in practice ... One thing is *tariki*, *tariki* of the True Pure Land denomination, I apply it to management too. Everything is *tariki*. I don't put my ego forward, well, I do, but when I look back, I see that everything was *tariki*, management-wise.

Tariki (the power of the other) is a concept specific to the Pure Land denominations of Buddhism in Japan that refers to the belief that one's salvation, or reaching the Pure Land, is not determined by the effort of the self but happens as a result of buddha Amida's benevolent compassion. It is often expanded to refer to the life in this world as a string of encounters (*en*) that are offered to people by Amida as well. Conceptualizing his approach to the management of the bar in terms of *tariki*, the owner withdrew himself as the ultimate decision-maker and placed the agential powers with buddha Amida. He once explained his overall managerial principles in the following way:

As I see it, everything is revolving on the top of Buddha's palm. There, we are made to chance upon different people ... I think people do realize that, but I'd like everyone to really comprehend it. It is a great discovery [laughs]. Once you realize this, everything becomes so easy. You don't need things like strategy and so on, really ... it is not something you do yourself.

He therefore relies on "coincidences" opening up new possibilities that shape the bar he runs. For example, he usually does not advertise vacancies when these come up. He explained that people typically approach him just at the right moment when there is a need for a new staff member. Similarly, although the owner has been thinking of introducing nonalcoholic warm drinks to the bar's menu for a while, he did it only after one of the customers who became a regular in 2016 asked if he could install a coffee machine from the company he worked for. The customer working as a salesman in one of the coffee shop chains needed to sign more contracts to meet the quota and asked the owner for a favor. After a while they struck a deal.

Such reliance on *tariki* transpires also in the training offered by the Cram School for Abbots of the Future (*Mirai no Jūshoku Juku*).[28] Established in 2012 by a duo of an MBA-holding priest and a former financial advisor, the school has been offering year-long courses in business strategy, marketing, leadership, public relations, and accounting to temple abbots and their families.[29] As part of the course, the school supports the participating temples in formulating a business plan that would "preserve the essence" of a temple as a Buddhist institution. One past attendee who shared his business plan with me concluded that the overall message he got out of the exercise was that in the end it all came down to putting to use what the temple already had, rather than chasing and creating new opportunities. Using the temple's existing resources to sustain and boost its financial situation once again guarded against turning the priest into an active agent in pursuit of economic gain.

Conclusion

The head priest of one of the branches of True Pure Land (*Jōdoshin*) denomination, *tōmonsama*[30] suggested in an interview that I ask at a *konbini* (convenience store) about the future of Japanese Buddhism. The idea was that soon enough people would be able to purchase Buddhist services in ways similar to the many ready-to-go products offered by *konbini* to customers who might have no time or inclination to search for more bespoke options. The suggestion was of course a joke, but a wry one, giving away *tōmonsama*'s awareness that a society expecting quick and clearly priced solutions to their consumer needs is not an easy space for temples to operate on donations.[31] He believed that the Priest Delivery service would be used by "people who like it cheap and hassle-free, those who have no time, and those who don't know Buddhism" (*yasui no ga ii hito, mendōkusai hito, jikan ga nai hito, bukkyō o shiranai hito*).[32] However, the emergence of such services was not a surprise for him, just as it was not a surprise for the abbot of Dentōin that he would lose the tax court case. These were the signs of the times when commodification achieved "total victory [...] over all spheres of life" (Cwiertka and Machotka 2018, 15).

As we have seen, with the traditional system of familial affiliation under duress from a combination of demographic, social, and ideological transformations, the view of temples as businesses is commonplace. Keiko's slip of the tongue gave away that much. Similarly, the meticulous scrutiny of the tax office that ultimately defined what is to count as religious activity and what not laid bare the more widely spread sentiment that funerary and related rites have stopped by and large to provide a religion (Buddhism)-inspired sense of solace. If that is the case, then a Buddhist temple accepts the remains not for the sake of the deceased and/or their families but for its own. At the same time, as paying customers, people can simply purchase a "place to throw away the bones," as Kuno-san put it.

This of course does not imply a complete disengagement with what Buddhism or Buddhist priests have to offer. The demand for a final resting place operated in a Buddhist idiom as well as the popularity of the Priest Delivery service bespeak the need for a ritual presence (see also Ukai 2016, 159), even if it is perceived as a product conveniently (and comparatively cheaply) purchased on Amazon. The difference is in the increasingly open calculative approach to transfers that traditionally have gone by the name of donations, whether the shift is welcome or not. That abbots attend temple-specific business courses or that some of them decide to put up price lists is a sign that the "spirit of donation" animating the Japanese sangha economy is being replaced by a need for and an expectation of calculation both on the part of the temples and their patrons/customers.

In some ways, this calculative approach is nothing new, as shown by Goodwin (1994). However, the difference with the practices of the Japanese past is that even though during the *kanjin* campaigns the donations were solicited by individual monks (*hijiri*) typically operating outside the temple organization, the accumulated resources directly benefited wider communities. As we saw earlier, not only were the donations expected to bring spiritual benefits (or build temples), but they were also commonly used to construct bridges, irrigation ponds, roads, and so forth (ibid.).[33] Significantly, too, "religious and secular projects ... were not necessarily distinguished or viewed as contradictions" (1994, 141). Modernity's discursive separation of economy and religion, material and spiritual, has produced powerful idealizations that although rarely (if ever) possible to realize, inform today's conceptualizations of the world in Japan and elsewhere. With the temples stripped of much of their former social functions, the flow and accumulation of assets resulting from religious rituals are now firmly located within the modern (secular) notions of private gain.

Alongside those who openly embrace the new realities, we see, however, priests who set prices for activities they organize and who operate businesses but who renounce the calculative approach. Whether as a corollary of a sense of mission or belief, as a sign of unease or a rhetorical device to assuage critics, these priests conceptualize and sustain an ideal of non-agential involvement in economic exchanges while they act in their religious capacity. By withdrawing themselves as active agents, the priests change the nature of the exchanges that they are a party to: unlike recipients of donations, they offer services and goods in the expectation of financial returns, but unlike usual recipients of remuneration, they disown the actions for which such payment is made. As claiming reliance on donations and disinterest in returns for the services offered is difficult to uphold and the pursuit of individual economic interests by priests is still viewed with suspicion, the withdrawal of economic agency makes possible an engagement in exchanges and profit-making that upholds the Buddhist ideal of individual detachment from the riches of this world. For some, it offers a business model suited for the challenges of a consumerist society shot through with secularist ideologies, a model that nevertheless maintains a distance from the pursuit of profit.

With the dawn of the "post-*danka* era" (Rowe 2011, 224) and as Buddhist priests increasingly engage with the laity outside of the funerary enclave (Nelson 2013), there comes a time for the Japanese sangha to change the terms of reference in their relations with the laity. Appealing to the institution of donations and to the conscience of lay adherents no longer confers a sense of respect, but rather gives rise to not much more than a suspicion that insincere priests are hoping to obscure the interest they have in profit-making. Under such circumstances, an openly calculative (and precise in pricing) approach presents itself as a viable, if still controversial, alternative. The calculative transparency can convey credibility and fulfil expectations of the laity. But even then, a degree of detachment from the transactional nature of the exchanges confers an ease of mind to some priests. No single model fits all. As the negotiations over the terms of relationship between the Japanese sangha and the laity are ongoing, the cases presented here might give us a hint at what some of the emerging modes might look like.

CHAPTER TWO

Merit, "Corruption," and Economy in the Contemporary Thai Sangha

Thomas Borchert

In May 2017, I stepped into a *wat* (temple) in the Phra Khanong neighborhood in Bangkok, one of the many *wat* that are situated along the canals of the capital of Thailand. I was interviewing monks about their views on politics, the new *sangha-rāt* (supreme patriarch), and whether or not they thought monks should be allowed to vote (which they cannot).[1] My conversations were somewhat eclectic; some monks were happy to talk about politics, while others had no interest in doing so. This meant that I never quite knew what I was going to find when I entered the grounds of a temple. On this particular day, I was looking at some statues that surrounded a *sān* (pavilion) that was separate from the *vihān* (worship hall) and surrounded by trees, creating the effect of a "forest" in the middle of the city. An older monk was sitting outside the pavilion, reading a comic book, and I asked him if he minded chatting with me for a few minutes. He invited me to sit and I asked him a few general questions about the temple, how long he had been there, and so forth. There was a lot of construction going on at a building across the alley and it was difficult to hear him. After a few minutes, I decided that this was probably not worth the time and I stood up to go. As I did so, he asked if I wanted to be blessed for good fortune in the future. Sure, I said, and the two of us went inside the pavilion. He chanted over me, probably one of the standard *paritta* from the Mangala Sutta. He took a bamboo whisk, dipped it into perfumed water, tapped me with it, and then blew on my head. He repeated this sequence with both of my hands. I put my hands to my chest in a *wai* of thanks and was about to leave when he lifted up a tray and said, "Now you should put some *satang* in here." I was a little taken aback by this, as a monk had never asked me for money so directly. Reaching into my pocket, I pulled out a ten-baht note (approximately US$0.30) and put it on the tray. He looked at it and said, "Hmmm, that's so small." I asked him how much I should give, and he said, "100 baht," smiling broadly when I put it on the tray. Having paid up, we then proceeded to talk for a short time about life in the *wat*.

Most Thais, both lay and monastic, would say that this monk acted in a fashion that was deeply inappropriate (*mai somkhuan*), if not outright corrupt (*tujarit*). When he initially mentioned the need for me to contribute some *satang*, I presumed that he was trying to teach me how to be properly respectful. Although we were speaking in Thai and this temple is not in a neighborhood that foreign tourists come to very often, I am a white American and it is not unreasonable to think that I would have little idea how to act properly.[2] Yet it was his actions that were out of the ordinary. Most Thai monks use money, notwithstanding Vinaya injunctions against handling silver and gold. But they do not ask for money for the most part, at least not directly, and if they do, they very rarely say how much. Indeed, it is a minor infraction (*phit*) of the Vinaya for a monk to tell someone how to donate. Moreover, if we think of the paradigmatic act of charity between monks and laypeople in Thailand, the morning alms round (*pindabāt*), it generally entails little to no communication. A monk walks by and stops when there is a layperson waiting to give him food. He does not ask and they simply offer him food.

My encounter with this monk is not the only example of impropriety (financial and otherwise) that we see in contemporary Thai temples. Since the start of the twenty-first century there have been quite a few monks, some quite prominent, who have been accused of corruption. One of the most consequential of these was faced by Somdet Phra Mahā Rajjamangalacharn, more commonly known as Somdet Chuang.[3] Somdet Chuang has for many years been the abbot of Wat Paknām in Thonburi, just outside of Bangkok city limits. He has also been one of the most senior members of the Mahā Thera Samakhom (Supreme Sangha Council or SSC), the institution that is responsible for governing the Thai sangha. Indeed, when the previous *sangha-rāt*, Somdet Phra Ñāṇasaṃvara, died in 2013, Somdet Chuang's name was forwarded by the SSC to the Office of the Prime Minister to be the next supreme patriarch. However, his nomination lingered in limbo for several years, and ultimately, in early 2017, the Thai king, Rama X, appointed Somdet Phramahā Muniwong to be the new *sangha-rāt* of Thailand. While there were several reasons for this failed nomination, perhaps the most prominent was that Somdet Chuang had a tax problem.

Several years earlier, Somdet Chuang had built a large *stūpa* at Wat Paknām that had a small museum inside. One of the displays at the museum contained several imported luxury vehicles. The problem was that it was not clear if Somdet Chuang had ever paid the import fees on the luxury vehicles. Monks are not usually subject to paying taxes in Thailand on their income,[4] but they are technically responsible for paying import duties. While normally a minor issue, in this case, it seemed to have profound consequences. The failure to pay taxes might be interpreted as taking something from the government. At worst, this might mean that Somdet Chuang had committed a *pārājika* offense, a rule that—if true—could cause him to be disrobed. Even if this were not the case, at a bare minimum, this tax problem left a significant stain on Somdet Chuang's candidacy (King-oua 2016).

While this was the surface reason for the stalled candidacy, not very far beneath there were political reasons. These events were taking place at a particularly fraught period in recent Thai history. Since the early years of the 2000s, the Thai population has experienced significant political instability. In 2006, protests against the democratically elected prime minister Thaksin Shinawatra led to a coup and his eventual flight from the country. In the time since the 2006 coup, there have been several different mass protests in Bangkok, rounds of elections, governments invalidated by judicial fiat, two constitutions, and an additional military coup. Many of the protests were indexed by colors, with royalists (anti-Thaksin) wearing yellow shirts and pro-democracy activists (mainly pro-Thaksin) wearing red. The red and yellow shirts also represent deeper factions within Thai society, mapping partly to geographical and class conflict across Thailand. The red shirts have generally been associated with working-class (whether in manufacturing or farming) communities of the north and northeast, while the yellow shirts are most often identified with the Thai center (including Bangkok) and south, and middle and professional class.[5] At the same time, the instability has perhaps been exacerbated by the progressively failing health and eventual death of Rama IX in 2016, who had been king since the 1940s. While Thailand is a constitutional monarchy, and the monarchy is "in the center, above politics," is a common phrase, the palace and the royal family have significant if indirect influence in Thai society (an influence increased by the uneven application of laws about *lèse-majesté*). The late king's decline created a power vacuum that gave oxygen to the factional conflict already in evidence.

These general statements about the Thai political context since the start of the twenty-first century had a very specific consequence for Somdet Chuang's candidacy for the office of *sangha-rāt*. As noted above, Somdet Chuang is the abbot of Wat Paknām which was the temple of Luang Pho Sot, the monk who presumably discovered the meditation method that is at the heart of the Dhammakāya movement. While there is no formal relationship between Wat Dhammakāya and Wat Paknām, most people see Somdet Chuang as having been an ally of the former abbot of Dhammakāya, Venerable Dhammachayo. According to rumors, when the late *sangha-rāt* wrote a letter ordering that Ven. Dhammachayo disrobe in the early 2000s,[6] it was Somdet Chuang who intervened. And in the current moment, when Dhammakāya is under investigation in part because it is presumed to have connections to deposed former prime minister Thaksin Shinawatra, these connections, real or imagined, meant that Somdet Chuang's candidacy became stalled.[7]

These two cases, my experience in Bangkok and the events (and rumors) around the appointment of the supreme patriarch, are of course very different and would seem to have little in common. One is a small, quotidian act and interaction that many Thais would see as inappropriate and unseemly. If it is an infraction of the Vinaya, it is simply a minor one. The other is a set of accusations about tax evasion that had a profound effect on the development of the Thai sangha. Yet they both point to the possibility of corruption in the sangha, of (alleged) acts by monks that are related to financial improprieties. Acts like these bring up the specter of corruption in the sangha.

Discourse about corruption has played an important role in Thai society since five months of protests organized around "corruption" in the government led to a coup in May 2014. While the military coup makers were not explicitly part of the protests, after the coup they took up the claim of corruption as a source of legitimation. At the same time, corruption in the Thai sangha became a more common trope in journalistic accounts. Many of these accounts presume that "true" and "proper" monks should not be concerned with wealth and that finances have a corrupting influence. This is an assumption that we should resist. While it is perhaps uncomfortable for some, it is important to recognize that Buddhist sanghas in Thailand and elsewhere have always been involved with finances, and Buddhists, monastic and lay, being human, have from time to time committed financial improprieties. However, there are moments when these (real or alleged) improprieties gain greater traction as part of a broader narrative about corruption in society or the decline of the sāsanā, the teachings of the Buddha.[8] The 2010s have become such a moment, and this has an impact on the lives of Thai monastics.

In this chapter, I want to consider the economic activities of Thai monks such as donations and merit-making in the context of the political discourse of corruption. Monks regularly engage in a variety of economic activities, but because of their status as having "left home," these activities are always potentially suspect. The current political climate in Thailand means that monks such as Somdet Chuang have become vulnerable to accusations of corruption whether or not they have committed crimes or offenses against the Vinaya. While monastics have developed strategies of distancing that separate them from the appearance of contact with money, these strategies have become far more important in the midst of the effort by the Thai state to reign in monastic financial practice in the name of "good governance" (Larsson 2016b, 25). In order to make this case, I begin with a consideration of monastic economies in Thailand.

FIGURE 2.1 Statues of monks, used to collect donations at a temple in Chiang Mai, 2013 (Photo: Thomas Borchert).

Dāna and Economy

In July 2018, I was walking through the Pratunām neighborhood of Bangkok, and I encountered a group of people lined up in front of a small hotel and restaurant who were waiting with trays of food. To the side was a group of monks who were chanting. As I watched, the monks finished chanting and then walked over to the people in front of the hotel, carrying the bowls (*bāt*) that they used to receive alms. One by one, the monks walked by each person and received food. After this was completed, they got into a van with the offerings and drove off. Later, I spoke with the organizer, the owner/manager of the hotel. She told me that she had organized this alms-making opportunity every Friday for eighteen years and had only missed a week in 2010 when the government cracked down on "red shirt" protests that had taken over the city center (less than a mile from the hotel). The practice had begun because the hotel had been having some conflicts between its employees and she thought that perhaps a weekly experience of listening to the monks and making merit (*tham bun*) would help resolve these conflicts. While she did not go into a long disquisition about the importance of gifts (*dāna*) and merit in contemporary society, she clearly saw tangible benefits to sponsor it, enough to justify a 3,800 baht investment each week for eighteen years.[9]

The act of making merit, such as I witnessed in Bangkok in 2018, is a central part of contemporary Theravāda societies, and Thailand is no exception. Indeed, making offerings to Thai monks, whether in a planned, formal way such as the above description or as a part of the acts of monks going on their alms round (*pindabāt*) around city or village, is a daily part of life for many if not most Thais. The *dāna* that Thais provide to monastics comes in many forms: food, land, goods, and money. It is well known that Theravāda monks following the Pāli Vinaya are not supposed to own anything beyond the eight requisites;[10] it is equally well known that male and female monastics do own things beyond the requisites and probably always have. This has produced something of a conundrum within the study of Buddhism, especially that of Pāli Buddhist societies: How are we to think about the goods that come to monks and nuns, especially those that are referred to as *dāna*, gifts which are said to produce merit? The conundrum has been exacerbated by Mauss's (in)famous footnote about South Asian religions, which suggests that gifts in this context are free of obligation to pay back or reciprocate, an obligation which Mauss argues as universal except for this one exception (Sihlé 2015, 353). As Sihlé notes, there has been much confusion over how to think about these interactions, with language of *dāna* being used to describe a variety of actions, some of which have a market logic while others do not (Sihlé 2015, 355, 357, 362, 367). He has argued, rightly, that while scholars sometimes refer to *dāna* interactions as "exchange" (e.g., Swearer 1995, 22), there is at most a "weak form" of reciprocity as the monk does not give the merit to the lay donor (Sihlé 2015, 365).

Even if monks are not responsible for paying anything back, *dāna* interactions help structure relationships between monastics and laity. In Thailand, merit-making interactions such as the daily *pindabāt* are often anonymous and lacking in personal content (Bunnag 1973, 60). However, they can also be an important part of a broader relationship. In Bangkok in 2014, while taking my son to school, I observed a monk stop at the same house several times a week. On a number of mornings, this monk would even ring the doorbell to let the lay supporter know that he had come. Such an action seemed out of the ordinary to me and perhaps even unseemly because it meant he was asking for a donation (like the monk telling me that my donation was too small). However, when I asked several monks about it, they all told me it was more likely that this monk knew that the laywoman was physically incapacitated in some way. By ringing the doorbell, he made it easier for her to make merit. That merit-making is only one aspect of the *dāna* relationship is evident in the literature. Joanna Cook (2010), for example, has shown how *mae chii* (female renunciants) and monks will sometimes use *dāna* interactions to "reset" their relationships, using a formulaic and "anonymous" act of giving as a mechanism to clear the relationship of whatever conflict had developed. Similarly, Charlie Carstens (2020) has written how *dāna* becomes the basis of a richer relationship between a monk and a lay family in Myanmar. What had once been an obligation-less gift from a lay donor to a monk became the basis of a patron-client relationship (and inverted in the process) when the monk disrobed. Part of what these observations imply is that there are a variety of gifting interactions within Theravāda contexts, some of which are anonymous and some of which are not; some of which are seen by the actors as *dāna* and some not (Borchert 2020; see Sihlé 2015, 360, on the diversity of these gifts).

There is a significant amount of opacity regarding *dāna*, wealth, and the sangha in Thailand. In terms of sheer numbers, the vast majority of *dāna* are small. Monks receive food and sometimes small amounts of money, as described above, and every *wat* has a number of boxes throughout the grounds (for example in the *vihān* or in front of images) which are for people to donate money for the upkeep of the facilities, to pay for the education of novices, or for similar purposes. These boxes are not seen as inappropriate because they are not for individual monks and there is no direction about them; they only provide the opportunity to make merit. The amount of money that flows into them varies significantly. Most donations are small, but in the aggregate, these donations present a significant flow of wealth into the sangha. *Wat* are varied places and many receive funds that are insufficient for the upkeep of the grounds, let alone the service projects that a temple may undertake, but others are clearly quite wealthy. Nonetheless, there are not robust mechanisms of accounting; or rather, there are not system-wide (sangha-wide) practices of accounting. Indeed one of the primary findings of a 2012 report from the National Institute of Development Administration was that "most temples do not have a systematic financial management structure," and that rules and regulations that foster the principles of good financial governance in temples were lacking (Nada 2012, 2). Instead, individual *wat* engage in accounting practices with significant variation in its quality and "very little accountability and transparency" (Larsson 2016b, 22). Until quite recently, there have been very few controls over the flow of wealth into and out of the Thai sangha.

Regardless of whether *dāna* is a "free gift" or of the nature of the exchanges, Thai monks are embedded in economies. They are "paid" for services even if they do not use the language of payment, as when they perform funeral rites (again Sihlé 2015, 355–6); they serve as both patrons and clients within networks of exchange;[11] and they are embedded in the modern economy of Thailand. They either use money or it is used on their behalf. They are responsible for paying bills or seeing that they are paid, even if they are naïve about economic matters (Bunnag 1973, 207–9). As Larsson notes, while "abbots are not supposed to handle money and finance personally ... they very often take direct charge of temple finances" (Larsson 2016b, 22). There are exceptions and limits to their engagement in the Thai economy, and some Thais decry this participation (e.g., Thammapāla 2018), but Thai monks are clearly engaging in economic activities (Suraphot 2018).

Similarly, individual monks have extremely varied economic conditions. Variables include the socioeconomic background of the monk, their level of education before and after ordaining, the wealth of their home *wat*, their time in robes, and the number (and wealth) of their disciples (*luksit*).[12] Thai monks and novices do not have to pay for lodging at a *wat*, and they receive their food either through the daily alms round or through donations to the *wat*. Novices who are attending a monastic high school generally do not go on the daily alms round, but rather *wat* have a cafeteria that prepares the food for them. In contemporary Thailand, it is rare that monks do not have enough food; indeed, the opposite is more likely to be the case (Suhartino 2018). They generally have smartphones, many of them have bank accounts using their monastic name, though many also have bank accounts in their preordination name that follow them into the *wat*. Monks also have credit and debit cards and many of them have their own computer that they keep in their dorm rooms (*kuti*). Monks receive an income from a variety of sources, only some of which are embedded in religious duties and relationships. Prior to making a few general comments about the economic conditions of monks, I will describe the situations of three different monks.[13]

Phra Khru is in his late twenties. A Mahānikāya monk from the North, he is currently studying marketing at Rajabaht University. He is also a social studies teacher at a public school that is adjacent to the temple where he lives. His primary income comes from this school, where he earns 2,500 baht each month. He told me that he rarely receives any money when he goes on *pindabāt* each morning, just food, and while there are occasional opportunities to attend rituals such as funerals, teaching or studying takes the vast majority of his time. When I asked, though, he thought that his income was probably about 35,000–40,000 baht each year. He receives a salary from the school for ten months; the remainder comes from the occasional ritual he attends or by going on *pindabāt*. He described his expenses as fairly minimal. He has a phone, he buys books, and he normally takes a taxi to attend classes at Rajabaht (his parents pay the university tuition). These expenses are about 1,000–1,500 baht a month. His biggest expense is for accident and life insurance, which is about 15,000 baht a year (the recipients of the life insurance, he said, are his family).

Phra Asa is a Mahānikāya monk in his late thirties from the Northeast, who is usually engaged in some sort of volunteer activity. He teaches in prisons and returns to his home village not infrequently to teach at the middle school he attended. I have also gone with him to craft training sessions where he would give a dharma talk. When he does this, he is often given a monetary gift in response, with varying amounts. As with chanting at funerals, these depended on the layperson. Some gave 200 baht to each monk, others as much as 1,000 baht, and so it was impossible to say with certainty what he might receive with any given activity. He was the least certain of the monks I discuss here about his annual income, thinking that it was probably about 50,000 a year, but I suspect he really does not know.

He pays about 500 a month for his phone and said that he sometimes goes to restaurants (when I attend events with him, I always pay for the taxi) but couldn't think of other regular expenses. He also has a life insurance policy (with his parents, brother, and his brother's children as the beneficiaries) of 40,000 baht per year (in other words, this takes up most of his income).[14] He has a bank account and uses a debit card.

Phra Annam is a monk from the Annam Nikāya, the group of monks who follow Vietnamese forms of Buddhism. He is a PhD student and has lived in Bangkok for about fifteen years. He has the highest income of the monks that I discuss here, suggesting that his annual salary was about 100,000 baht. His primary source of income is translation work that he does for a company that makes and sells statues to Buddhists in Vietnam. Several times a year he travels to Vietnam for this company, for which he would receive 10,000 baht per statue. He also supplemented his income through chanting at funerals, where he said that amounts vary from 200 to 2,000 baht per performance. When the monks at his temple went to a funeral or other such ritual, the abbot of the temple supplemented the gift from the lay sponsor by giving 800 baht to each monk. He estimated that he needed about 3,000 baht each month to cover phone and utilities and food. He also pays his own university tuition of about 2,000 baht a year, though previously it had been covered by a relative.

There are several points to be made here. None of the monks felt particularly well-off but they also recognized that they were relatively comfortable. As noted above, their housing and food needs were all taken care of through the *wat* they lived in and by going on *pindabāt*. All of them had traveled abroad and did not express feeling cash-strapped in any way. They all referred to performing at funerals as a possible source of regular income even though they never knew what they would receive because it was up to the lay donors. All three also expressed that they tended not to engage in this work too much, because they were busy with other activities and did not need the income. None of them expressed any concern with using money in their daily lives (cf. Thammapāla 2018).

Most of them also described the money they received as *dāna*, not as a salary (*ngen-duean*, literally the "month-money") which implies a fixed and regular amount of money. While Phra Khru received a salary and referred to it as such, the three monks and others I have talked with during these interviews say that Thai monks do not receive a salary unless they have a job such as being a teacher in a public school.[15] Some monks, primarily high-ranking monks who are abbots (or deputy abbots of large *wat*), receive a monthly allowance from the National Office of Buddhism. This is referred to as *nittayaphat*, and according to Jane Bunnag, is meant to relieve senior monks of the responsibility of going on a daily alms round (Bunnag 1973, 61, 197–8). The amount of this stipend varies according to the monk's educational attainments, rank in the sangha, and the size and type of temple. Abbots whose temples have schools attached to them, for example, receive a higher stipend. For example, an assistant abbot at a temple in Bangkok with a public school attached told me that the abbot received 4,000 baht a month (the assistant abbot himself did not receive anything perhaps because he did not work at the school). Another monk, the abbot of a small temple with five monks just outside the walls of the old city in Chiang Mai, told me that he received 2,700 baht per month but only for ten months a year (during the other months, this income would go to a local hospital).

Monks strongly objected when I referred to this monthly income as a "salary." They told me that it was money that it was not really even for the monk to use himself but was to be used for the upkeep of the *wat*.[16] Moreover, they told me, the allowance is completely insufficient for this capacity. According to the assistant abbot in Bangkok, the abbot's *nitthayaphat* barely covered the utility bills at the *wat*, let alone other problems encountered in the maintenance of *wat* facilities. In order to defray these costs, *wat* often have to diversify their activities. Temples may own significant land, donated by lay supporters, that can be sold or leased. Many *wat* in Bangkok end up using temple grounds as parking lots. Most of the monks that I have talked to about this, however, do not know how much money these enterprises bring into their *wat*'s coffers. This may bespeak genuine ignorance,[17] that they are uncomfortable talking about temple finances with strangers or simply that the economic aspects of the lives of individual Thai monks are at best obscure. Indeed, Phra Khru mentioned with a combination of chagrin and humor that laypeople had no idea of the financial difficulties monks sometimes faced.

The Appearance of Corruption and Governing the Thai Sangha

This does not mean that the Thai state has not been concerned with monastic finances. This became clear in May 2018 when the government sought to arrest six well-known monks of the Thai sangha. Five of these monks were quite senior, including three who had been members of the SSC until their arrest. These five monks were being called out on charges of embezzling funds from temples (Matichon 2018; Styllis 2018; Wassayos 2018).[18] The embezzlement charges are all associated with a plan that has been in place for a number of years to maintain *wat*. According to a *Bangkok Post* report from 2017, the National Office of Buddhism apportions 500 million baht each year for the maintenance of temples. In the case in question, the senior monks have been charged with accepting money for the maintenance of *wat* but then improperly handling the remainder. While the timing of the arrests may, perhaps, have been a surprise,[19] this step on the part of the national police is simply a key moment in a campaign that has gone on over several years, focused on how *wat* are funded and managed. While historically the Thai political system has been more concerned with limiting monastic involvement in politics rather than commerce (Larsson 2016b), this case implies that the government is now more explicitly concerned with adding transparency to sangha accounting practices and "cleaning up" the sangha.

However, as with the case of Somdet Chuang's candidacy to become supreme patriarch, there is a political subtext to these efforts to eliminate corruption. The 2014 military coup that brought the current government into power was preceded by six months of protests led by an organization called the People's Democratic Reform Committee, a royalist organization that argued that the government under Yingluck Shinawatra was hopelessly corrupt. Their slogans were about "reform before election" and a need to "Shut down Bangkok, Restart Thailand" (complete with pictures of power buttons on computers). The coup leaders similarly talked about the need to root out corruption as a justification for the coup, and they have justified their continued control of the country through their capacity to overcome corruption.[20] Over the course of the last four years, the government has sought to extend their control over individuals and institutions that may oppose them, and certain parts of the sangha have been an ongoing source of attention. In particular, in 2016, the police shut down Wat Pha Luang Ta Bua Yannasampanno, called the "Tiger Temple," for practices of breeding tigers for sale, and in 2017, they invaded Wat Dhammakāya for ongoing financial improprieties. On the surface, these are reasonable actions. For decades, the Tiger Temple has been the target of conservation groups for its practices, and the Dhammakāya organization has been the subject of concern since at least the late 1990s (Fedde 2016; Scott 2009). At the same time, the widespread presumption of the links between the Dhammakāya organization and Thaksin Shinawatra (referred to in the introduction) also makes it a likely target for a government that sees the Shinawatra family as the height of corruption. In other words, although the Dhammakāya organization might handle its finances in ways that are problematic and perhaps illegal, they are also on the wrong side of the current government. It is no coincidence that the proposals to reform the sangha's financial management practices echo the government's rhetoric of "good governance" (Larsson 2016b, 25).

While the current government of Thailand may or may not have been targeting certain monks when they focus on monastic finances, many monks themselves believe this to be the case. In July 2018, I interviewed fourteen monks in Bangkok and Chiang Mai about changes taking place in the Thai sangha, and the arrests of the monks in May figured prominently in our conversations.[21] All of the monks saw the arrests as motivated by politics at least as much as by alleged illegalities on the part of the monks. They agreed that the monks had acted improperly, but only two thought they were guilty of anything that resembled embezzlement. The other twelve were convinced that the monks had not stolen money but were guilty of nothing more than improper paperwork. They disagreed about whether it was because these monks were ignorant, naïve about politics and finance, or lazy but they were convinced that those arrested had not broken the second *pārājika* precept about taking that which is not given. They said it was political in part because on the same day, another monk was arrested, *Luang Pu* Buddha Issara. This was a monk who had been a central part of the political protests of 2014 and in general was supportive of the military government. He was not a part of the embezzlement of *wat* reconstruction funds but was arrested on a variety of charges stemming from the protests four years before. The monks I interviewed claimed that Buddha Issara was arrested as a pawn in a game of chess and as a balance to the other monks who were arrested. The logic, I was told, is that it showed the government was not just against monks who were seen as "red-shirt" monks. Whether or not this is the case is unclear but not relevant to the point. What matters is that a number of monks think that political actors in Thailand (and in particular the military government, though perhaps also the new king) were using the excuse of financial improprieties to pursue a political agenda.

Monastic Finances and Anxiety about "Corruption"

While the events of May 2018 would seem to be fairly distant from the lives of most monks, it becomes clear in conversations that Thai monks are concerned that they themselves might well become the targets of demands for religious purification with regard to finances. This became evident in a conversation with a Chiang Mai abbot regarding a new building being constructed at his *wat*. While the monk handled the day-to-day management of the construction project, he had a disciple (*luksit*) handle all of the finances for the building. It is common for a *wat* to have a layperson be responsible for finances either partially or in total so that the abbot does not have to touch money if he prefers not to (see, e.g., Bunnag 1973, 131), but this *luksit* was not a member of the temple committee. Rather he was financing the construction of the building. The monk told me that whenever a bill came, for either materials or services, he would simply forward it to his *luksit*. This provided him with great relief, as it meant that he would never be put in the kind of position that *Somdet* Chuang was in.

The feeling of pressure about financial improprieties is not limited to this monk. One Dhammayut monk in Bangkok told me that he loves going out to Suvarnabhumi, the international airport, because it is like being in a foreign country. He can buy things and use the ATMs to get his money without difficulty. He told me that although there were many ATMs near the *wat* where he lived, he would never use them because people would criticize him for doing so. He imitated their comments, saying, "Oh, the monk has so much money!" and "Why do you need to use all that money?"

It was not clear from our conversation if he had ever received this criticism or it was simply an anxiety. However, this same monk also told me that the internet had transformed his life once he figured out how to utilize it properly for e-commerce. He told me that he used to ask lay supporters to do everything for him, but when studying abroad in India, he realized that he could do many things for himself without compromising his spiritual state. Still he had to hide these actions, not because they were illegal or even inappropriate but because he was concerned about lay criticism. Michael Chladek (2018) has argued that monks use an "imagined lay voice" when trying to discipline novices. These monks will often tell their student-novices that if they act inappropriately it will hurt the faith of lay supporters. The airport loving monk seems to have this same imagined voice, but for him it is oppressive, rather than a source of disciplinary strength.

Perhaps in light of the arrests in May 2018, laypeople have begun to think more explicitly about how much money monks should be allowed to keep. When I was interviewing monks about the arrests in July 2018, one of them told me about a rule being discussed that would limit a monk's personal bank account to only 3,000 baht. The rationale for this was that monks should not have money of their own. However, when I asked other monks about this proposed rule, they clarified that the first monk had himself misunderstood what was happening. There was no rule—at least not yet. Rather, there had been chatter on Facebook criticizing monks for their wealth and that a rule limiting their capacity to accumulate money would be valuable. When I asked Phra Khru what he would do if his bank account were limited to 3,000 baht per month, he got an impish smile on his face and said that he would spend it all on books and speakers and electronic equipment until he had so much stuff there would be nowhere to put it. The point is less about the constraints that are actually being put on monks in the current moment and more on the sense among Thai monks that the current political conditions are increasingly restrictive for them, and that they are under surveillance in ways that they had not been several years ago.

Conclusion

The issue at the heart of this chapter is really less about the finances of monks and more about the context in which these finances are being used. A number of years ago, Frank Reynolds observed that "Theravāda interpretations of the Dhamma from the very beginning, have incorporated a more or less positive valorization of wealth, including material resources, goods and services" (Reynolds 1985, 63–4). While monks were generally precluded from gaining wealth, there have been "periods of cyclic oscillation between periods that justified monastic accumulation of wealth, and periods of monastic reform accompanied by the condemnation of monastic wealth"

(Reynolds 1985, 73). This is consistent with the argument being made by the Thai scholar of Buddhism Suraphot Taweesak in light of the May arrests. Suraphot (2018) observes that according to the *dhamma-vinaya*, monks should not accumulate wealth, but he also notes that these regulations are reflective of the context of India several millennia ago and not of the current lives of Thai monks. In order to function in the current moment, he says, monks have to use money.

If this is the case, it helps to make sense of the two monks with which I began this chapter. The monk who asked me for money was acting inappropriately perhaps, but his action was unremarkable. It probably happens many times a day as monks work their way through the days trying to function within the constraints of the discipline, as well as gossip or criticism of the people. Yet because at the heart of the discipline there are claims that money causes problems, it means that monks are always vulnerable to claims that they are acting inappropriately. Somdet Chuang may not have committed a great crime with the taxes of the luxury cars (and he may not have committed a crime at all), but the finances of these cars made him vulnerable to accusations of impropriety. In other words, the problem is not money but rather the politics of money in the current moment.

CHAPTER THREE

Ritual Virtuosity, Large-Scale Priest-Patron Networks, and the Ethics of Remunerated Ritual Services in Northeast Tibet

Nicolas Sihlé

The provision of Buddhist domestic ritual services (individual- or household-level apotropaic rituals, healing rituals, propitiation of deities, etc., carried out in a Buddhist idiom by Buddhist religious specialists) and the patronage relations within which this activity unfolds constitute an understudied domain in the larger field of Buddhist studies. As we will see, under certain circumstances, providing such ritual services can become the object of ethical critiques, even in strongly ritual-centered forms of Buddhism such as Tibetan tantric Buddhism. The emic value hierarchies that these critiques reflect (soteriological vs. worldly orientations, etc.) may have influenced the choices of a Western scholarship sometimes prone itself to Protestant biases (which express partly similar value hierarchies: higher valuation of the soteriological, the doctrinal/textual, etc.). In any case, if the rituals' "internal" ritual/religious logics in themselves have been deemed worthy of interest,[1] the economics and social embeddedness of this "lesser" dimension of Buddhist religion has received, on the whole, only much more modest scholarly attention.[2]

As I have argued in a recent overview of the anthropological treatment of the "gift" and other religiously inflected modes of economic transfer in Buddhist contexts (Sihlé 2015), there are also significant empirical complexities in conceptualizing the economic dimension of the provision of ritual services. In emic terminologies, in particular in Theravāda contexts, one finds a strong tendency to euphemize the remuneration of ritual services, with preference given to terms like *dāna* (a Pāli/Sanskrit term which primarily refers to Buddhist "gifts" in the sense of alms or donations) or its vernacular equivalents (2015, 355, 370–1). Here Bourdieu would speak of a "euphemization" or "misrecognition" of the economic nature of the interaction (1998, 114, 118–19). Following Testart, who has critically reexamined the anthropological conceptualizations of the "gift" and emphasized in particular the need to distinguish more rigorously between "gift" and "exchange" (Testart 2007, 2013), I have argued that the paradigmatic Buddhist "gift" (alms, donations) is largely devoid of reciprocity (Sihlé 2015, 358–69), whereas the exchange nature of the transactions centered on ritual services needs to be recognized, even if the provision of ritual services and their remuneration do not align on all counts with the features of market exchange (2015, 355–6).

This chapter aims at introducing an example of religious patronage networks (in the northeast of Tibet)[3] that is striking in terms of demographics, the spatial scope, and the prestige involved. There is here something unique, possibly unequaled in the ethnographic record, in terms of the size and geographic scope of the phenomenon, but I do not wish to dwell on this idea of uniqueness. The question is: How should we deal with the ethical critiques that are prompted by some of this (sometimes substantial) income-generating ritual activity? In keeping with anthropology's disciplinary basics, I eschew a narrow focus on these ethical discourses and stress how essential it is to contextualize them within what underlies the priest-patron networks and relations: essentially, a thick, more complex, partially integrated bundle of different registers of value.

The Repkong Ngakmang: A Massive Pool of Ritual Specialists in Northeast Tibet

The socioeconomic organization of the type of Buddhist clergy to be examined here is strikingly different from standard monastic patterns. Quite unlike other forms of Buddhism, Tibetan Buddhism is marked (and has been so throughout most of its history) by a twofold clergy:[4] on the one hand monastics and on the other householder religious specialists, commonly called *ngakpa* [sngags pa][5] and most often referred to as "tantrists" in Western languages. These non-monastic religious figures are primarily male and most often belong to patrilineal family lineages; they strongly specialize in tantric ritual practice (Figure 3.1).[6] Whereas monks and nuns reside primarily in cenobitic monastic institutions belonging to more or less structured religious orders, *ngakpa* constitute a less organized and more decentralized form of religious clergy. The monk versus tantrist duality (in terms of mental categories, if not of actual religious persons) is present throughout Tibetan areas—with linguistic variations however: although *ngakpa* is the most commonly used term across Tibet, the terminology for tantrists varies from region to region or sometimes even locally (Sihlé 2013a, 288–92). (The same twofold clergy is found also in the Tibetan Bön [Bon] religion, which is religiously and sociologically very similar to Tibetan Buddhism and in particular to the Nyingma [rNying ma], the order of the "Ancient [translation of the tantras]," with which most tantrists are associated. Only a small minority of Tibetans, however, are Bönpos [Bon po], or adherents of Bön.) Monks and tantrists share to quite some extent a common religious universe and their practices overlap substantially. Thus, monks are generally trained in tantric practice; however, tantrists are more exclusively so, and when it comes to ritual power, and in particular to its more violent uses, such as when a powerful exorcism is deemed necessary, across Tibet it is rather to tantrists that one typically turns. As for spirit mediums (an important presence in Repkong County; cf. Buffetrille 2008; Makley 2014; Reb gong pa mKhar rtse rgyal 2009; Snying bo rgyal and Rino 2008), most of them in this part of Tibet are laymen, but in rare cases they can be simultaneously tantrists (one will be briefly mentioned below).

FIGURE 3.1 The dual clergy of Tibetan Buddhism: tantrist (here in the form of a virtuoso adept) and monk, Khyunggön [Khyung dgon] temple, 2012 (Photo: Nicolas Sihlé).

Sociologically, the general picture, in most Tibetan areas, is one of more or less isolated family lines of tantrists (e.g., Sihlé 2009). In some Tibetan-speaking areas of the Himalayas as well as in parts of Amdo (northeast Tibet), one finds what can be called "village communities" of tantrists (Sihlé 2013a, 78 and passim): villages with substantial proportions of such family lines, often centered—at least for a large part of the community's religious life—on a temple functioning as the main place for the local tantrists' ritual gatherings. In some cases, virtually all of the village's family lines—or "houses," as they are often referred to—are associated with a tantrist identity, which does not mean, however, that in each one there is a tantrist at every generation. In Amdo some of these villages are known precisely as "*ngakpa* villages," *ngakdé* [sngags sde].

One county in eastern Amdo, called Repkong [Reb gong, Reb kong],[7] is particularly renowned for its large numbers of tantrists. With perhaps 1,500–2,000 tantrists out of a population of roughly 80,000 ethnic Tibetans, the density of tantrists is equivalent to that of monks—in a Tibetan context already known for its "mass monasticism." This demographic mass and density are unparalleled in other Tibetan areas. Beyond the similarity in demographic weight, it should be noted, however, that the monastic clergy is much more organized. Furthermore, most monasteries belong to the dominant Geluk [dGe lugs] order, which has enjoyed for centuries, in Repkong and throughout large parts of the Tibetan cultural area, privileged associations with the centers of political power—when the Geluk hierarchs and monasteries were not in fact the actual wielders of power. Tantrists have thus generally occupied a sociopolitically somewhat subaltern position in Tibetan societies. This is nuanced, however, by their associations with strong ritual power.

In this respect, the Buddhist tantrists of Repkong have been well known since the early nineteenth century under a prestigious collective designation, "the Repkong Tantrist Collectivity, the 1,900 Ritual Dagger Holders," Repkong Ngakmang Purtok Tong dang Gupgya [Reb gong sngags mang phur thogs stong dang dgu brgya]—or often just "the Repkong Tantrist Collectivity," Repkong Ngakmang, for short.[8] The ritual daggers, *purpa* [phur pa], that occur in this name are key implements used in violent ritual activity such as that aiming at the destruction of demonic forces (or other enemies) and, as such, these objects are symbolically associated with the figure of the tantrist. The Repkong Ngakmang is, in Anderson's sense, only an imagined collectivity. It consists of individuals living in several dozens of villages across the county (and even somewhat beyond its contemporary boundaries) and is largely devoid of centralized hierarchy or other mode of overall structure. Beyond the shared designation and identity, this collectivity manifests primarily (and metonymically, as never more than a fraction of the tantrists take part) in a number of large annual ritual gatherings (Sihlé 2013b). Partially in relation with this prestigious collective designation, the Repkong tantrists have a reputation of great numbers and (collectively and individually) of impressive ritual power; and thus, they are sought after, well beyond the bounds of Repkong, for their ritual services.

The economy of tantrists' households is a mix of secular activities (like any other households—although selling livestock is seen as sinful and frowned upon) and religious forms of income: primarily the remunerated provision of ritual services to others, as well as, occasionally, donations received at distributions in the context of ritual gatherings (on this latter domain, see Sihlé 2013b). To give a sense of the orders of magnitude involved here, based on figures from 2015, one should note that the most substantial annual income in most Repkong households is derived from the collecting, in May–June, of "caterpillar-fungus" or *ophiocordyceps sinensis* (a mushroom that is sold for high prices on urban Chinese markets); this income may reach figures like 10,000 yuan (roughly 1,400 US dollars) per household. In comparison, donations received at the largest ritual gatherings of tantrists rarely go beyond 500 yuan (70 dollars), and the total of such donations probably never exceeds twice this sum over the course of one year. The income derived from ritual services is generally much greater. For one day of ritual service, a modest patron may offer his priest 40–50 yuan (6–7 dollars), but a more affluent patron might offer ten times more or, for instance, invite the priest to officiate for one week and remunerate him with up to 2,500–3,000 yuan (350–400 dollars). The latter figures are considerable sums for local standards: only somewhat successful businesspeople or higher-level officials (one should add here also figures of the higher religious clergy) earn that much (or more) on a daily or weekly basis. (Of course, it is only occasionally that tantrists would make such an income.)

Providing ritual services to the laity and deriving part of their sustenance from the remuneration they receive on such occasions are part of Tibetan tantrists' typical profile. If one were to adopt a "religious market" approach to the Repkong Ngakmang phenomenon, one could suggest that, due to its demographically massive character, the local (Repkong County level) offer of ritual expertise greatly exceeds the local needs. In effect, the patronage relationships that have appeared over time between Repkong tantrists and lay households from other counties (located sometimes within more distant prefectures) generate a substantial part of many local tantrists' activity as providers of ritual services. Two main scenarios are described by my local interlocutors: some tantrists, in need of income, have actively sought patrons in other areas, but sometimes they have been contacted by laypersons with ritual needs who have turned to Repkong on account of the great renown of its tantrists. When patrons are satisfied with the first encounter and have a long-term need for a reliable provider of ritual services (on both an annual and possibly occasional basis), a lasting relationship can develop. The result is a massive pool of ritual specialists endowed with various degrees of virtuosity and/or prestige, whose activity spreads across a wide region, up to several hundred kilometers away from Repkong. The Repkong tantrists also provide ritual services within their county itself: for instance, they virtually all take part in funerary rituals in their own village communities and a number of them are called for a variety of other ritual services in their own communities and, for some of them, in other villages or in Rongwo (Ch. Tongren), the main county town, as well.

Methodologically, this is a challenging object of study, due to its size and the necessity of multisited investigation (both within Repkong and far beyond), not to mention the usual difficulties of fieldwork in Tibetan areas within the PRC. My fieldwork on the Repkong Ngakmang, in and around the county, has spread so far over a period of more than fifteen years (2003–18), with a total of eleven months on-site. It has involved countless hours of conversations with dozens of tantrists from many parts of Repkong, focusing on individual experiences and perspectives, including village-level assessments offered by certain informants, as well as observations of their ritual activity, primarily within the county but also further afield, by following close acquaintances among the Repkong tantrists.

The data presented here offer a picture that is incomplete but indicative of a number of major trends. Figure 3.2 gives a rough overall view of the main counties outside of Repkong in which the Repkong tantrists are active, with the arrowhead sizes giving a sense of the relative importance of the ties with these areas. The main points I wish to highlight here are the following:

1. The main destinations are pastoral areas, in particular the Tsekhok [rTse khog] County right to the south of Repkong, as well as the much more distant Temchen [Them chen] County in the far north of Amdo. The lower-lying and less pastoral areas to the north of Repkong have a substantial *ngakpa* presence themselves; furthermore, pastoralists have a reputation for being pious and generous patrons.

2. As exemplified by the case of Temchen (a major destination of Repkong tantrists), these ritual specialists are called to officiate, often annually, in places that are several hundred kilometers away. I know of no other comparable case in which a massive and prestigious local pool of ritual specialists numbering in the hundreds has such a wide sphere of activity.

3. A few Repkong tantrists have set up relations with affluent (mostly Han) lay patrons living in large Chinese cities. (This still limited phenomenon is represented by the thin arrow pointing "out" of the map, eastwards.) This echoes a pattern that has developed perhaps more substantially in Tibetan monastic contexts (see Caple 2015; Jones 2011; Smyer Yü 2012).

4. With regard to the Bönpo tantrists in Repkong, the only substantial patronage links with areas outside the county that I am aware of are with another Tibetan area that counts a sizeable Bönpo population, namely the high pasturelands of Nakchu [Nag chu], in the north

of Lhasa—an area more than a thousand kilometers away by road, where Amdo dialects are not spoken. Generally speaking, some Bönpo tantrists have Buddhist patrons, but in Repkong this is today less often the case than it used to be in pre-1950 society.[9] (In this chapter, the predominant focus will be on the Buddhist tantrists.)

The case of one particularly active Repkong tantrist, with quite a reputation as a ritualist, will give a more individual-level view of the preceding elements. This tantrist, whom I will call Dorjé Gyel [rDo rje rgyal],[10] belongs to a renowned village community of tantrists of Repkong. I have known him in his late forties, an age in which many key household duties can be left to the adults of the younger generation (one of his daughters is married and lives with her husband and young children in the house). This explains partly the impressive proportion of his time that Dorjé Gyel is able to devote to his ritual activities: he takes part in village-level as well as larger, supra-local ritual gatherings roughly 100 days per year and is busy with providing ritual services during a substantial part of the remaining time. (On some years he also devotes part of the winter to retreats for personal practice.) He has well-established, long-term patronage relationships with more than 100 households within Repkong itself, including a cluster of more than seventy composing an entire village in one of the outlying parts

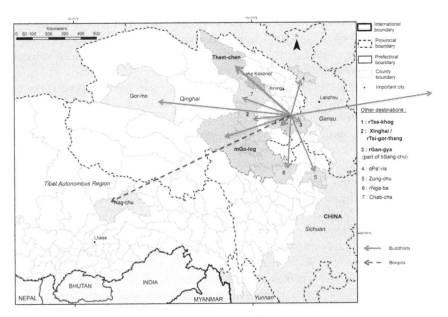

FIGURE 3.2 Spatial extension of the Repkong tantrists' ritual activity (main destinations, copyright Nicolas Sihlé and Jerôme Picard, CNRS, used with permission).

of the county. His main concentrations of patrons outside of Repkong are found in Tsekhok (number 1 in the map) and Temchen counties, in which he has roughly thirty patron households each—but he has also officiated in a number of other counties. He is very frequently solicited and often has to decline requests for ritual services. This activity is, in his case, a substantial component of the household economy.

In Dorjé Gyel's activity one finds also a special, rather rare, variant of the patronage pattern based on domestic ritual services, namely ritual services provided to (ad hoc or institutionalized) groupings of houses. Thus it may happen that in a *tsowa* [tsho ba], or residence-based village subunit (cf. Langelaar 2017), a number of untimely deaths occur; a powerful tantrist or a group of such tantrists are typically called to exorcise the agents of misfortune that are responsible for the calamity.

One of the reasons for Dorjé Gyel's solid reputation as a ritual specialist lies in his active involvement in the large-scale ritual gatherings of the Repkong Ngakmang. His mastery of the texts and their chanting, as well as of the rituals' structure, and his powerful voice have led him to occupy at various (local or supra-local) levels the key position of the ritual's chant master, *umdzé* [dbu mdzad]—the one who intones alone the first line of each section of the ritual and guides the ritual performance from the beginning to the end. This has surely contributed to establishing his reputation as a ritual expert. His personality—for instance his confident style—has probably played a role as well.

There is, however, a question of hierarchy and balance between the major components of one's activity: from a purely religious perspective, personal practice and, to some extent, collective ritual practice are far more valued than the provision of ritual services, which should not occupy most of one's time. It is striking that the most general term for domestic rituals performed for a patron, namely *drongchok* [grong chog, lit. "house ritual"], is often associated, at least in my experience of the Amdo/Repkong context, with ethically problematic overtones (with regard to the priests).[11] Along the same lines, a slightly derogatory term for a tantrist who devotes a large amount of his time to the performance of ritual services is *drongchokpa* [grong chog pa, lit. "one (who performs) house rituals"]. Thus, in terms of fieldwork methodology, the more cautious way to start a conversation with a Repkong tantrist about his own activity in such matters is to studiously steer clear of the word *drongchok*—something that took me some time to understand and which definitely impacted my first, embarrassingly awkward attempts to explore this topic. With regard to the ritual activity of interlocutors that one knows well, the word *drongchok* can be used, but one still needs to delicately steer away from unpleasant potential overtones—or, alternatively, if one so wishes, to tackle headlong the topic of the ethical questions raised by (inordinately active) involvement in this domain.

One is thus here in an ethically ambiguous domain, marked by both the strong value attached to ritual mastery and expectations of moderation on behalf of the ritual experts, but the relations between priest and patron are based on a much thicker bundle of values than these two simple factors. In order to provide a measure of ethnographic depth, let us follow a party of Repkong tantrists to a small locality in Chapcha [Chab cha], a county some 400 kilometers to the west by road, high up in the Amdo pasturelands.

Three Ritual Heavyweights and an Assistant on the Grasslands

The party of four men was gone before I even knew it. In early July 2015, having just recently arrived in Repkong, I got in touch by phone with one of my main local tantrist acquaintances, Shawo Tsering [Sha bo tshe ring], only to hear that he was far away in Chapcha, officiating for patrons with three other tantrists. I realized that this was again an occurrence of a patronage modality that I had not yet been able to observe first-hand: something like the "Premium" or "Platinum" offer for tantrists' ritual services, consisting ideally of three ritual heavyweights plus an assistant. When a patron desires to have rituals carried out in a more full-fledged mode than is usually the case, or with a stronger concentration of ritual power, or with a higher (and hopefully thus more efficacious) level of investment on his own behalf, he may ask his usual priest to find three other officiants who can accompany him that time. If his usual priest is—as in the present case—a ritual expert of some reputation, the typical pattern is that he will find two other good experts, plus one younger officiant, who will be given some of the subaltern ritual tasks, such as preparing or handling the offerings or other ritual devices during the ritual. In this case, the information about the four tantrists' coming was passed along by the main patron, and at least three others in the same locality lined up, ready to seize the occasion, one after the other, of inviting the group of four tantrists.

I asked Shawo Tsering whether I could join them—I was a bit hesitant, as the next upcoming ritual was a powerful exorcism, which might mean that the patron's situation was delicate (there might be, for instance, serious health issues in the household)—but he quickly assured me that I was welcome, and so a few days later I left for Chapcha myself, by car and by bus, following the same route as the four men had taken, thanks to my acquaintance's instructions. As Amdo is a mountainous terrain, the quickest and easiest route is actually a long, 400 km drive passing through the provincial capital Xining, with highways for much of the way (Figure 3.3).

The patron for whom the four tantrists were officiating by then was a prosperous pastoralist in his early forties. The wooden house was new and spacious; the patron's family had moved into it just a year before. The exorcism was a Purpa *tong-dok* [Phur pa stong zlog], "The Thousand-fold Repelling [based on the deity] Vajrakīlaya (Adamantine Dagger)," lasting

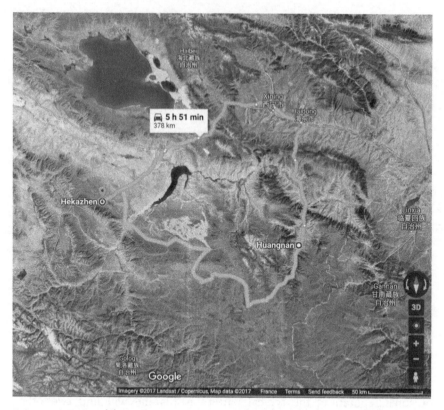

FIGURE 3.3 Road from Rongwo (Huangnan Prefecture seat and Repkong County seat) to Chapcha (Google Maps image, adapted by Nicolas Sihlé).

five days. It is a powerful ritual, but in the present case I was informed that its performance was not a response to any particular misfortune; rather it had been prescribed to the patron as a ritual to be carried out in the year. (At every New Year, Amdo households solicit from their lama or from a respected astrologer indications—obtained through divination in the first case, through astrological calculation in the second—regarding rituals that should be carried out in order to ensure a safe and successful year.) Indeed, the atmosphere around the ritual performance was relaxed and devoid of the tension that may otherwise accompany exorcisms.

The composition of the group of four tantrists illustrated well the pattern that I have referred to above as "three ritual heavyweights plus an assistant." The household priest, a tantrist of some stature and experience, had invited a younger tantrist from his own village, as well as two ritual experts (including my acquaintance Shawo Tsering), both of whom like him had already served as chant masters in various collective settings. The three experienced ritualists all hailed from villages in the northeastern sector of Repkong and knew each other well from their common participation in large-scale ritual gatherings.

The ritual took place in a large room used mainly for special events. During the periods of ritual performance, the senior-most of the three elder tantrists (which happened to be the household priest, although this is not necessarily always the case) officiated as the tantric master (designated in Amdo commonly as *lama* [bla ma], or *dorjé-dzinba* [rdo rje 'dzin pa, lit. "*vajra*-holder"]). Sitting at the top of the right row, he was in charge of some of the more critical phases of the ritual. The second senior-most of the three officiated as chant master—a trying task for an intense ritual lasting five days. The third of the senior tantrists had no specially designated task; he and the junior tantrist simply took part in the chanting—apart from moments when the latter was called by his more subaltern tasks, such as the preparation of further ritual cakes, *torma* [gtor ma]. On occasion, however, the household priest or the officiating chant master was called for other business: the latter was asked to perform a short ritual for a sick child at the neighbor's house, while the former was asked for advice regarding the plans for the new shrine-room of the house. During these periods when only three tantrists remained to officiate, the head roles of the Vajrakīlaya ritual were passed down according to seniority.

The structure of the ritual was rather repetitive: one same core sequence (with offerings, requests directed at the main deities, and a variety of actions aiming at eliminating malevolent beings) was performed once on the first day, then four times a day for each of the following three days, and finally twice on the concluding day. The whole ritual was brought to a close after the final expulsion of the main ritual devices. Throughout, the periods of ritual performance were punctuated by tea breaks, copious meals, and relaxed breaks on the pasturelands outside—if not occasionally by phone calls and various discussions. The atmosphere alternated between periods of concentrated ritual performance or more mechanical recitation, short phases when the family was brought in to receive the blessings of the ritual and sat or kneeled in devotion (Figure 3.4), and moments of lightness, of commensality and socialization.

During the second half of the last day, one external element was putting a bit of pressure on the officiants: the presence of the next (and final) patron, a young man in his thirties who lived a few kilometers away and who was firmly hoping that the tantrists could start still on the same evening the ritual that he had requested. He helped the hosts serve the officiants the last meal they had to offer; then at last the head of the house offered a remuneration to the four tantrists. The priests answered with last blessings, particularly to the children, and as quickly as patronage relationship decorum allowed, the men (and their ethnographer) were escorted to two cars outside and driven away. The remuneration was generous: 500 yuan per day per person—thus an expense of 10,000 yuan, or roughly 1,200 euros, for the remuneration alone. The expense for food—in particular meat—had been substantial too.

FIGURE 3.4 Ritual atmosphere: from right to left, the officiants with the patron sitting next to them and the rest of the family, assembled in order to receive blessings (one young man taking pictures from behind the stove), 2015. The altar is further to the left, opposite the area occupied by the officiants (Photo: Nicolas Sihlé).

The next ritual that awaited the tantrists was of an entirely different character: this was a Dé-gyé *gyak-ngen lhapsang* [sDe brgyad brgyags brngan lha bsang], or "fumigation [offering] to the gods, a gift of provisions for the eight classes [of deities and spirits]." The aim of the ritual is to secure the goodwill and protection of all the worldly deities and spirits, as well as, to some extent, of the higher, Buddhist protector deities.[12] Here again (in particular with the very worldly character of the main beings addressed in the ritual), as with the preceding powerful exorcism (and its violent mode of activity), we are dealing with a type of ritual action that in Tibetan ideas is associated primarily with tantrists, even if, on occasion, monastic ritual specialists may be called for this kind of ritual services. This fumigation ritual was to be carried out in a particularly ample mode, and it took the officiants eight solid hours of work (four on that very evening, until midnight, and four again on the next morning) to prepare the material basis for the ritual: a massive pyramidal—cosmological—structure, with a large number of dough figures representing various classes of spirits and deities arranged all around it.

The fumigation was held on a grassy slope not far from the patron's house. Lay assistants carried the massive structure to the spot and piled up juniper twigs and various offerings (silk scarves, flour, fruit, sugar, yogurt, etc.) all around it. In due course fire was set to the branches and the officiants performed the textual component of the ritual in a white tent that had been pitched right next by. Here again the ritual was interspersed by breaks—drink, foods (particularly festive and lavish), and simply relaxing in the grass or even trying out for fun the young patron's powerful motorbike. In the late afternoon, everyone returned to the patron's house and the tantrists could rest at last, chatting and laughing among themselves and with their hosts, who managed to force yet another meal upon them.

In the morning, the tantrists carried out a concluding sequence of ritual actions with blessings and a *yangguk* [g.yang 'gugs], "calling for prosperity," component. They were (again) munificently rewarded: the patron offered each one of them 800 yuan (or roughly 100 euros), holding deferently the crisp 100-yuan bills with a good-quality ceremonial scarf, *khata* [kha btags]. As always, the amounts were the same for all four officiants but simply offered in order of decreasing age. The priests then blessed the children, exchanged some last friendly words with the host family, and departed. (Two cars had been arranged by them and myself.) The patron accompanied us to the township seat and offered each one of us drinks and further generous amounts of money for the meals along the way. "Those were good patrons," the tantrists remarked with genuine appreciation as we drove toward Xining and Repkong.

The ethnographic glimpse we are afforded here suggests that the relations between priests and patrons are predicated upon much more than purely (if at all) an ethically problematic question of remunerated services—a point we will come back to shortly. Starting with this window into what we could call the "high end" of the spectrum of Repkong tantrists' ritual services, let us first broaden our view somewhat: How do the relations observed here fit into the larger picture of patronage relationships with the Repkong tantrists? We will then return to assess the economic dimension of this domain of activity, along with the tensions in values that are associated with that dimension.

Sociology of Patronage Relations and Dynamics of Reputation

One of my Repkong acquaintances suggested in an informal discussion a threefold classification of modes of patronage that provides a good point of departure. There are, first, established relations or, as he put it, relations that are renewed by the patron. Other relations are new and come into being after a patron contacts a priest who has been recommended to him or her. Yet other relations are the temporary results of chance encounters between a patron and an itinerant tantrist who is actively searching for houses with ritual needs—some Repkong tantrists go off for months to pastoral areas in search of such employment. One may add that chance encounters sometimes also happen simply in the streets of Rongwo town: tantrists are often clearly recognizable due to their distinctive hairstyles (and, to a lesser extent, clothing)—this is particularly true in the case of senior tantrists, many of whom wear a coil of bulky dreadlocks wrapped around their heads (a feature that may be perceived as related with ritual power) and can be spotted at a distance (Sihlé 2018).

There are also functional equivalents of interpersonal patronage relationships in which a patron comes to a monastery or to the temple of a tantrist community and asks that ritual services for his household be performed there. According to one of my Repkong research assistants (a former tantrist himself during his young adult years), the first of these modalities may be increasingly favored by pastoralists, for reasons of convenience: as opposed to individual tantrists, a community of monks can always be found at the same place.

The great improvement of roads and road transportation has led in the current generation to the establishment of numerous new patronage relations. (On the whole, the tantrists have been comparatively less affected by state policies than their monastic counterparts, but this is clearly a domain in which there has been an impact.) As we have seen, however, there also exist lasting associations between a family line of tantrists and a patron house (or set of houses), associations that can be maintained over several generations. For a tantrist, such patronage relationships, which involve a whole history of trust, esteem, hospitality, and generosity, complemented on the other side by availability, concern for the patrons' welfare, religious support, and, implicitly, ritual efficacy, are a source of pride. Some patron families cultivate these key relations with their priest also by paying him a visit, with gifts, on the New Year—this is, however, rarely systematic. (One observes similar, and more systematic, patterns of that kind with regard to a household's *lama*, who provides guidance, through divination, meditation, or simple discussion, as well as religious teachings in some cases.) Finally, some patron families try to further strengthen their relations with their priests by seeking marriage alliances with them.

These enduring relationships are perhaps particularly prevalent in the case of patron communities that are at some distance from their priest's place of residence; patrons who live closer—and in particular patrons living in the same village as the tantrist—are better informed about the local availability of capable tantrists and their patronage relationships may be more fluid, variable, and multiple. As we have seen with the case of Dorjé Gyel, according to whom all of the approximately 70–80 houses of a village in an outlying part of Repkong are his patrons, it is also striking that tantrists often have local (village- or even township-level) clusters of long-term patrons. This often starts with a single patronage relationship, which then extends to relatives, neighbors, and others living in the vicinity.

In the case of certain Repkong priests who, as with Dorjé Gyel, are in high demand and do not have the time to travel in order to respond to all of the occasional requests for services they receive (increasingly now by cell phone), one observes a modality of provision of ritual services that I had never come across in my previous research experience with tantrists. If the tantrist has some limited availability but cannot afford time-wise to travel, he may agree with the patron that the latter come to his own home, where he will be hosted for a few days if necessary and where the tantrist will perform the appropriate ritual services for him. Besides this modality, in some cases there is no direct contact: when a tantrist is considered to be very powerful, some patrons are willing to employ his services from afar, confident that his power can have effects at a distance.

One analytically intriguing question is that of the possible correlation between a tantrist's reputation as a ritual expert and the distances over which he travels for his ritual activity. The situation is however complex. On the one hand, certain reputed tantrists are called to officiate in very faraway places, if the patron has the means to invite them that far. One very special case here is a tantrist from the northeastern part of Repkong who at the same time is a medium (a rare case where these two powerful forms of religious specialization are held by the same person). He is a local celebrity of sorts and is invited (often with a few tantrists who will officiate with him for the textual, tantric part of his activity) by patrons far beyond Repkong County. In cases such as when an illness is involved, he resorts also to his mediumistic skills. It has happened that he is invited to a very distant place, like Golok in the south of Amdo, by a patron who even buys airplane tickets for him. His daily remuneration is said to reach the 600–2,000 yuan (80–300 dollars) range—up to four times as much as what each tantrist officiating for the Chapcha patrons received in the example presented above.

But long distances do not necessarily imply a strong reputation: it may boil down to chance encounters and, ultimately, to the faith of the individual patron. A few Repkong tantrists, for instance, have affluent Han Chinese patrons, living in cities like Beijing or Guangzhou. Chinese patrons, as non-Tibetans and non-Tibetan speakers, may have, however, a very incomplete picture of what counts as ritual expertise and of who's who among the Repkong tantrists. Furthermore, as my Amdo colleague Chenaktsang Hungchen [lCe nag tshang Hūṃ chen] once astutely observed, in an informal discussion of ours, the most reputed Repkong tantrists are strongly in demand among their own local communities, or beyond that in Repkong itself, and often (although not systematically) they hardly have the opportunity to accept other requests from further afield. Tantrists of lesser reputation may receive some local requests for ritual services but on the whole have to fall back on patrons living further away.

How ritual power is evaluated is, however, even within the Tibetan context, a complex question. Ultimately, how powerful or efficacious a tantrist is cannot be known with certainty. Receiving initiations into certain tantric cycles and then performing retreats dedicated to the ritual service of (or *nyenpa* [bsnyen pa], "familiarization" with) the high tantric deities on which these cycles are based is technically considered as the primary way of developing ritual power—at least, provided everything is done correctly and successfully. However, patrons, especially from outside Repkong, may know nothing about a given tantrist's training; reputation heard by word of mouth as well as appearance, demeanor, ways of talking are all important in a first encounter. The collective reputation of wielders of great ritual power enjoyed by the Repkong Tantrist Collectivity (Ngakmang) is also a key element in the perception of Repkong tantrists outside of their quotidian social environments. Finally, and importantly, post hoc events may be read by the patron as signs of the efficacy of the priest's ritual intervention and, by implication, of his ritual power. The following account illustrates some of these points well.

Tamdrin [rTa mgrin], a rather unassuming and almost timid Repkong tantrist in his sixties, is well known among tantrist circles of Repkong for being a good ritual technician. Approximately ten years ago, when he was in Golok to meet a famous master, he heard that a ritual specialist was needed nearby and he ended up officiating for a local hotel owner, performing both an exorcism and a *gyak-ngen* offering ritual (see the example mentioned above). A few days later, the patron's daughter was the only passenger of a vehicle to escape unharmed in a bad accident in which the seven other passengers were all injured. The patron developed as a result great faith in his Repkong priest and he asked him to come back to perform a *gyak-ngen* offering ritual on an annual basis. Every year, on the agreed date (in the second lunar month), he sends his own car to pick him up and then drive him back for the long Xining-Golok stretch of the road. To me, however, Tamdrin claimed that he is not particularly powerful: the event was only the result of the grace of the lamas and protector deities he had invoked. He had been confident, however, in the outcome of the rituals he was to carry out: before accepting the hotel owner's request, he had performed a divination, and the result had been excellent. He always performs such a divination before setting out to Golok, to make sure that he should go. (Another tantrist mentioned paying attention to his dreams before he sets out on similar business.) Tamdrin pointed out to me that it is not only he and the patron who will be impacted: the "name" (i.e., reputation) of the Repkong Ngakmang—a priceless asset for the Repkong tantrists—is also at stake.

In recent years, Tamdrin was also called once to officiate in Golok after the theft of several horses. Upon hearing that a Repkong tantrist had performed two powerful exorcisms, a Sengdong *dokpa* [Seng gdong zlog pa, lit. "repelling (based on) Lion-Face" (a wrathful *ḍākinī*)] and a *dradrup* [dgra brub, lit. "imprisoning/burying the enemy"], in fear the thieves promptly brought back the horses.[13] Here again, to me Tamdrin insisted that he had only invoked the lamas and protectors, and that it simply worked out well.

In the present discussion of the sociological dimension of the Repkong tantrists' patronage relations, a last point should be mentioned, lest the reader be left with the false impression that the tantrists' patrons are always laypersons. In a Repkong (and more widely Tibetan) context marked by the recurring theme of (Geluk) monk versus (Nyingma) tantrist antagonism, the existence of more symbiotic links should not be overlooked. Thus, as specialists of tantric ritual power, some tantrists have occupied the position of providers of ritual services for Geluk hierarchs (a position that in some cases was not devoid of military associations).

FIGURE 3.5 The priest of the Shar incarnate master, on the day of his enthronement, in 1991 (photo of the original photo by an unknown photographer, kindly supplied by the son of the now-deceased priest).

One particularly striking example in Repkong is a family line of tantrists from the Tsozhi [mTsho bzhi] village that is said to have provided priests (Amdo: *xön* [dpon]) for centuries for the most preeminent line of Repkong Geluk incarnates—the Shar [Shar] lineage of masters of Rongwo Gönchen [Rong bo dgon chen] Monastery. When the current Shar master was enthroned, the tantrist of that priestly line was asked to be present. He was standing in the first car of the traditional procession that brought the new Shar master from his main hermitage to his main monastery, and one of my close assistants told me he remembered vividly the scene, although some twenty years or so had passed. The tantrist was an impressive figure, with his dreadlocks wound around his head, his beard, the special red clothes he wore on that day, and his large ritual dagger: his duty was to "open" the way for the Geluk incarnate (Figure 3.5). In the monastery's vast assembly hall, during the enthronement ceremony, the tantrist occupied a specially designated seat next to the master's throne.

Thus, the overall picture is marked by some ambivalence: the main term used for domestic ritual services, *drongchok*, is marked at least for a number of people, in Repkong and beyond, by ethically problematic associations, to the extent that in a number of situations one prefers to avoid it, but this domain of activity is also one of beneficial ritual power, of important social relationships, and sometimes of great prestige. We turn now to the economic dimension, where the tensions in values are felt the most clearly.

Economic Dimension and Ethical Tensions

The primary justification for carrying out domestic ritual services is obvious: they constitute a culturally stipulated response to a number of situations involving uncertainty or misfortune—a response that leaves many patrons, on the whole, rather (and sometimes very) satisfied, which leads them to renew, year after year, the relationships they have built with their priests. Generally speaking, tantrists being householders who (aside from periods of more intensive religious practice, like retreats) live in their village homes, they are also characterized by their proximity to their fellow villagers: it is often easier and quicker to call a tantrist than a monk. As we have seen, they also have a religious profile that distinguishes them partly from the monks: when powerful exorcisms or rituals addressing certain classes of worldly spirits and deities are needed, it is preferably tantrists who are called. Some tantrists also have multiple competences—such as in matters of ritual, divination, astrology, or sometimes traditional Tibetan medicine— that make them particularly useful people to call on.

As far as the tantrists are concerned, there is quite general agreement that individual religious practice (such as retreats of "familiarization," *nyenpa*, with high tantric deities), or even collective practice (such as the monthly or yearly ritual assemblies dedicated to the cult of these tantric deities), constitutes a "higher" mode of religious activity than providing domestic ritual services. However, there are ideological affinities between the ritual activity that is carried out for patrons and a core value of Tibetan religious culture—universal altruism. In moments of dire need (such as when medicines fail to cure a seriously ill person), tantrists may accept to drop other important plans in order to officiate. Tantrists sometimes refuse to take the entire sum that is offered to them as remuneration for their services (the patron will then insist adamantly and sometimes they end up settling on some intermediate count, the priest leaving a bill or two on the table). Tantrists also frequently carry out certain small ritual acts, like blowing protective or healing mantras on a baby or on an ill person, without expecting anything in return. On the whole, however, even if the amount is left to the appreciation of the patron, remuneration is expected and, in many cases, is a conscious objective of the tantrist's activity (even if they should not focus mentally on that aspect). It is understood to constitute a legitimate source of income for tantrists (or monks, for that matter).

This is all the more so in cases of economic hardship—a not uncommon occurrence, in particular in the early 1980s, when religious practice was allowed again, after two decades of devastation wrought by Maoist policies and the Cultural Revolution. Due to the hierarchy of religious activities outlined above, as well as to individual inclinations, some tantrists who preferred to abstain from carrying out domestic ritual services have felt literally compelled by poverty to resort to this mode of generating income. The biography of one renowned Repkong tantrist, Bendé Gyel [Ban de rgyal], a rather bookish, erudite religious man, who served as the tutor to one of the Repkong Nyingma masters, makes it quite clear that it was only his poverty and inability to pay for medical treatment for his wife and himself that ultimately led him, following his own master's insistent advice, to engage in such activity (Ban de rgyal 2018: 238–42). Thus, for a number of years, he traveled to Tsekhok, the county located just south of Repkong, to officiate for a period of one month, twice a year, for local pastoralists.

As we see yet again in this case, numerous tantrists have sought patronage among pastoralists (whether in the higher-altitude, outlying areas of Repkong or in other counties), who have a reputation for being pious and generous patrons—as well as often rather affluent. Traditionally, pastoralists would remunerate their providers of ritual services with meat, hides, butter, or live animals. Many tantrists would spend one or several months, starting right after the New Year period (or slightly later, in the second lunar month, once the fields were plowed), in a given pastoralist area. A number of them went to visit their pastoralist patrons twice per year. Sometimes these patrons would bring themselves to Repkong, at a later point in the year, the large quantities of products or numerous animals that they had given to their priests. Today, this religious economy has been very largely monetized (see, for instance, the case, presented above, of rituals performed in Chapcha).

Beyond the historical shifts and individual inflections, we are dealing here obviously with an institutionalized religious economy. But the renunciatory and soteriological ideals of Buddhism can inspire critiques of tantrists' engagement in the income-generating performance of domestic ritual services. (In what follows, unless mentioned otherwise, the critiques were voiced spontaneously by tantrists themselves.) It is rare, however, that this mode of activity is critiqued wholesale. A first distinction that needs to be considered is that of the type of rituals performed. Thus, involvement in funerary rituals is irreproachable and even a tantrist who is reluctant to engage in the provision of ritual services would not think of refusing a request of that nature, especially if he already has social or religious ties with the house of the deceased. Healing or apotropaic rituals are perfectly legitimate too; we are here, however, in a (as we have noted above, relatively less valued) domain of religious activity which can potentially come to occupy a very large part of a tantrist's time and detract him from other, more valued involvements, such as personal religious practice. As one tantrist put it, with a slightly sarcastic bite: "eating people's food does not make a tantrist advance towards enlightenment." Some local lamas are also known to have publicly encouraged tantric practitioners to focus more on their personal practice. In any case, the above-mentioned hierarchy of religious activities may well guide a tantrist's choices in matters of how he organizes his time, but it never does so in an absolutely systematic way: there is always room for negotiation and, as we have seen, pressing ritual needs (as in the case of serious illness) mentioned by the patron may lead the priest to alter his plans in order to accommodate those needs.

In actual practice, beyond the implication that the tantrist is privileging less valued modes of activity, what is really critiqued most of the time is *excessive* involvement in domestic ritual services. Devoting inordinate amounts of time to such pursuits inevitably opens the door to the (implicit or explicit) suggestion that the tantrist is driven by greed. There is thus a fine balance between the generally accepted notion that tantrists draw part of their income from this kind of activity and the idea that they should not be motivated too strongly, or beyond a reasonable investment of their time, by the promise of material gain.

Some voices, however, go beyond and imply that tantrists' greed may lead them to rejoice in other people's misfortune, as that generates more requests for their ritual services. A local saying (that, truth be told, I heard only very rarely) has it that "Buddhist tantrists and Bönpos have a bad (literally 'dirty') spirit," *ngakpa bönpo zhegyü tsok* [sngags pa bön po zhe rgyud btsog].[14] Of course, actual individual motivations vary greatly. One tantrist living in Rongwo town is known to have become quite affluent through his extensive practice of domestic ritual services, to the point that he now also lends money. Another reputed ritual expert is known to be really greedy; potential patrons know that they will have to remunerate him very well—if not, he will never come again, one says. These accounts should be seen, however, in the broader context of a critical scrutiny that also assesses monks and even lamas' adherence to ethical principles of nonattachment, compassion for the plight of the suffering, and so forth.

Ethical critiques sometimes also aim at some of the consequences or modalities of the provision of domestic ritual services. As we have seen in the Chapcha example above, the officiants are treated by their patrons to the best of food, which in Tibetan contexts generally means meat—and, if the patron can afford it, large quantities thereof. Animals may need to be slaughtered (a highly sinful activity) in order to provide food for the priests. This aspect is already clearly critiqued in texts such as Zhapkar's biography (Ricard 1994) and was echoed by a lay acquaintance of mine, a vocal vegetarian militant (who otherwise has very close ties to Nyingma tantrists).

A final important ethical subtext of critiques of tantrists' involvement in domestic ritual services is related to the points made above regarding the relative unknowability of an officiant's ritual power. Some local voices (both tantrist and lay) suggest that, occasionally, certain tantrists may accept ritual tasks that they in reality cannot master. (In that case, one might say that the ritual "service" boils down to "eating people's food," as we saw one of my interlocutors formulate it just above.)[15]

Perhaps in relation with these critiques (possibly as a modernist ethicization?—but my data here only allow for speculation), a few tantrists I know claim to abstain from any involvement in ritual services. Such a claim needs to be taken with caution, as at the very least they cannot avoid participating in funerary rituals; one of these tantrists actually does accept in some cases to officiate when patrons insist convincingly that they really need him. To what extent similar discourses or attitudes were present in previous generations is, however, unknown to me.

Basically, if we sum up, tantrists are expected to provide the ritual services they are trained to perform (and to be remunerated for their labor), but they should do so with moderation and in a state of mind that focuses on providing beneficial effects. As for patrons, they can voice critical perspectives on certain excesses or ethical lapses; however, when they actually invite a religious specialist to officiate for them, they are expected first and foremost to stick to an active practice of faith ("doing faith," *depa jé* [dad pa byed]) that is understood to be conducive to positive ritual outcomes. At that point, the issue of the priests' appropriate degree of involvement in such activities is not what matters primarily—and with most priests the patrons probably never find a reason to harbor doubts.

Closing Words: A Complex Bundle of Value Registers

What appears clearly, if we contrast these various strands of ethical, sometimes critical, perspectives with the larger range of economic and sociological elements that have been brought here and with the account of the four tantrists' activity in Chapcha, is that there is vastly more to the ethics and values of performing domestic ritual services than the simple theme of ethically problematic income-oriented activity. An excessively narrow focus on the strands of critical discourse within the local society would blind us to the much richer bundle of value registers involved in these interactions and ultimately prevent us from giving these elements of ethical tension their due weight.

Ethical assessments regarding the providers of ritual services are but one slice of a much thicker culture of ritual patronage. This culture is built around several registers of values, roughly distributed in clusters around the two figures of the priest and the patron. Beyond disinterestedness (which applies to both), there is also, on the one hand, ritual virtuosity and religious power, coupled with a concern for the welfare of fellow *saṃsāra* denizens, and on the other, faith and generosity. Between them, there is furthermore the quality of multilayered social relationships constructed over time (sometimes generations) and involving ritual and other services, but also socializing and hospitality extending sometimes over several days and often repeated annually. This culture is also constructed on bodies of knowledge (tantric ritual, divination techniques, etc.) and a distinct lore, associated with the prestige and fame of the Repkong Tantrist Collectivity, that for two centuries have been spreading out through Amdo, and today constitute a shared strand of religious culture from the faraway pasturelands of Temchen to those of Golok or Nakchu.

In the above-mentioned article (Sihlé 2015), one of the arguments put forward was that the transaction composed of the provision of ritual services and its remuneration by the patron often has a misrecognized economic dimension in Buddhist contexts and analytically needs to be seen as in some ways similar to market exchange. In light of the data assembled here, some specific features of this mode of exchange appear more clearly. For instance, a significant aspect is the above-mentioned tendency to refuse, at least at first, to take all the money that is offered—a sort of inverted mirror-image of bargaining, in a context where patron generosity and priestly disinterestedness are strongly valued. One should also particularly highlight the strongly valued modality of the transactions taking place within a thick nexus of prolonged/repeated social interaction. Here, the economic transaction is visibly part of a complex interaction, informed by a partially integrated bundle of different registers of value. As I have argued, contextualizing the exchange within this larger set of values and practices is key to a balanced understanding of the ethics and, *in fine*, of the very nature of the economic transaction—something that a narrow focus on certain strands of critical discourse (or, for that matter, a narrowly Testart-inspired, overly juridical focus on the status of individual material transfers; cf. Sihlé 2015, 365–6) would obscure.

*

The author expresses his profound gratitude for the generosity and insight of his many interlocutors and hosts, as well as of his precious assistant—all of whom will have to remain unnamed.

CHAPTER FOUR

"Bad" Monks and Unworthy Donors: Money, (Mis)trust, and the Disruption of Sangha-Laity Relations in Shangri-La

Hannah Rosa Klepeis

Many scholarly works on Buddhism are devoted to practices of giving and their meanings in various times, contexts, and places, as well as notions of reciprocity within the social and economic workings of Buddhist societies. As Ivan Strenski notes, "giving defines the very relationship between the sangha and lay society" (1983, 470). Unlike other chapters in this volume (see Jonutytė and Mills) that challenge the assumption of laity and sangha in Buddhist giving as two separate groups and question the presumed reciprocity of exchanges between those two groups, this chapter addresses how ready access of the sangha to outside resources leads to doubts about the central act of giving, accompanied by feelings of suspicion and mistrust, which have a *disrupting* rather than a *binding* effect on the relationship between laity and sangha. Fueled by increasing economic growth and social inequality, giving in Shangri-La has become central to questions of morality and to debates about the worthiness of both the donor and the receiver. Focusing on donations and remunerations that the laity gives to the sangha in return for ritual services, I will reflect on how money itself is perceived in these debates and the meanings it can take on.

This chapter is less concerned with questions of reciprocity and does not distinguish between gifts in the strict sense of the term and donations and remunerations (for a typology and in-depth discussion, see Sihlé 2015). Rather, I propose to look at the role notions of trust play in these exchanges and how money and the accumulation of wealth create mistrust. I hereby do not employ the term to simply describe a complete lack of trust but rather a situation of ambiguity and doubt; furthermore, I have chosen the term "mistrust" over "distrust." While very close in meaning, distrust tends to be based on past experiences, whereas mistrust refers to a more general sense of the unreliability of a thing, person, or group (Carey 2017, 8). Based on twelve months of ethnographic research in Shangri-La between 2015 and 2017, I look at the ways both laity and sangha reflect on these moments of mistrust and the role money takes on in these discourses.

Changing Sangha-Laity Relations in Shangri-La

Since 2001, Shangri-La is no longer just a fictitious paradise but also refers to an actual place in the north of the southwestern Chinese province of Yunnan. The decision for renaming the county formerly known as Zhongdian, or Gyalthang in local Tibetan, was backed up by semi-scientific interpretations of events and the origin of the name (Hillman 2003, 177–8). As the official recognition of Shangri-La coincided with the central government's goal of economic development and the promotion of interethnic harmony, it was granted without much contestation. Despite having received county-level city status in 2014, most of Shangri-La still consists of rural villages and grasslands; local estimates suggest that only one-third of Shangri-La's population of 130,000 resides in the urban center and county seat Jiantang. The region's rapid economic growth and its integration into the Chinese market in recent decades have been built largely on the back of state-supported ethnic tourism, which has tapped into the mystical exoticism surrounding Tibetan Buddhist culture (see further Hillman 2003; Kolas 2008).

The restructuring of the local economy and attendant processes have had a significant impact on the region's demography, which has changed rapidly since its renaming—a change that has affected the relationship between laity and sangha. For one thing, the Ganden Sumtsenling Monastery's development into a "scenic area" (*fengjingqu*) for tourism attracts millions of visitors every year and the entire tourism infrastructure of the monastery, including the revenues made from entrance tickets, is controlled by the county's tourism department. As a consequence, government involvement in monastic affairs is eyed with great suspicion and is likely to extend into the monastery's internal affairs. Furthermore, new business opportunities have encouraged immigration from both Han and Tibetan regions and have also given rise to new aspirations among Jiantang's local population. Through this, Shangri-La has once again become a nexus of Sino-Tibetan and intra-Tibetan connectivity, a role it had played for much of the past few centuries.

Located in the Sino-Tibetan border area of southern Kham, Gyalthang was a trading post on the southern Silk Road, or Ancient Horse and Tea Road. Although Tibetans make up the majority of the population, the region has always been shaped by the interactions of its different ethnic groups (such as Bai, Naxi, Yi) as well as its location between the Chinese empire and the Dalai Lama's polity in Lhasa. While these different ethnic groups have lived in the region without any major conflicts, discussion about ethnic distinctions and authenticity dominates the local public discourse. Tibetans from other regions often blame the borderland location for Shangri-La Tibetans' receptiveness to Han influence and lack of cultural and historical awareness. Among Tibetans, Shangri-La has become imagined as a place of moral and cultural degradation. Much of the debates on both sides center around the standing of the monastery and the developments around it. The monastery is seen to lie in the heart of Tibetan society, as a protector and guide of the Buddhist dharma as well as moral integrity. Further, religion and its institutions have always been conceived as a crucial ingredient in the process of acculturation or "Tibetanization" in the borderland regions from the sixteenth century onwards.

Tourism development over the past two decades has resulted in economic inequalities that are particularly pervasive between Shangri-La's urban center and rural areas. The urban population largely consists of people not just from outside but also locals running their own businesses or in relatively middle-class professions, such as office clerks, shop assistants, teachers, tour guides, and civil servants. Many villagers, on the other hand, still predominantly live of cash crops and subsistence agriculture, and may substitute their income by having a family member working in the city; however, villagers commuting to Jiantang often tend to work on construction sites or as drivers, earning much lower and less reliable income. Urban families tend to hope for their sons to go to university and earn a lot of money in the future. For rural parents, in comparison, sending a son to the monastery is still an economically viable option. Although religious convictions are often the main motivation, for many rural, young men joining Ganden Sumtsenling offers opportunities, such as access to education, financial security, and proximity to the urban center, that may otherwise be unattainable to them. As many of their families live a several hours' drive away, monks enjoy a certain level of anonymity when moving around the city.

Whereas the majority of the 700 monks at Ganden Sumtsenling still depends on their own kin for food and basic subsistence, tourism and economic growth have provided monastics with several substantive income sources. One main source of income are the donations collected at each of the khamtsen[1] temple halls, which get divided among the khamtsen's monks at the end of the year. Another main source of income are the remunerations received in return for ritual services most commonly held at laypeople's homes. These may vary according to the monk's status and the hosting household's financial situation, and do not tend to be openly negotiated between the parties. In village households, they normally range from 100 to 200 yuan, whereas in the city the households are expected to compensate monks with up to 500 yuan for their services. Additionally, each monk receives a subsistence allowance (Ch. *dibao*) of 400 yuan from the government each year. Besides these income sources that are available to all monastics at Ganden Sumtsenling, highly educated or reincarnated lamas (Tib. *tulku*; Ch. *huofo*) often receive additional monetary donations for divinations (Ch. *suanming*) or gifts in kind such as mobile phones or prepaid trips by disciples from all over the country who come to seek their spiritual advice (see also Smyer Yü 2012). A minority of Ganden Sumtsenling's monks also employ the charisma and trust they hold as

FIGURE 4.1 Money offerings at a small altar in the entrance hall of the Shambala Tibetan Culture Museum in Shangri-La, 2016. The museum was built to showcase Tibetan religion and culture and also contains a small temple (Photo: Hannah Rosa Klepeis).

members of the sangha to engage in various entrepreneurial or (largely illegal) money-lending activities (Ch. *gaolidai*).

Although both monks and local laity insist that it is only a minority of monastics who engage in these illicit or improper means of wealth accumulation, rumors abound in Shangri-La of monks drinking in bars, visiting prostitutes, or breaking up families by handing out high-interest loans to gamblers. As a result, Ganden Sumtsenling's reputation has suffered both locally and beyond its region in recent decades. People used to explain the lack of discipline with market integration, government influence, and the growing presence of Han visitors and migrants, as well as the monastery's proximity to the urban center which is considered an inappropriate environment for monastics. While residents from Amdo region tend to refuse to talk badly about any member of the sangha, among Shangri-La locals the topic "bad monks" tends to dominate the discourse around Ganden Sumtsenling. It leads to lively and thoughtful debates about how a "good" monk should behave, in particular about the proper and correct ways for monks to accumulate and spend money. These debates, however, rarely result in any consensus and to discuss them at length would exceed the scope of this chapter. In the following, I will therefore concentrate on the effects these changes in sangha-laity relations and economic circumstances in Shangri-La have on Buddhist giving.

Giving as a Market Transaction?

During one of our conversations, Tsering, a young business-owner, reflected on the ritual performances undertaken during a ceremony he held when opening his new business. In his home village just outside of Jiantang he had set up a youth hostel in an attempt to promote a more sustainable form of tourism in the region. A former NGO worker with a university degree, Tsering cares greatly about the protection and preservation of local culture and spends some of his free time engaging in discussions with high lamas in order to further his own understanding of Buddhism. In order to ensure the success of the opening ceremony, Tsering had contacted a senior lama who now lives at one of the main monastic universities in the Indian diaspora to inquire about the proper procedures and scripts required for a successful ritual. At the opening ceremony itself, the rituals were then carried out by four local monks he knew personally in accordance with instructions given by the lama. Tsering recalled hearing them chant, but throughout the entire ceremony he had doubts that they were chanting the entire scripture from start to finish, thinking that perhaps they were leaving out significant parts of it. Close to confronting them about it, he in the end let it go and rather unwillingly handed them money. Yet, in Tibetan Buddhism, he explained, doubt is one of the worst feelings one can have toward monks.

Expectations of the Buddhist gift resembling the Maussian "free" or "unreciprocated" gift that bears "no visible fruit within this world" and "can be presumed to result in an unseen and transcendent reward in the form of spiritual merit" (Ohnuma 2005, 104) are of little concern to both laity and sangha in Shangri-La. Quite the contrary: exchanges between the laity and the sangha are often talked about in terms of transactions, with rituals acknowledged as services that demand remuneration. The most common ways in which my interlocutors referred to the act of handing money over to monks were in terms of paying a *mu-wa* (Tib.) or a *xinkufei* (Ch.), meaning a payment given in return for good service, rather than a *yön* or the Chinese *bushi*, which literally refers to remuneration or almsgiving in the religious context. Similarly, monks themselves may describe the act of visiting a household to carry out a ritual as "going to work" (Ch. *qu gongzuo*) and their obligation to the laity to provide ritual services as a "contract" (Ch. *hetong*). Nicolas Sihlé points out the risk of losing some of the nuance by employing labor market vocabulary in regard to ritual services. He presents us with the example of a conversation with an elderly layman who refers to remunerations as trade (Tib. *tsong*) or a salary (Tib. *yok-la*), which "unmistakably suggests a proximity with the domain of remuneration of services and market exchange" (2015, 358). Sihlé describes the interlocutor as being "irreverent and challenging common codes of etiquette" (2015, 358). We nevertheless might wonder how it affects people's views of these exchanges when labor market terms have become dominant.

Tsering's example illustrates that remunerations of ritual services appear to be transactions and are often talked about in these terms, but they are never merely instrumental and are rather part of a larger and long-term transactional cycle with its own social and moral obligations. Whereas in straightforward, purely economic exchanges—money in return for a service—the giver could withhold the payment until the service has been carried out to his or her satisfaction, the exchange between laity and sangha is still defined by the very act of giving, which is an intrinsic part of the Buddhist social system and moral universe. Although Tsering's doubt was partly built on his general mistrust of local monks and their capability in general, in this specific case he also suspected them to perform the ritual not out of a feeling of duty and obligation but rather out of an economic motivation. The suspicion that monks do not abide by the moral rules led Tsering to render them unworthy receivers in this exchange. As historical accounts demonstrate, the ideology of *dāna* has often served the demonstration and solidification of power positions and wealth (Kieschnick 2003, 191–9), with lay beliefs evolved around rivalry, jealousy, and pride, rather than corresponding to understandings of "purified giving." Gift giving has thus always had important economic consequences (Benavides 2005, 89–91) and is not secluded from the sociopolitical conditions it takes place in but is deeply embedded within them.

Even though large donations are often associated with Han or Western donors (see also Caple 2015), people complain that the prevalence of money can also be observed among fellow Tibetans. The general consensus in Shangri-La is that tourism and the increasing integration into (and dependence on) the capitalist market economy in recent decades have corroded local Tibetans' value system and have—like elsewhere in China—led to a new money craze (see also Caple, this volume). The omnipresence of money is considered to affect all sectors of society and exchanges and other forms of sociality taking place between people. Many of my interlocutors voiced their concerns over the effects of money on Buddhist practices and beliefs among Shangri-La locals. According to one of my interlocutors who had moved to Shangri-La from Amdo region, people in Shangri-La are prone to say that because they donated 10,000 yuan to the monastery last summer, they are good Buddhists. "People here don't really know much about Buddhism," he explained, "they don't ask any questions, just donate money." Another common criticism is the increasing size of donations and remunerations, mainly driven by wealthy locals who reimburse monks with up to 10,000 yuan for their religious services. In her historic study of Tibetan monastic rules, Jansen (2015, 158) references a set of monastic guidelines from 1848 that warns monks against treating benefactors differently on the basis of their wealth. This suggests that this problem is not a new one but has likely existed in many times and places. In Shangri-La it is not necessarily the large donation as such that is being criticized; rather, it raises monks' expectations about their level of renumeration. Indeed, a former monk admitted to having experienced feelings of disappointment toward unexpectedly low remunerations. Just as laypeople cannot withhold the remuneration when monks fail to carry out a service to their satisfaction, monks cannot criticize the amounts they receive. Nevertheless, I have heard accusations that monks were unwilling to return to households from which they had received a seemingly inadequate remuneration in the past. This particularly affects low-income households who may struggle to find monks for ritual services. Instead, monks are said to go where the money is.

The Abstract Qualities of Money

In an article on Han Chinese patronage relationships and the ways they are reflected upon in a Tibetan community in Amdo, Jane Caple (2015, 464) highlights that there are certain values and "rules of the game" that underpin the ethics of transferring wealth and goods to the monastery, regardless of whether these are classified as gifts or remunerations. She finds that what is central to these rules and values is the category of faith. While discussions about the donors' intentions and faith are similar in Shangri-La, the main concern among laypeople is usually the impact those gifts can have on their receivers. The gift in this context is nowadays—with few exceptions—money. Bloch and Parry have argued that money itself does not necessarily change everything; instead, existing worldviews give "rise to particular ways of representing money" (1989, 19). Unlike in other (Buddhist) contexts, money is not considered to be inherently bad or polluting in Tibetan Buddhism; only in certain situations money is spoken of as problematic and dangerous. Unlike described by other researchers,[2] Shangri-La residents do not consider the danger to be attached to the substance itself; rather, it lies in the context in which money is given and the intention and worthiness of the giving and the receiving party. As pointed out by Bloch and Parry's (1989), it may thus be more fruitful to whole transaction systems and their transformative processes instead of focusing on the meaning of money itself.

In my view, the context of Tibetan Buddhist monasticism being integrated into the capitalist market economy, marginalized by the Han majority and facing repressions by the atheist state at the same time, has led to a reevaluation of money among Tibetans. My interlocutors in Shangri-La would often reminisce about a past when money only played a modest role in daily life, and the exchange of goods was still a central part of the local economy. Similar to what Erik Mueggler describes for the Lijiang area in the early 1990s (1991, 209), Shangri-La's residents attribute the rise of money and market exchange to both urbanization and ethnicity, specifically the immigration of Han, who in return are being associated with corruption and disorder. Unlike other parts of China where major socioeconomic change is linked to the beginning of the Reform and Opening Up policies of the early 1980s, people in Shangri-La claim to have been spared by any major transformations until the beginning of mass tourism brought about rapid urbanization and a radical reconstruction of the local economy in the late 1990s. The acceleration of economic and urban development in recent years and the growing influx of Han entrepreneurs and visitors into the county seat have caused worries about the future of Tibetan cultural traditions and moral values, especially among the younger generation—a point I will return to in the end.

Webb Keane (2008, 29) questions the notion that money necessarily threatens the "long-term cycles" of reproduction in exchange-based societies. The ethnographic accounts that Keane refers to clearly demonstrate that the problem with money is rarely that it has alienating and erosive effects per se but that it is unequally distributed (see Foster 2002; Meyer 1999). While money may change social relations, it does not simply abolish them. Pointing to the relationship between money and the Saussurian concept of the linguistic sign that had already been observed by Marx, Simmel and Saussure, Keane compares money to indexical signs which have "causal relations with a heterogeneous diversity of things," inevitably "embedded within contexts of moral evaluation and political action" (Keane 2008, 70; see also Gregory 1997, 25). Ipso facto, "money as a sign is also ... a material part of and participant in the moral world of social agents"

(Keane 2008, 70). When Shangri-La Tibetans thus talk about it, "money" rarely refers to the actual material substance as such but signifies a complex set of social, moral, and political relations and their transformations. We may therefore understand money as having a dual nature in the sense that it does not purely represent economic value but also acts as an agent of social relationships (see Simmel 1990).

Paraphrasing from a discussion on hoarding, David Graeber returns to the distinction Marx made between "money" and "coin": that is, money in its abstract and concrete aspects. The "coin" that stands for the physical object offered in exchange only becomes money when it is withdrawn from circulation and no longer is an "immediate object of anyone's action but instead represents a kind of universal potential *for* action." By holding on to it the hoarder preserves her power—the power to buy anything she wants. Marx reasons that money becomes a kind of ascetic religion to the hoarder "in which the owner tends to develop an intensely personal ... relationship with the source of his powers" (Graeber 1996, 10). Indeed, since the economic reforms, materialism is considered to have resulted in filling a "spiritual vacuum," and money as a representation of power is pervasive and ever-present in twenty-first-century China.

In his ethnographic account on the spread of Tibetan Buddhism in China, Dan Smyer Yü even goes as far as to state that money is becoming China's "second nature," a development that Tibetan Buddhism is not immune to. He states that in the past large-scale monetary donations were a rare occurrence (2012, 16). Nowadays, the revitalization of Tibetan Buddhism in China is undeniably and "intimately entwined with the dual nature of money," meaning that Tibetan monks are no longer seen as merely embodiments of the Buddha's teachings but have also become objects of acquisition: "On one hand they are subject to commercialization; on the other hand, their objectification reflects both the internal moral and spiritual values of Han as well as the social conditions of religion in contemporary China" (Smyer Yü 2012, 14). Yet, for my Tibetan interlocutors, monks are not merely subjected to commercialization but have become active agents that further these processes. Much of the debates around this issue revolve around a moral conundrum in which on one hand the necessity of monks generating a monetary income in order to sustain their own livelihood is acknowledged; on the other hand, money also bears the danger of leading the monks astray from their spiritual pursuit as their economic status leads to powers beyond that of the monastic realm.

Making "Bad" Monks through Money

As one would probably expect, the accumulation of wealth by monks is seen as particularly problematic when it is assumed to have been generated through means other than donation, such as business ventures or illegal gambling and money-lending activities. A reincarnated lama at Ganden Sumtsenling complained to me that these days some of the monks refuse to carry out rituals for the laity as it is too much hassle and they no longer depend on the extra money these services bring. Seemingly at odds with the lay criticism directed against monks as "ritualists for hire," the lama's comment also demonstrates the discrepancies in expectations and values between laypeople and monastics. Whereas laypeople may question a monks' motivation for carrying out ritual services and consider the value of such services to be dependent on the monk's purity and intention, monastics themselves derive the value of such services primarily from a sense of obligations (toward the laity), on one hand, and necessity (to maintain their own livelihoods), on the other.

Many of my interlocutors reasoned that increasing donations and the large amounts of disposable income nowadays enables monks to engage and invest in such improper, profit-oriented activities in the first place. While a certain respect was usually voiced for those willing and able to give sizable donations of money, few people hesitated to declare their disrespect for rich monks. A certain level of wealth is considered desirable in order to prevent monks from being distracted from their soteriological duties but wealth that threatens to erode the reciprocal relationship between laity and sangha is met with disapproval.

Drawing on Simmel (1907), it might be argued that having access to large amounts of money destroys social ties and "frees" the monk from his social obligations. For Parry and Bloch (1989) the analysis of money and the morality of exchange always needs to be seen in relation to their transactional cycles. The authors distinguish between two such cycles, the first one being based on short-term, instrumental relations and the second one on long-term, transactional ones. The latter often plays an important role in the reproduction of ideological systems. The ongoing relationships encompassed within these cycles are protected by the morality embedded in institutions such as religion or in social relations based on hierarchy, kinship, or trust.

It is when the monk is seen as having "freed" himself from this long-term order of reciprocity that laypeople refer to him as being a "bad" or "improper" monk. Since he no longer relies on their trust and support, he is considered more likely to engage in forbidden this-worldly pleasures, thus threatening the long-term stability of an "enduring social and cosmic order" (Bloch and Parry 1989, 28). Large monetary gifts and donations thus further erode the already strained relationship between Shangri-La's laypeople and the local sangha. Rumors about the embezzlement of money by Ganden Sumtsenling's administrative elite have also made some locals wary of giving donations to the monastery.

Dorjee, a local businessman and tour guide, told me about an incident when he guided a group of fourteen businessmen from Lhasa around Shangri-La. When they arrived at the monastery, the men decided that they wanted to leave a donation. They went to the little office booth on the side of one of the main temple halls and informed the monks there about their intentions. When the businessmen had handed over the money, Dorjee felt the need to intervene. As they had donated a total of 28,000 yuan, he felt they should know where the money went and requested a receipt from the monk who had taken the money. The monk excused himself for being unable to write, so Dorjee offered to write it for him. When this was done, he asked the monk to put the monastery's official stamp on it, which he knew every Tibetan Buddhist monastery has, but the monk claimed he did not know about it. Dorjee continued to insist, knowing that the monk would eventually call the abbot of Sumtsenling Monastery for assistance. The abbot sat down with them, issued the proper receipts, and eventually carried the money away himself. Only then did Dorjee feel sure that the money would be properly used, as he suspected the monk of keeping the donation for himself. He emphasized that this just applied to Shangri-La; had this happened at a monastery in Amdo or Central Tibet, he would have trusted the monks there to handle the donation appropriately. Dorjee then recalled guiding a delegation that included Prince Andrew of Britain. When they arrived at Ganden Sumtsenling all the monastic leaders and the governor of Shangri-La were present and waiting. Later that day, a big banquet was held for the honorable guest for which several Russian oligarchs were present as well. Large donations were made that night—a total of one million yuan as far as Dorjee remembers. "There, of course," Dorjee said, "proper receipts were handed out and they had the proper stamp and everything." Generally, one could argue that donating large amounts to the sangha is acceptable; it is when these large amounts end up in the pockets of individual monks that they become problematic.

Dorjee's criticism toward the way donations are handled at Sumtsenling Monastery did not end here. "Rich businessmen come here and they [the monks handling donations] don't even care about the intention of the person donating the money," he complained. In comparison, Dorjee told me about the way donations are handled at Serta, a monastery located in Ganzi Prefecture, Sichuan. There, potential donors receive a list of ten rules as not drinking alcohol for three years, not lying, not killing, and so forth, and are asked to choose up to three which they think they can follow. If they cannot even commit to one of them, the donation will be refused. Praising Serta's solution to this issue, Dorjeeopenly voiced his mistrust over Sumtsenling Monastery and its willingness to accept anyone's money. Even though he still visits Sumtsenling to worship Buddha, he never donates any money to it. If he goes on a private occasion, he usually brings some yak butter, which he concludes "is really the same thing."

Dorjee's story raises several issues that I have come across in various conversations during my fieldwork. While giving money to the sangha or a monk is considered acceptable, and equivalent to giving objects or groceries, there is a point when money becomes dominant in the transaction and in doing so, changes the nature of the exchange. It is then that it is seen as breaking the rules of the game, corrupting not only the transaction itself but also the recipient. When Dorjee says that giving yak butter is the same as giving money, he does not claim that these two substances are equivalent in their economic value. What he means thereby is that in soteriological terms the giving of either of these two objects is equally effective. For him, the karmic consequences remain the same, yet, as he does not trust the recipient, by giving yak butter he effectively prevents the monk from any temptation to put the donation toward illicit means, thereby better controlling the destination of his donation.

The idea that money corrupts monks and destroys their moral integrity is widespread in Shangri-La but certainly not specific to the region. Particularly those holding positions within the Monastic Management Committee (the administrative unit responsible for handling donations to the monastery) are suspected of becoming selfish and immoral soon after taking office, have they not reached this position through these vices and abuse of political connections in the first place. Relatives of monks whom I spoke with took pride in telling me stories of their brothers or cousins who refused large sums of money offered to them by Han businessmen. This suggests that despite the general understanding of the monk's obligation to act as a field of merit and receive and use any gift that is offered to him, he must refuse it in certain circumstances in order to maintain his integrity as a monk. Large amounts of money thus do bear a danger of corrupting not only the purpose or intention of the gift as such but also the two sides of the transaction. On the one hand, the monk or receiver may fear that the gifted money has been accumulated through unethical means and can thereby affect his integrity as a respectable member of the sangha; the layperson or giver, on the other hand, may fear that an unethical receiver could misuse the money instead of spending it according to the giver's wishes, thereby depriving the donor of his meritorious benefits. On each end, the money that is feared to be accumulated by or encouraging corrupt behavior is tainted by it; through its contamination, it carries the potential of reciprocating corruption.

So which ways are there to mitigate these threats and dangers? The mistrust is not only voiced in regard to the "undeserving-ness" of the receiver and his misusage of the donation. In times when money has become the main object of both desire and soteriological benefits, trust between laity and sangha is further distorted by the potential threat of deception by illegitimate members of the sangha. The phenomenon of "fake monks" is not exclusive to Shangri-La; rather, with the global commercialization of Buddhism, fake monks have become particularly common at religious sites that have been turned into tourist attractions across East and Southeast Asia. With its reputation of wealth and its large tourist industry, Shangri-La is not an unlikely place for this phenomenon to occur. Fake monks are mainly found at a square inside the old town and are largely assumed to be young men coming from rural areas nearby, trying to make money off gullible tourists by begging them to throw some cash into their cardboard boxes. However, there are also some who claim to come from poor areas in Qinghai and Sichuan and use less blatant strategies, generating uncertainty even among Shangri-La's residents. In moments of confrontation, locals have employed different strategies of dealing with the possibility of "fake-ness." Once during a dinner with one of my informants, a Tibetan high school teacher in his thirties, a middle-aged man dressed in monk robes entered the restaurant with a pile of small notes in his hand and asked for money. When the teacher spotted him he pulled out his wallet and when the man arrived at our table, he handed him some change. As soon as the monk left he said that he was probably a fake monk and most definitely comes from another area. Asked why he still gave money to the man, he reasoned that in Tibetan culture, asking other people for something and not simply grabbing it was a legitimate way of obtaining things. In his opinion, Buddhist monks should not have their own possessions but should beg from other people. In the end, he did not care whether or not the monk was "real," as there was always the chance that he was and one would be worse off by denying a donation to a monk than giving to someone who is just pretending to be one.

Opinions on this matter, however, vary greatly and most of my interlocutors found the idea of fake monks receiving donations more problematic. Damo, a former monk who is now a student at the local Thangka Centre,[3] recalled an incident when a small group of monks came by and asked them to donate money for the rebuilding of a temple. Explaining how he knew they were fake, Damo said that as a former monk he was immediately able to tell by simply talking to them; for definite proof, he asked them to produce the proper certification. If monks are sent out to collect donations for construction or renovation purposes, they always carry an official note from the monastery's abbot, stating the intended purpose.

Before returning to these examples, I will briefly discuss a moral dimension that has come to dominate all of these exchanges. Even though they remain a minority, more and more young people in Shangri-La refuse to visit the monastery or engage with local monastics due to monks' demonstrating their wealth and a growing body of stories of Ganden Sumtsenling's monks breaking their precepts. They made explicit references to Buddhist values on non-attachment on occasion but often seemed to draw on them only as a last resort when trying to explain their discomfort with some monks' behavior and accumulation practices. Jarrett Zigon notes that morality is more than "just another term for socially approved habits" (2008, 1) and should therefore be treated as distinctive from religious beliefs, etiquettes and values (ibid., 5). I have come across several instances of moral reasoning that are not necessarily in accordance with Tibetan Buddhist teachings, such as the refusal of certain kinds of gifts or the criticism directed toward large donations. Similar to post-Soviet Ukraine, notions of morality in Shangri-La often concern individual and collective interests in the face of the pursuit of wealth (ibid., 515). Following Catherine Wanner, if, as is often the case, competing moral ideals are present at the same time, it is the ethnographer's obligation "to contextualize the specific forms of sociality that give rise to different understandings of morality and the variety of cultural practices that interconnect with moral imperatives" (2005, 516). The moral codes applied to economic exchanges in Shangri-La should thus not be seen as a way of reinforcing and maintaining the status quo. They do not only concern the advantages or necessity of economic growth in the face of increasing inequality; they are also tied to questions of how Tibetans can and should participate in a Han-dominated market economy without having to betray their own cultural values.

As in other postsocialist contexts, moral contestation mainly centers on the creation and consumption of wealth. In Ukraine, for instance, this has led to the replacement of Soviet-era economic practices by cash transactions, leading to the remaking of social and familial networks and their corresponding obligations (ibid., 515–16). As to Buddhist economic exchanges in Shangri-La, we firstly have to place them in a context in which everyone expects to receive money in exchange for services rendered and money is considered to buy you anything you want. Secondly, moral conflicts must be seen as a result of the transformations in the social and economic sphere in which roles and functions are no longer as clear as they used to be. In a situation where the sangha is no longer reliant on its local laity for economic support and when support by some of the laity becomes more attractive than others, this can be seen as breaking a moral code. At the same time, laypeople become less reliant on the local sangha for their proper practice. Particularly the young and educated use their mobility and social media networks to seek spiritual guidance from elsewhere. Like in Ukraine, "the growing dominance of money and monetary forms of exchange are the primary engine of change" (Wanner 2005, 533)—a change that most individuals in Shangri-La are hesitant to embrace. It is in these times of uncertainty that the laity turns to the sangha, considered the backbone of Tibetan society, in expectation of moral guidance, only to find that the sangha has been influenced by the very same dynamics—or even worse, has taken on the role of a driving force. Further, their integration into a Han-dominated economic market forces Tibetans to negotiate their own marginal position in the context of contemporary Chinese society.

Conclusion: A Matter of (Mis)trust?

With regard to Sino-Tibetan patronage relationships Jane Caple notes that "examining when and how [they] are understood to break the rules of the game tells us as much (perhaps even more) about values and concerns underlying Tibetan conceptions of the ethics of lay–monastic relations as they do about the actual dynamics of Chinese sponsorship" (2015, 463). Similarly, I believe that looking at when and why giving money to the sangha is considered as "breaking the rules of the game" tells us more about the perceived social and moral impact of China's market economy upon the local laity and sangha and their relationship to each other than about Buddhist understandings of donations and money. In Shangri-La it is not the giver passing on pollution onto the receiver, nor is it the giver necessarily seen as being inefficacious for the receiver as described in similar exchange contexts elsewhere (see, for example, High 2013b; Parry 1986)—what if the problem lies in the gift itself? What if it signifies danger brought from outside into the transaction due to its association with the very dynamics that are reconstructing and transforming the reciprocal exchange between laity and sangha? The problem may thus not be simply that "with money, one can exchange anything with anyone, and thus enter social relations with anyone, without careful manipulation of obligations and relationship" (Mueggler 1991, 213; on the impersonality of money, see also Hart 2007); instead money only becomes the problem when these traditional obligations and relationships between laity and sangha are perceived to have been compromised.

The focus here, however, is on perception rather than on reality. Even the strongest critics of Shangri-La's sangha admitted that only a minority of monks engage in new forms of exchanges and wealth accumulation. Similarly, we can assume that many of those who donate large sums do not simply have their own status in mind or see the money as a form of making up for their bad deeds. As I have suggested in the beginning of this chapter, I believe the issue is one of trust or rather of mistrust. The ethnographic vignettes above demonstrate that when given to an individual monk, it doesn't matter so much what the money is spent on; yet when the donation is not made as a remuneration for a particular service but as a general donation, it does matter how the money ends up being used. In either of these cases, the central issue appears to concern whether or not the receiver of the donation can be trusted. When I asked my friend Lhamo, a NGO worker in her early thirties, who has been living and married in Shangri-La for over six years, whether she would seek the services of local monks she negated my question firmly:

> No, because, to be honest, I really don't really trust them and I don't really have any respect towards them—because monks here are really different. Of course there are also good monks, but so far the monks here they are giving [me the impression] that they are playboys; they are not trustworthy people, because they are not good monks. Even at night they're in bars. I never saw that, but I heard. So, I believe what I heard.

The ruptures in the exchange relationship between laity and sangha may therefore not simply be caused by the presence of money and the structures of inequality it tends to uncover, but rather by the lack of trust that would be necessary for these exchange relationships to be sustained in the first place.

Feelings of mistrust toward the local sangha are even stronger among urban lay society in which personal relationships with members of the sangha as well as with one another tend to be less intimate. Forms of bureaucratization may help to eliminate feelings of mistrust and can create certainty that the money will land in the reach its legitimate recipient: Dorjee felt reassured that their donation would not end up in the pocket of a potentially corrupt monk; for Damo the monks' inability to produce a certain letter was the ultimate proof that he was dealing with imposters rather than legitimate members of the sangha. Dorjee's insistence on receiving evidence for the transaction in particular shows how proper bureaucratic procedures can be seen to mitigate the likeliness of fraud and can compensate for the lack of trust placed by the giver in the receiver.

Although the anonymity of urban spaces should not be entirely dismissed as part of the explanation, Tsering's example in the beginning of this chapter showed that despite knowing the monks who carried out the ritual service and having invited them personally, this did not prevent feelings of doubt. Unlike the Tibetan householders in Repkong who maintain close associations with tantrists (see Sihlé, this volume), in Shangri-La the pervasive socioeconomic and demographic transformation of its urban center has resulted in a situation where degrees of intimacy and proximity between monastics and laypeople do not necessarily overlap. Although Tsering's example reminds us that "proximity and familiarity do not necessarily equate to knowability or certainty" (Carey 2017, 8), Sihlé's example also prompts us to consider whether trust in relations between laity and sangha is also dependent on the active maintenance and investment in the social aspects of these relationships.

Likewise, the trust put into members of Shangri-La's sangha by outsiders, as well as the trust put by Shangri-La residents in members of the sangha in other regions and the Tibetan diaspora, invites us to further challenge the widespread assumption that there is a fundamental connection between proximity, familiarity, and trust (Carey 2017, 8). It also encourages further enquiries into the disruptive forces that money and unequal economic development can have on relationships built on such values. Thus, Strenski's assumption mentioned in the beginning of this chapter—"giving defines the very relationship between the sangha and lay society" (1983, 470)—cannot be taken at face value: it is rather that "giving" defines the premises upon which the relationship between laity and sangha is negotiated in any given time, circumstance, and place.

PART TWO

Beyond Reciprocity

CHAPTER FIVE

Donations Inversed: Material Flows From Sangha to Laity in Post-Soviet Buryatia

Kristina Jonutytė

After more than half a century of violent repressions against religious practices and institutions, what is commonly known as a Buddhist revival started in the late 1980s in Buryatia, a multiethnic republic in the Russian Federation along its border with Mongolia. Since then, over a dozen temples have been built in its capital city of Ulan-Ude: a significant undertaking in terms of money, time, and effort. While some were constructed on money raised during live TV fund-raising shows (Rus. *telemarafon*), others relied on foreign or regional ties (Rus. *zemlyachestvo*), door-to-door fund-raising, and other networks of gathering money, materials, and labor. One temple, however, stands out from the rest in how it was funded. It was built on a mortgage loan taken out by the founder, who is also its abbot (Bur. *shireete*). Lamrim temple, named after a Tibetan Buddhist textual form that discusses the path to enlightenment, is a project of a middle-aged Buryat lama Choidorzhi Budaev. Starting off as a driver at Ivolginsky *datsan*,[1] the only functioning Buddhist institution in Buryatia at the time, he went on to study at a Buddhist institute in Ulaanbaatar in the 1980s. He subsequently returned to Buryatia to take on several important positions in the local Buddhist administration. In 1993, he was elected the Khambo Lama[2] but was soon removed, allegedly with accusations of embezzlement. Budaev then established his own local Buddhist organization "Lamrim," and later regional and federal Buddhist umbrella organizations, contributing to the changing institutional landscape of the previously centralized Buryat Buddhist administration. His efforts, however, have been rather marginal and have not challenged the prevalence of the Traditional Sangha, the dominant Buddhist organization which runs most *datsany* in Buryatia, and its current leader of over two decades the Khambo Lama Damba Ayusheev.

In fact, Budaev embraces his marginal position in the local Buddhist hierarchy and uses it to criticize the current state of the sangha, which he sees as degenerate because of what he sees as overly worldly preoccupations, as well as issues with discipline and education. Indeed, Buryat lamas[3] have often been criticized both from within the sangha and by laypeople for lack of right motivations, poor education, and flawed discipline. This was particularly so in the early post-Soviet years when many temples were being rebuilt simultaneously while there was still a very limited number of lamas. Since a Buddhist institute was only opened in Buryatia in 1991, many started working without having finished a full course of education. Discipline, too, was then lacking and it was not uncommon to see inebriated or otherwise inappropriately behaving lamas in temples or outside. This, however, is rather rare today: while the majority of lamas do not adhere strictly to the Vinaya monastic code, their misconduct is not as visible, and their temple and private lives are kept separate. As most lamas in Buryatia remain non-celibate, many Buddhists have come to consider it a local tradition rather than a failure in discipline.[4] In terms of education, it is now rare that a lama is accepted to a temple without having graduated from a Buddhist institute, and dozens studied in highly respected Tibetan monasteries in India. Several Buryat lamas recently earned the *geshe* degree in Buddhist philosophy there and returned to Buryatia—a fact that many take pride in as a sign of improvement in education and virtue of the sangha.

As Budaev claimed in my interview with him, it was indeed a wish to purify the sangha in Buryatia that was among the main reasons for building the Lamrim temple. Even though he ran several urban temples over the last two decades, lamas there were just like elsewhere in Buryatia in terms of limited knowledge and non-celibacy. Budaev does not deem himself a role model, and while he often wears lama-like robes,[5] he admits to being beyond change as a result of his time when there were few opportunities for monastic life. Instead, he wants to be a facilitator: build a "proper" temple and bring in well-educated Tibetan monks, a move which he hopes will gradually help reform the Buryat sangha.[6] With this in mind, Budaev started the construction of Lamrim temple in 2007 in a quiet area not far from the city center (Figure 5.1). He later took out a private loan of 45.5 million roubles, opening a restaurant in the temple complex so that its profit would cover the loan payments. A hotel had also been planned but was not opened by the time of my fieldwork, and the whole temple complex, while open to the public, was still under construction. As the economic crisis hit Russia in 2014, it became difficult for Budaev to keep up with loan payments, which

FIGURE 5.1 Lamrim temple interior, 2016 (Photo: Kristina Jonutytė).

had at times been 1.2 million roubles a month but fell that year to around 200,000.[7] The restaurant, with its rather high prices and fancy interior, was not particularly popular, as it was out of the way and did not meet the standard of much of the well-off clientele that it targeted. After several unsuccessful attempts to restructure the debt, Lamrim temple was put up for auction—an unprecedented event in Buryatia that was shocking to many. Unsurprisingly, no buyers volunteered, and Budaev was judged bankrupt in the summer of 2016. An air of uncertainty that was present in the temple throughout my stay in Ulan-Ude prevailed especially that summer. While a small group of lamas had split off from Budaev's organization over financial uncertainties half a year earlier, lamas who remained loyal were far from assured of the positive outcome and were considering various options for the future.[8]

Using the story of Lamrim temple as a case study, in this chapter I will unpack the kinds of flows that are rarely discussed in the literature on Buddhist exchanges: namely, material flows from the sangha to the laity. The Buddhist economy is often imagined as transfers of money, goods, and labor from the laity to the sangha and the provision of ritual support and merit in the other direction. Using the example of contemporary Buryatia, I will argue that this is not always a productive model for understanding sangha-lay relations. Instead, I will argue that Buddhist economy might be seen as a social field with a variety of flows rather than as static relations between two clearly separated groups of the sangha and the laity. I will start by giving a brief overview of the literature on exchange in Buddhism and move on to discuss flows from the sangha to the laity in Buryatia today. I will argue that these flows can be understood as a particular system of exchanges, reciprocities, and gifts, namely pooling, directed toward reestablishing a strong and visible presence of Buryat Buddhism in this multiethnic region. Finally, I will look at Buddhism in Ulan-Ude as a social field, arguing that the different actors within it each pursue their own moral-political projects. These projects are future-oriented, while often selectively drawing upon history and the "moral authority from the 'deep past'" (Humphrey 1992).

Buddhist Gifts and Exchanges: Overview

Exchange between the laity and the sangha has often been argued to be at the core of Buddhist institutions, practices, and societies. This exchange is usually conceptualized as the laity giving material support to the sangha and the sangha giving ritual support and merit to the laity. According to Strenski (1983, 470), "Buddhist society was formed in the process of ritual giving ... Giving defines the very relationship between the sangha and lay society." He argues that in early Buddhism, it was indeed this exchange with the laity that led to the "domestication" of the sangha, by which he means the adoption of sedentary life by previously wandering renouncers, as well as their entering of ritual, social, political, and economic relations with the laity. Strenski sees this relationship as involving elements of restricted exchange and sacrifice, but mostly based on generalized exchange whereby the gift is not reciprocated immediately and not necessarily by the same person. While agreeing with the centrality of exchange to the domestication of the sangha, Carrithers (1984, 322) objects that the relationship between monks and laypeople is mostly that of restricted exchange; it is personalized because donors are often friends or relatives of monks.

The complexities of Buddhist exchange have often been discussed in the light of Marcel Mauss's (2011 [1954]) seminal work on the gift, where the social constraints of the gift are explored. Among other aspects of the gift, Mauss discusses the immanent social obligation to repay it. Scholars of Indian religions have debated whether *dāna*, that is, various forms of almsgiving and charity without expectation of reciprocity such as the laity giving to the sangha in Buddhism, constitutes a truly free gift. Two apparent paradoxes have been of particular interest to scholars: first, if the act of giving is selfless, but merit is gained from it, is it still a "free gift?" And second, if the laity gives "selflessly" to the sangha, but monks perform rituals for them, is this a case of mutual gifts or an exchange of a different kind? In the Jain context, Laidlaw (2000) contends that the Jain gift to renouncers comes close to being a "free gift"—it is not reciprocated and not recognized as a gift by donors nor recipients—but is not quite free as karmic merit is gained from the act. Ohnuma suggests for Buddhism that a "pure gift" is only possible among the highest Buddhist realms (e.g., bodhisattvas), as they are not guided by self-interest like humans are, although ordinary Buddhists do "partake in the character of pure gift" when donating (2005, 119). Some authors argue that the "free gift" only happens in theory and in reality all Buddhist exchange is that of reciprocity (Falk 2007, 142), while others claim that "in philosophical Buddhism, ... the meditating monk becomes the model of non-reciprocity" (Tambiah 1980 [1970], 68). Yet others distinguish between transactions that are reciprocal and non-reciprocal, claiming that the latter are associated with soteriological goals while the former with this-worldly and profane ones (Ames 1966, 37–8).[9] In a recent attempt to review the debate, Sihlé (2015, 363) concludes that "there is no reciprocity in any strict sense of the word" in the context of giving *dāna* to members of the sangha, because it is not the recipient that produces merit but the very act of giving itself.

But should all Buddhist giving be understood as free gifts? Sihlé (2015) suggests that discussion of exchanges in the Buddhist context has often been simplified and unrefined. Instead of sticking to the strict distinction between "gift" and "commodity" and uncritically positing the idea of reciprocity as universal, he argues for the complexity of the modalities of gift-giving and other exchanges. When reciprocity is indeed present in the Buddhist context, he suggests that a distinction between weak and strong reciprocity should be made. Sihlé (ibid., 373) also draws attention to the fact that it is not just (free) gifts that are at the core of lay-monastic relations—as has been argued by, for instance, Strenski (1983, 470) and Ohnuma (2005, 104)—but various kinds of other exchanges, including also remunerations of religious services.

Apart from the question of reciprocity, scholars have explored what Buddhist giving does, other than producing merit and sustaining the livelihood of the sangha. In Myanmar, Buddhist monks refused to accept alms as a form of public political protest (Gravers 2012). In Thailand, through mediating exchange, Buddhist nuns—although only partially ordained and hierarchically below monks—reaffirm themselves as an integral part of the monastic community (Cook 2008). In Sri Lanka, selective donating shapes the religious experiences of the donors by dismissing monks who, for instance, subscribe to discriminating caste categories, thus transforming non-satisfactory lay-sangha relationships (Samuels 2007). These and other examples point to not just the multiplicity of effects that the variety of exchanges between the laity and the sangha has within and beyond the strictly religious context but also the fact that these exchanges—and thus the relationship between the two groups—are dynamic and multifaceted.

Temple Building: Sangha to Laity

In the literature on Buddhist exchange it is often merit and ritual that are highlighted as the basis of flows from the sangha to the laity. They are also crucial in the case of Buddhism in Ulan-Ude. In what follows, however, I will discuss cases of giving that vary beyond merit and ritual in their type and aim. The first one is Lamrim temple as a gift to the laity, the second one a gift of sheep through a herding project run by the Traditional Sangha. While they may seem to be special, one-off projects, in fact they are indicative of a larger undercurrent very much present among Buryat Buddhists. This is the idea that the sangha is not just a religious, ritual-providing institution, but that they also have to be useful in more direct, pragmatic ways and carry responsibility for the well-being of the people (as well as nonhumans) in Buryatia in spheres beyond religion.

To come back to the case of Lamrim temple, its founder Choidorzhi Budaev sees it largely as his gift to the people of Buryatia. The new temple with its envisioned "correct" Buddhist activities was to be an offering to both the Dalai Lama and the local people. The gift-like rhetoric around it focuses on two main points. One is giving local people an opportunity to practice what Budaev sees as a more authentic version of Buddhism, where monks would have completed substantial Buddhist education and would keep their vows. This would in his opinion not just provide laypeople with better and more varied ritual services and produce more merit but also inspire people to strive toward the Buddhist ideal thus transforming their behavior and attitude toward life. While such "correct" Buddhism is, according to Budaev, very much needed in a socioeconomically depressed place like Ulan-Ude, it is not possible now due to the current deteriorated state of the Buryat sangha. Budaev therefore risked his own material well-being and security in order to provide this opportunity to the local laity.

Another part of the gift-like rhetoric is the fact that he is building the temple using his own funds rather than gathering donations from laypeople. This happens rarely in temple building because donating toward such projects generates merit and often prestige, and people engage in it keenly for a variety of reasons (for instance Fisher 2008; Samuels 2007; Scott 2009). One Ulan-Ude lama shared a widespread sentiment when he told me that it seems not just odd but unfair not to accept lay donations for such cause because this deprives laypeople of a merit-making opportunity. Even more, he carefully added, this implies motivations that are not desirable in a lama: pride, narcissism, and a cry for acknowledgment. In contrast, Budaev highlights that he does not collect donations on moral grounds: people in Buryatia are poor and he does not wish to burden them by asking for their money. Instead of stripping them of their last roubles, he argues that they themselves need support, and this is what he was trying to achieve with the new temple. Many laypeople saw the good intentions in his undertaking but disapproved of his stubbornness. As a laywoman told me in Lamrim temple, she did not see why he would not put a donation box in the temple or organize a fund-raiser—while she personally could not give much, many small contributions would still make a difference. However, even after the financial difficulties became public and seemingly overwhelming to Budaev, he insisted as previously on not collecting lay donations.

Budaev—like others in his temple and some laity—highlighted the good intentions as inscribed into the materiality of the temple. In many conversations, people pointed to the beautiful Buddhist art painted on the walls by a Tibetan artist, the quality furniture imported from Europe, or the imposing Buddha statue from Nepal. Taking journalists on a tour,[10] Budaev lingered on the rubbish bins, windows, and bathroom tiles—of which he was proud because the place was not built and furnished *kak papalo* (Rus. for "randomly," "without sufficient attention") but was carefully thought through and expensive. Its quality was supposed to demonstrate Budaev's dedication to the matter and to materialize his offering that would be purifying and transformative. Having been active in Buryat Buddhism for over three decades, this was to be his most significant contribution to its revival: in his words, a "pure" temple, where Buddhism can finally be "properly" practiced. To him, this involves both material and immaterial forms: a temple that adheres more strictly to the canons in terms of physical space (for instance, having monastic quarters within the precincts as well as hosting a residency for the Dalai Lama in case he visits) and in terms of the kinds of people, knowledge, and practices that are present there.

Sangha to Laity: The Social Flock Project

Another kind of giving pertinent to understanding the flows in Buryat Buddhism today is a project run by the Traditional Sangha, called the Social Flock (Rus. *Sotsial'naya otara*). Through this project, the Buddhist organization gives out flocks of sheep to selected families across Buryatia. As flocks grow with years, some of the newborn sheep have to be given back to the headquarters. New flocks thus form, and these are given away to newly selected families. This way, more and more families have flocks, and herders in neighboring villages can herd sheep communally, which facilitates cooperation. Moreover, as the Khambo Lama explained, he hopes that this will facilitate settlement of remote areas and thus the extension of telephone, electricity lines, and other amenities there. The aim of this project is not just to support rural, traditional herding lifestyle, increase its prestige, and encourage rural migration[11] but also to bring back the endemic breed of sheep. These *Buubei* sheep are smaller and their wool is somewhat lower in quality, but they handle the harsh steppe climate well, digging up old grass from under the snow and requiring little extra food and care. In the Soviet period, these sheep were largely substituted for a more productive but less adaptive breed. This reviving of the "Buryat" sheep is not just an economic undertaking but also an ideological one: getting rid of Soviet heritage and reestablishing the link with the deep past. To quote the Khambo Lama (in Makhachkeev 2015, 31, my translation from Russian):

> Our ancestors left us our partners—Buryat horses, *Buubei* sheep, cows and *Khotosho* dogs. Then the communists came and said: "You have bad partners, the Buryat horse is small, the cow gives little milk, the sheep gives little wool." That is why they made us change them to Simmental cattle and Merino sheep, and we became their slaves. Because we need to feed them year-round!

The Social Flock project is different from the traditional *jisa* mechanism in Mongolian monasteries whereby cattle donated to a monastery is loaned to the laity, and the monastery receives a large part of the produce (Miller 1961, 435–6). Instead, families selected for the project are *given* sheep and only have to return a part of the newborn sheep, which is effectively a gift and not a *jisa* kind of loan. This kind of giving would possibly eventually bring benefit to Buddhist temples, especially those in the countryside: if people are well-off, they will also support the *datsany* which helped them attain material stability. This consideration, however, is not vocalized and even if it was among the reasons for initiating the project, such outcome is rather distant—if at all attainable—and dependent on a number of additional factors. Social Flock is therefore by and large understood by the public, as well as by those who partake in the project, as a gift from the Buryat sangha to the local people. In fact the gift extends beyond the laity, as the project does support not only Buddhists or Buryats but others as well.

Social Flock is a project that is representative of the sangha striving to be of tangible, material help to the laity. Time and again during my fieldwork, I heard both lamas and laypeople talk about how the sangha is a "pillar" (Rus. *opora*) in society, and there are several ways in which this was said. From the point of view of the laity, the sangha provides—among other things— ritual support, practical advice in the setting of private consultations, a link with the past, a significant part of national identity, and representation of the Buryats on local and federal levels. This is especially so as politicians are not trusted, and the Khambo Lama is seen by many as being the "real power" in the republic. The herding project in particular gains him support, with many praising the fact that there is "more than just words" and admiring the Khambo Lama as a good manager. From the point of view of the sangha, this project is part of a larger tendency to be a "pillar" not just in the religious sphere but in economic, political, and other matters as well. This striving is present in discourse and in undertaken activities. One urban lama, for instance, insisted that *datsany* should be of more direct help to the laity than they are now: they should not just provide ritual support and consultations but also employ laypeople and establish businesses where laypeople could work. In his opinion, it is the responsibility of the sangha to offer help (Rus. *okazyvat' pomoshch'*) to people in whatever ways it is needed. An abbot of a rural *datsan* that I first met in Ulan-Ude was running errands in the city for the benefit of his parish villagers, the main task being to get the regional administration to send a sports coach to work in their area. That, however, was only one of many things he had done for his parish community, others including teaching locals agricultural techniques, providing them with seed potatoes, and helping them deal with bureaucratic matters. While the young lama had hoped to spread Buddhist teachings when he was initially selected to be the abbot of a freshly rebuilt temple, he said that much of his time now is taken by caring for the laity in other spheres of their lives. While initially he found it frustrating, he now sees such practical help as necessary in order to sustain the Buddhist community. Other examples of such attempts of the sangha to offer "non-religious" help to the laity are organizing republic-wide competitions of Buryat language, projects to rehabilitate addicts and homeless, and a Buryat-language radio station.

The Social Flock and other projects mentioned above are a kind of Socially Engaged Buddhism insofar as they are efforts of a Buddhist organization to tackle economic, social, political, and other problems in contemporary society (cf. King 2009). Like many other cases of engaged Buddhism, they can be seen as endeavors by Buddhist actors to make up for a weak, ineffective state in certain spheres or pitch in where the state is seen as tackling issues in an unsatisfactory manner (for instance, Darlington 2012; Jacquet and Walton 2013; Main and Lai 2013, 26). However, as Ip (2009, 151) argues, similar forms of social engagement are attempts not just at reforming society but also of reforming Buddhism itself. This is also critical in the Buryat case. As I argued above, these projects can be seen as a way of redefining the role of the sangha in society today and thus remaining relevant and prominent (more on the Buryat case in Jonutytė 2020; see similar discussions in Samuel 2013; Tedesco 2003; Watts and Okano 2012). At the same time, the Socially Engaged Buddhism label can only be used with caution in regard to the Buryat material. While many projects of engaged Buddhism are translocal and NGO-like and essentially a post–Second World War trend,[12] those run by the Traditional Sangha have no clear links or references to projects elsewhere and are presented and perceived as expressly local.

Giving and Receiving, Sameness and Difference

Discussing Buddhist exchange, Strenski (1983, 470) argues that "the monks are always the receivers, the laity always givers," referring to material flows.

In his understanding, giving to the sangha expresses difference between two separate groups and forges a relationship between them. Religious giving is taken to be one of the main practices that distinguish the two groups. Moreover, in theory at least, the sangha renounce productive activities and enter into a relationship with the laity whereby they have to be materially supported. However, in practice the line is not so clear-cut: nuns engage in wage labor (Gutschow 2004, 78) as do monks in some contexts (for instance, Miller 1961, 433). In Buryatia where the monastic code is not strictly observed, this distinction into monks and laity has little to do with productive activities, but it is drawn in a nontrivial way that I will discuss below. Significantly, what the Buryat case shows is that not all kinds of flows in Buddhism differentiate and separate the laity and the sangha, but some can instead express sameness and working toward the same cause. Both the Lamrim temple and the Social Flock project, rather than establishing the sangha as a distinct group of religious professionals, are initiatives that blur this distinction.

Across the Buddhist world, a variety of practices and observances separate the sangha from the laity. As already mentioned, dependence of the sangha on the laity for its subsistence is usually among the key aspects of such distinction. Mills (2001, 72–3) sees it as part of a wider division of productive and reproductive activities between the laity and the monks. Ordination and monastic vows strictly or loosely observed are also key in most Buddhist contexts. Some of the other aspects that have been noted as relevant by various authors are bodily comportment, discipline, and dress (Bunnag 1973, 29–36), and ability to manage chthonic spirits (Mumford 1989). In Buryatia, these distinguishing factors are relevant only to a limited extent. Instead, being a lama involves one or both features of having a formal or informal education in Buddhism and earning an income from religious services. Even then, these characteristics are rather fluid: if one graduated from a Buddhist institute and moved on to a lay profession, one may or may not be deemed a lama. The income from religious services is, too, a vague factor: it does not have to be steady or sole income and a lama may hold another job in addition.[13] It can be said that being a lama today in Buryatia has been to a certain degree professionalized. This has tangible implications for sangha-lay relations: they are thus compartmentalized. Lamas are lamas insofar as it is their specialization that (usually) brings income. Remunerations for rituals and consultations are a recognition of such specialization and thus express a degree of difference between the giver and the receiver. However, this recognition of difference is compartmentalized in that it does not spill over into other flows between the sangha and the laity. In other words, these remunerations are not definitive of sangha-lay relations but are part of the many kinds of flows in the social field of Buddhism in Buryatia.

In what ways do Buddhist giving practices create sameness (if not unity) among a variety of actors in this field? By and large, this giving—both by laypeople and lamas as well as by other actors—contributes toward the rebuilding of Buddhism in Buryatia. These transfers are inputs toward the reestablishment and further spread of Buddhism where it was once impeded, obstructed, and even demolished. Three aspects of this Buddhist revival are particularly relevant here: revitalizing Buddhism as a teaching and a practice, (re)formulating the role of the sangha in society, and establishing a strong, visible Buryat-Buddhist presence in a multiethnic region. While some of these are intentionally pursued by some of the actors involved, others occur as unintended consequences. The first two are not unexpected in a Buddhist revival, but the third perhaps needs clarification. In the context where religion is seen as coinciding with—or stemming from— one's ethnicity (see, for instance, Amogolonova 2014), the public presence of Buddhism is also part of identity politics. In multiethnic Buryatia where due to imperial, Soviet and Russian policies many feel that Buryats have lost power in their republic and that Buryats are rapidly "losing their culture," a strong presence of Buryat Buddhism is an important way of reclaiming not only social standing and prestige but also power in the region.

Fisher (2008) discusses temple building in contemporary China, where monks and nuns travel across the country and abroad to collect donations for building new temples. They "becomes a powerful outward symbol of the religious community" of Buddhists and are "a powerful testament to the efficacy and rightness of the practitioner's belief in a country where Buddhism—and religious practice in general—is still often criticised" (2008, 148). Similarly in Buryatia, Buddhist building projects—undertaken by lamas and laypeople alike—are a way to publicly express the strong presence of Buryat religion (as well as ethnic identity with which it is intertwined) in the context of increasingly centralized Russia and increasingly Russified Buryatia.

While I primarily focus in this chapter on the material flows from the sangha to the laity since they are less common in discussions on Buddhist giving, I consider transfers from the laity to the sangha as part of the social field of Buddhist giving as well. Based on my interviews and conversations with laypeople, remunerations for consultations with lamas or for rituals are variously considered as expressions of gratefulness (Rus. *blagodarnost'*), payments (Rus. *oplata*), and offerings (Rus. *podnoshenie*). However, at the same time my interlocutors often highlighted that their support of temples and lamas is necessary for the reestablishment of Buddhist infrastructure which the common good of the Buryat people is hinged upon. One interlocutor, for instance, compared Buddhist temples and the specialists and rituals within them to public toilets. In her view, they are "normal human needs" (Rus. *normal'naya chelovecheskaya potrebnost'*) and should therefore be widely available and accessible to all. Another interlocutor told me that she considers various kinds of offerings obligatory (Rus. *obyazatel'no*) when visiting a *datsan*. In her view, they are "necessary for the development of

Buddhism and *datsan*, as well as separately [given] for the lama." These examples point to donations, remunerations, and other kinds of transfers being conceptualized emically not only as directed at their immediate aim (e.g., thanking the lama), but also contributing to the larger projects of rebuilding and sustaining Buryat Buddhism.

Pooling and Projects in a Social Field

The various flows in Buryat Buddhism such as remunerations for rituals or donations toward temple building—especially those of a material kind— can be better understood not as an exchange between the sangha and the laity as two distinct groups but as a common project of pooling. In arguing this, I diverge somewhat from Strenski, Carrithers, and others who interpret exchange, reciprocity, and/or gifts between the laity and the sangha as the core of Buddhist economies or even "Buddhist society" (Strenski 1983, 479). While I see a model of exchange between two separate groups as not quite fitting in the Buryat case, pooling is nonetheless "an organization of reciprocities" (Sahlins 1972, 188). The significant difference, then, lies in the fact that "pooling is socially a *within* relation, the collective action of a group. Reciprocity is a *between* relation, the action and reaction of two parties" (1972, 188; original emphasis). In other words, while there are certain links of generalized exchange, reciprocity, and gift-giving within the Buddhist economy in Ulan-Ude, altogether they can be seen as a set of relations *within* the group of Buryat Buddhists that result in a pooling of resources toward a common cause.[14] This cause, then, is the revival— and expansion—of Buddhism in Buryatia, which encompasses a variety of concomitant processes such as establishing a link with the pre-Soviet past, asserting a public and political presence of a minority ethnic group, and strengthening social unity and its boundaries.

Pooling, as Sahlins (1972, 189) argues, "stipulates a social center where goods meet and thence flow outwards, and a social boundary too, within which persons (or subgroups) are cooperatively related." Pooling in Buryat Buddhism, while it creates a sense of unity within and draws social boundaries, is not "chiefly" and does not have a central authority. Instead, I find it more fitting to consider it a social field, as this helps see Buryat Buddhism as dynamic and diffuse, rather than a static hierarchy. To be clear, I do not argue here that the Lamrim temple building or the Social Flock project are individual instances of pooling: funds for them may (in Social Flock) or may not (in Lamrim temple) be pooled, but this is beyond the point. What I highlight here is that all these projects together—and the donations that go into them—are a kind of pooling on a greater societal level. Thus, pooling occurs at the larger scale of the social field of Buryat Buddhism en masse and incorporates a wide variety of material and immaterial flows. A social field, as defined by Bourdieu and Wacquant (1992, 97), is a network, or a configuration, of objective relations between positions. These positions are objectively defined, in their existence and in the determinations they impose upon their occupants, agents or institutions, by their present and potential situation (*situs*) in the structure of the distribution of species of power (or capital) whose possession commands access to the specific profits that are at stake in the field, as well as by their objective relation to other positions (domination, subordination, homology, etc.).

The institutional landscape of Buryat Buddhism is rather complex today, with different organizations having differing access to lay donations, public funds, as well as differing outreach. Those that associate with the Traditional Sangha, for instance, have more (and more substantial) sponsors at hand due to both belonging to the most prominent Buddhist organization in Buryatia and to the successful efforts of the current Khambo Lama. Lamas outside of it, like Budaev, who are further removed from state authorities and influential contacts, have to rely on narrower network of sponsors or alternatively—as with the Lamrim temple—on themselves and their commercial initiatives. Still others rely on *zemlyachestvo* regional ties, which may be more or less fruitful depending on the number of rich businessmen or politicians who come from that region. In some cases, lamas who are charismatic or otherwise exceptional forge their own networks of financial support, often extending across Russia. In temple building and similar projects, all these strategies are available to both lamas and laypeople, and are utilized by both. Humphrey and Ujeed (2013, 319) also argue that the division into two groups—monks and laity—is insufficient in the Buddhist "gift economy" in the Inner Mongolian context, and it should instead be seen as a "three-cornered relation," which also includes political authorities who substantially supported monasteries both historically and in contemporary Inner Mongolia. However, I would like to extend the scope even further and see the gift economy as a whole field, where not just political authorities take part alongside sangha and ordinary laity but also commercial actors (for instance, sponsors who are not laity), academics (such as those who made the case for the "scientifically proven miracle" of the early twentieth-century Buryat Buddhist monk Etigelov, see Quijada 2012), those in between strictly defined spheres (such as lamas-businessmen), and so on.

What is at stake in this field is, firstly, building a temple or implementing a different project that one undertook. Secondly, it is shaping the geo-temporalities of Buryat Buddhism: not only its current social and material landscape is in question but also its pasts and futures. Budaev's project, while being a Buddhist temple seemingly like any other, is also an attempt to transform and purify Buryat Buddhism by adhering more strictly to the canons and inviting the presumably more disciplined and virtuous Tibetan monks. This is not only an act of shaping the future of Buryat Buddhism but also a statement about the past. While the current Khambo

Lama Ayusheev refutes the significance of Tibetan connections in Buryat Buddhism historically and today (for instance, Bernstein 2013, 80), Budaev sees Buryat Buddhism as stemming from and bounded with the Tibetan Buddhist world and calls for more integration into it. He does that through cultivating contacts with the Dalai Lama, regularly inviting Tibetan lamas, but also framing the "purification" project as inherently Tibetan—not only was a Tibetan artist invited to paint the temple walls, Tibetan monks would also be invited to reform local Buddhism. Undermining the Tibetan link, Ayusheev and his Traditional Sangha instead draw legitimacy and authority from a link with prerevolutionary Buddhism. As in Mongolia, in Buryatia the "deep past" is "the source of moral authority in the present … [and it] is being called upon to provide inspiration for a discontinuity with the immediate past" (Humphrey 1992, 375). This is done through a number of means such as sacred objects and sites, and amounts to envisioning an autocephalous Buddhist church, which is imagined not only as uniform and continuous throughout history but also as developing unto itself. It is therefore both competing interpretations of history and competing visions for the future of Buryat Buddhism that are at stake in temple building and similar projects—and by extension in giving money, labor, and other resources toward them.

Giving in Buryat Buddhism, while prompted by a range of motivations and circumstances, is often part of "moral projects" undertaken by the givers, individuals, and institutions alike. As Cole (2003, 99) defines it, moral projects are "local visions of what makes a good, just community." She highlights that in them "people's private concerns and existential predicaments [are situated] within wider social and historical political ideologies and material contexts" (ibid., 122). Cole is interested primarily in the ways in which people's moral projects shape the way they narrate memories of an anticolonial rebellion in East Madagascar. In a radically different context, this concept also sheds light on practices of religious giving in Buryatia. It highlights the fact that gifts are not only motivated by personal and social considerations and situated in particular sociopolitical contexts, but that they also contribute to individual and communal efforts to interpret and shape the world around them.

I do not wish to argue that all donations are directed toward communal moral projects or even that all of them are explicitly moral. They can, to the contrary, be directed at constructing oneself as a virtuous person, be it in the eyes of others or not. They can, moreover, be primarily political or social rather than strictly moral projects, such as the Social Flock gifts of sheep to the laity, which rests on sociopolitical aspirations for self-reliance and the return to a traditional rural Buryat lifestyle. Importantly, however, giving in this context is not just a religious act aimed at merit-making or a quest for prestige and social capital, as it has often been described in the literature on Buddhist gift and exchange. Alongside, it is also part of moral, social, and political projects undertaken by the givers, which are directed as much at the construction of self (e.g., as a moral person by "doing good") as at shaping the surrounding world (e.g., making Buddhism and thus Buryat presence more visible in the multiethnic city).

Conclusion

In this chapter, I proposed that flows in the Buddhist economy in Buryatia can better be understood as pooling of wealth, transforming it via the sangha and recirculating it, rather than as strictly reciprocity between the laity and the sangha as two distinct groups.[15] This is because pooling is a collective action *within* one group, whereas reciprocity is a relation of social *duality* between two groups—a perspective that is not strongly supported by the analysis of flows in Buryat Buddhism. Having said that, pooling and redistribution occur not through a strong authoritative center but within a social field with multiple actors and complex power relations. Laity and sangha, individuals and institutions alike, are parts of this social field, where the stakes are not just the revival of Buddhism but the particular ways in which this is done. These ways concern authority both over interpreting the past of Buryat Buddhism and over its current and future developments and alliances. Religious giving is moreover a moral (but also political, social) project that is directed at shaping both oneself and the surrounding world.

The argument presented here is based on a particular ethnographic case—namely, a case where Buddhist practices and institutions, while having a long history in the region, were violently repressed and dismantled for over half a century. It is only in the last three decades that they have undergone a revival, drawing as much on earlier traditions as on translocal influences, other religions, socialism, current geopolitics, and other factors. The relevance of the case presented is then twofold. First, material and immaterial transfers—whether reciprocal or not—may be at the core of Buddhist institutions and practices, but they are not necessarily static, structural, or differentiating relations between two groups. Second, religious giving should not be seen as an isolated—and a distinctly lay—affair but as an act that a variety of actors undertake, guided by a range and mixture of factors, such as moral, social, and political considerations, and particular historico-political circumstances.

CHAPTER SIX

Exorcising Mauss's Ghost in the Western Himalayas: Buddhist Giving as Collective Work

Martin Mills

And what is the treasure of generosity? There is the case of a disciple of the noble ones, his awareness cleansed of the stain of stinginess, living at home, freely generous, openhanded, delighting in being magnanimous, responsive to requests, delighting in the distribution of alms. This is called the treasure of generosity. (*Anguttara Nikaya Sutta*, 7.6)

It is taught that when in giving, the giver, the receiver and the act of giving are empty, this is said to be a transcendent perfection [but] when attachment to these three is born, this is called a worldly perfection. (Chandrakirti's *Madhyamakāvatāra*, vs. 16)

Introduction

The *Anguttara Nikaya Sutta* above emphasizes openhandedness as the essential quality of the Buddhist notion of generosity, characterizing much of the normative stance of Buddhism's institutional view on religious giving to the sangha itself, or *dāna*. In both this and Chandrakirti's seventh-century *Guide to the Middle Way* (*Madhyamakāvatāra*), it is the quality of engaged perception, or motivation, that defines the distinction between worldly exchange and transcendent giving. The paradigmatic case of *dāna* is of course the daily village alms round by Theravadin monks, their bowls filled with rice by laity to silent non-acknowledgment.

The etiquette of non-acknowledgment is a vital aspect of the economic structure of *dāna*. In Buddhist studies at least, the openhandedness of religious giving by laity is seen as almost universally matched by *non-reciprocity* from the Buddhist monastic community (Ohnuma 2005, 105; Sihlé 2015, 352; Strenski 1983, 422–3), who may well perform rites and prayers for laity *but not in specific return for what the laity give*. As Heim summarizes in her review of Buddhist sources:

> Dāna, according to all formal discussion on it, is not obligated in any way. It does not evoke return from the recipient and is not premised on a notion of reciprocity and interdependence. As the Dharma śāstra author Lakmīdhara bluntly states: "reciprocal gifts are not part of dharma." Moreover, dāna does not and should not inspire gratitude from the recipient.
>
> (Heim 2004, 34)

Along with certain other South Asian renunciatory traditions, this is seen as a defining exception to the general anthropological dictum formulated in Marcel Mauss's *Essay on the Gift* that all giving requires reciprocity. Mauss concluded that just as there is an obligation to give and receive, there is also an obligation to give back (Mauss 1990 [1922], 16–17). This seems not only to be rejected by Buddhist monastics, many of whom assert a studious asymmetry of exchange in *dāna*, but is widespread enough in the Buddhist world to constitute a substantive falsification of Mauss's conclusion as a general anthropological truth. In answer to the Maussian question of reciprocity ("What do laity get in return for their sponsorship and support of the sangha?"), Buddhist orthodoxy tells us, very simply, that the answer is *nothing*.

Nonetheless, most anthropological analyses retain Mauss's cynicism regarding the widespread authenticity of such openhanded generosity. As Parry famously quipped:

> The gift is always an "Indian gift"—that is, one "for which an equivalent return is expected"—and the notion of a "pure gift" is mere ideological obfuscation which masks the supposedly non-ideological verity that nobody does anything for nothing.
>
> (Parry 1986, 455)

Parry's point, of course, is that there is an *expectation* of return by laity themselves, otherwise why would they support the sangha in the first place?

The view that Buddhist principles of unreciprocated giving are merely pious priestly ideology obscuring a reality of transactional exchange is certainly one shared in one form or another by many anthropologists (e.g., Cole 1998; Gernet 1995; Strenski 1983, 471; Walsh 2010, 18), for whom Marcel Mauss's general dictum that all giving *requires* reciprocity remains one of the few *idées fixes* of the anthropological canon. Like Banquo's ghost, Mauss's assertion lingers at the ritual feast, pointing a finger of suspicion.

In this chapter I will argue that much of this tension derives from the assumption that laity and sangha should be treated as analytically separate groups, and that *dāna* is therefore a form of reciprocal exchange in Maussian terms. This, I will argue, fundamentally distorts our understanding of communal ritual action in Buddhist societies. Instead, such actions are better understood as forms of collective work that bind laity and sangha together as a single social actor. Specifically, I will argue that in engaging with members of the Buddhist sangha through ritual-specific transfers, Buddhist lay practitioners are deploying the sangha as extensions of their own household action, a distributive act that voids the reality of exchange and therefore the need for reciprocity.

The principle of non-reciprocity of lay religious gifts to the sangha is firmly and near-universally asserted within Buddhism. That the sangha demand no set fee for their ritual work, and ritual work itself is not recompense for the offerings received.

Of course, in practice *some* lay-sangha engagements are clearly commodified forms of exchange, such as the "rent-a-monk" scheme available on the Japanese Amazon store (Świtek, this volume) or the fixed-price selling offices for the performance of Buddhist rites by monks at Ulaanbaatar's state-owned monasteries (Abrahms-Kavunenko, this volume). Nor is the monetarization of Buddhist monastic economics in any sense a modern phenomenon, as Gregory Schopen has shown in detail (2004). However, it seems perverse to deny the reality of non-reciprocity in Buddhist *dāna* when it is otherwise so prevalent and when such a doctrinal interpretation is so strongly asserted not just by members of the sangha but by laity too. This disinterested presentation of *dāna* is linked to assertions regarding the sangha's karmic value as an object of giving. In such terms, the sangha is doctrinally presented as the supreme object of offering, above animals, humans, even Buddhas (Ñanamoli and Bodhi 1995, 1105).

The idea that such free generosity creates karmic merit for future lives has raised speculation that such merit is *itself* the reciprocated object (Heim 2004, 34; Walsh 2010, 18), the returned commodity that the sangha somehow owns, in the manner in which the Catholic Church claimed ownership of the keys to heaven. Once again Buddhist orthodoxy denies this, asserting that, as Strenski puts it, "the sangha is an occasion of merit, as the scriptures put it a 'field of merit;' [but] it is not its origin, much less is it a private reserve to distribute to the worthy" (Strenski 1983, 473; see also Ames 1966, 31; Spiro 1970, 280, 410).

We are thus faced with two possibilities: either Mauss was simply wrong about exchange or *dāna* itself is not an exchange as Mauss conceived the term.

In what follows, I will argue for the latter: that *dāna* (as both normatively conceptualized and widely practiced within the Buddhist tradition) is neither an exchange nor a gift but *redistribution* and *transformation*. More specifically, it is a form of combined ritual "work" that chains individuals together into a collective process of ritual transformation that extends *across* the apparent divide between laity and sangha. This requires us to think carefully about what is meant by "the ritual actor" in such events and the degree to which we can see Buddhist monks and nuns as separate from householders—that is, as *anāgarika* ("homeless ones").

To look at this in detail, this chapter will examine Buddhist *dāna* between lay and sangha in Leh Dosmoché, a large-scale exorcistic rite carried out by Tibetan Buddhist monastic communities in the Western Himalayas. While this *looks* like reciprocity between laity (who provide economic offerings) and the sangha (who provide blessings in return), its ethnography of practice and prodigious indigenous exegesis both imply that the sangha are merely an extension of lay religious actions and desires; specifically, that such monastic exorcisms play a key role in the symbolic purification of lay wealth and inheritance as it moves between generations—a role which in part explains the ongoing public support for and participation in such otherwise highly esoteric Buddhist rites. Much of the ethnography here is taken from two performances of the Dosmoché Festival seventeen years apart in 1995 and 2012 by the Geluk school monks of Lingshed Kumbum Monastery (see Mills 2001), for whose advice, friendship, and hospitality I remain deeply indebted and which (ironically) I can never fully repay. Subsidiary and smaller forms of the described protector rites were attended on numerous occasions over thirty years. As we shall see later, this span of years brought changes to such performances, shifting the nature of giving between laity and sangha in important ways.

Leh Dosmoché: The Festival of the Thread Cross

Leh Dosmoché[1] is the annual expelling rite carried out at the King's New Year (the twenty-eighth to twenty-ninth day of the twelfth month, usually around February or March) in the city of Leh in the kingdom of Ladakh, a segment of Jammu and Kashmir, India, that crosses onto the Tibetan Plateau. At the time of writing, Leh was the regional capital, a city of some 30,000 inhabitants under the jurisdiction of the Ladakh Autonomous Hill Development Council (LAHDC). The city's origins probably date from the tenth century, but much of its historical architecture derives from the Namgyal Dynasty of the sixteenth to seventeenth century. The nine-story Leh Palace on Tsemo Hill was completed by King Sengge Namgyal (1570–1642), an adherent of the Buddhist Drukpa Kagyu school, and dominates the skyline of the city, surrounded by a cluster of temples that act as the ceremonial core of the Dosmoché Festival.

Dosmoché is a citywide exorcism (*torlok*[2]) in which the powers of the Buddhist protector deities (*choskyong*) are invoked to expel the *lhandré* (bad spirits) and *dud* (demons) from the "old city," the rectangular main bazaar area that was originally the king's fields. This invocation includes several monastic communities from Ladakh's various Buddhist schools—the Nyingma, Sakya, Kagyu, and Geluk—who perform parallel and separate expelling rites, each based in one of the various Old Palace temples into the city below.[3] After several days of monastic ritual invoking the protector deities within the temples, large expiatory votive cakes (one for each main monastic community) are carried through Leh's main bazaar. These are called *torma* and made of barley flour, butter, and vegetable dye, constructed on top of a large metal bowl. Each procession stops at the city's main crossroads to perform rites that summon bad spirits into each *torma*. It is at this point that the majority of public lay giving occurs, with members of the crowd placing cash or dough balls (*zan ril*) into the metal bowl. Reaching the lower end of the main town, the *torma* and offerings are carried to an unoccupied wasteland to the south of the central city. Here, large pyres had been prepared in advance, into which the various *torma* are thrown.

The centerpiece of this stage of the rite is the destruction of the great "thread cross" (or *dos*) by the local Nyingma monastery of Taktok, in addition to their *torma*. The *dos* is an elaborate cage-cum-hut made of multicolored threads and flags, into which demons had been summoned and trapped during the rite. The *torma* and *dos* are burnt to great acclaim and cries of "*Lhandré dud tsar!*" ("Spirits and demons are finished!") from the surrounding laity, whereupon the crowd converges on the pyres in a fierce melée, with the remains of the burnt dough collected as medicine (*sman*) and the remaining threads of the *dos* fought over as blessing (*chinlabs*).

Calling the Lord of Death

If the ethnography above was an "outer" public description of the rite, the monks themselves attend more privately to its "inner" aspects. The ritual performances of Dosmoché by the various Buddhist schools in Leh centered on the invocation of different tantric Buddhas. Since these were parallel rites, we will concentrate here on those performed by the monks from the Geluk school in Ladakh, founded in the fourteenth century by Je Tsongkhapa and closely affiliated to the Dalai Lamas.

Geluk involvement in Leh Dosmoché centers around the invocation of the Buddha Dorjé Jigjet (Skt. *Yamantaka Vajrabhairava*, "Terrifying Adamantine One, Subduer of Death"), the central tutelary Buddha of the Geluk school, a tantric form of Bodhisattva Mañjuśrī. Bull-headed with multiple arms, his wrathful iconographic form derives from his triumphant victory over Shinjé (Skt. *Yama*, the Lord of Death), who acts as his servant and executor. Here, wrathful deities are almost never referred to as being "angry" in the normal sense of the word but as being "compassionately wrathful"—that is, acting in a way motivated by compassion, but also in a manner which is unflinching in its desire to destroy *nyon-mongs* (Skt. *kleśa*), the mental afflictions which cause sentient beings' suffering. Because buddhas are regarded as otherworldly deities, however, they are not seen as interfering directly in worldly matters, a task which is delegated instead to their affiliated protector deities—in this case Shinjé. To give a sense of the logic involved here, a senior Geluk monk in Leh explained to me that while foreigners find it unsettling how they invoke the "Lord of Death" to cleanse monasteries, villages, and towns, the Buddhist understanding was that meditation on death served as an antidote to attachment to this life, to wealth, and to the body. He described such mental afflictions as being ultimately embodied in demonic forms which are both within people and present in the world. In this sense, "death" was a friend of the dedicated Buddhist practitioner, providing them with an object of contemplation and renunciation that cuts through their afflictive attachment to the world. The Lord of Death was therefore a protector of the Buddhist path and a servant of Mañjuśrī, the Buddha of wisdom.

The ritual invocation of Dorjé Jigjet and Shinjé is a standard part of the ritual calendar of most Geluk monasteries, being performed daily in its shortened form. It follows the standard structure of Buddhist protector rites (*skangsol*) in the Geluk school: the principal officiant visualizes himself as Dorjé Jigjet, in which guise he then summons Shinjé to purify any breaches of the monastery's tantric vows. In its more elaborate form such as Dosmoché, Shinjé's power is embodied in a specific *torma* offering cake called the *drugchuma*, representing the fiercesome weapon of Shinjé, a flayed and burning corpse in the form of a flaming pyramid—its red triangular form topped with a skull being a standard symbol for the entrapment of demons.

The invocation usually takes two to three days, preceded by several days given over to the preparation of the offerings and *drugchuma*. Once the invocation of Dorjé Jigjet and Shinjé is complete, the *drugchuma* is processed down the winding mountain paths from the Old Palace temples to Leh's main bazaar, carried by *rigs-ngan*—male members of Ladakh's "untouchable castes," such as the *mon* or *beda*—who are hired for the occasion. At the main bazaar, the procession stops at the crossroads in front of the main mosque, where the principal officiant performs a short rite summoning the negative forces and spirits of the place into the lower half of the *drugchuma*, effectively imprisoning them beneath Shinjé's power (Figure 6.1).

Arriving at the waste ground at the lower end of the Old Town, several triangular thickets of briar are arranged to receive the *drugchuma* and *dos*. The officiating lama from Lingshed performed the purificatory fire ceremony, a short ritual that invokes the deity Dorjé Khandro (Skt. Vajradhaka, an emanation of the Buddha Akshobya), who sits within the fire, waiting for the *drugchuma* with mouth upturned. This rite is often used during funeral ceremonies (see Mills 2001, 227), in which Dorjé Khandro "eats" black

FIGURE 6.1 Geluk monks summon obstructive spirits into *drugchuma* (center) in Leh Bazaar, winter 1994 (Photo: Martin Mills).

sesame seeds thrown into the fire, thus transforming the deceased's negative karma into emptiness (*stongpanyid*). The *drugchuma*, along with the dough balls and coins, is cast into this deified fire, followed by arrows shot by the officiating lama (acting as Shinjé) to "nail" the *drugchuma*'s accumulated demonic load to the fire. The elements remaining after the ceremony are deemed to have been purified by this fire and to have been transformed into purificatory medicine (*sman*) and blessing (*chinlabs*), which are left to be claimed by the younger male members of the surrounding crowd. After this, the monks return to the temple to perform prayers of aspiration (*smonlam*) and dedication (*sngowa*).

Now that we have seen this rite through, as it were, an "outer" lay ethnography as well as an "inner" sangha one, how are we to understand the patterns of exchange and transfer that occur within it?

The Giver and the Gift: The Significance of Barley and Cash

Lay giving in Dosmoché involves two main processes, in each of which offerings are intimately associated with the giver: they contain, as Mauss noted, something of the very personhood of the those who gift them (Mauss

1990 [1922], 16). In the first, households from the Leh area sponsored the performance of the rite in advance through donations to the All-Ladakh Gompa Association (ALGA) offices in Leh Bazaar, providing support, offerings, food, and drink for the initial invocation rites in the palace temples, as well as the materials for the construction of *drugchuma* and *dos*. Here, the names of sponsors were taken down by the monastic officers of the ALGA and donors given a written receipt. In the rite itself, the offerings of lay sponsors were signified by the use of *yugu*, small red offering cakes (effectively, small *drugchuma*, designed to capture the demonic afflictions of the donors) that were carried in a tray along with the main procession.[4] In the second (which we will attend to in greater detail), members of the crowd awaiting the procession hurriedly placed either barley dough balls (*zan ril*) or cash offerings into the base of the main *drugchuma* as it passes by the major thoroughfares of the town. This was purely informal: no names were taken and no receipts were given—indeed, no acknowledgment was provided at all by members of the sangha. Both forms of lay offering at Dosmoché—whether the initial formal offerings or the ad hoc procession offerings—were spoken of in a general sense as ritual sponsorship (*zhindak*) and are understood by both laity and monks as a participation in the general expiatory (*skangwa*—appeasement, amendation, correction) function of the rite.

The offerings given from the crowd during the procession include either *zan ril* or cash. In 1995, the majority of such offerings from local landholding Ladakhi Buddhists were *zan ril*, brought by members of the crowd from their homes, where they had usually been handed round from a dish to whomever was present, to be pressed to the eyes, ears, nose, mouth, throat, and heart, intended to "soak up" the negative thoughts, feelings, words, and sights of the person from the previous year. By contrast, resident Hindu (and occasionally Muslim) shopkeepers from the bazaar area tossed in rupee coins.

Seventeen years later, this dynamic had shifted almost entirely. Rather than throwing in *zan ril* dough balls, the overwhelming majority of such donations by both local Ladakhi Buddhist householders as well as Hindu and Muslim traders was in the form of cash. With the value of rupees having changed dramatically since 1995, this was mainly in the form of 100-rupee notes, although many gave larger denominations. While there were still a few who threw in *zan ril*, the shift to rupee notes meant that by the time the procession had reached the lower streets of Leh, the large *drugchuma* bowl was overflowing with notes, and one of the monks had to trail behind, picking them off the street as they blew away. This was not a task he relished, and as the cash blew around the street, onlookers stepped back to avoid being touched by it.

Dosmoché shares this overall ritual template with informal Tibetan Buddhist household rites at New Year that rarely involve members of the sangha. For the last meal of the year, households prepare a *gut'uk* stew containing nine ingredients, including *zan ril*, that are dished out to recipients, each containing an item that symbolizes their dispositions for the upcoming year: wool for kindheartedness, charcoal for miserliness, chilli for harsh words, and so on. Alongside the *gut'uk* are prepared a set of dry barley dough balls and a human figurine (*lud*) also made of barley dough on an outlying bowl or deep plate. This *lud* signifies all that is bad about the previous year. Over the course of the evening, spirits are chased from each of the rooms of the house, and householders and guests press the *zan ril* dough balls to their foreheads, mouths, and chests, as well as any part of their body that is injured or sick. These are then placed back in the plate that carries the *lud*, and a candle is lit next to it. At the end of the final meal, participants pour the last remnants of stew from their bowls onto the *lud* plate, which is then carried beyond the boundaries of the household and its fields by a family member who, not looking back at the house, takes it to the nearest crossroads, where it is thrown to the ground and left for animals to eat.

The use of barley dough in both rituals—the household and city exorcisms—was intimately linked to domestic household production. Barley flour (*tsampa*) acts as an item of personal and inter-household exchange and rent: rarely available commercially, it remains an important component of the nonmonetary economy in Ladakh and Zanskar, and an intimate index of wealth, hospitality, and commensality. At the same time, as Adams has discussed at length, *tsampa* acts as a principal ritual object of demonic desire (1995, 121–70). As with the new year feast in household exorcisms, *tsampa* is the primary ingredient for making a *lud* figurine designed to act as a simulacrum of household members and intended to draw malignant spirits away from their human hosts. In both the new year household and Dosmoché rituals, use of the *zan ril* serves to embody the internal "afflictive emotions" (*nyong mongs*; Skt. *kleśa*) of participants as externally present *lhandré* and *dud* (spirits and demons), who are drawn to it.

The apparent equivalence of barley and cash as offerings should be treated with some care here, because they are *not* equivalent but *parallel*, as demonstrated by the historical shift from the predominance of *zan ril* to that of cash offerings in Dosmoché between 1995 and 2012. In the seventeen intervening years, the incorporation of Leh into the tourist economy led to dramatic transformations in the local economy. Leh became a thriving hub of trekking and adventure holidays, doubling the size of the city and intensifying the hotel and guesthouse economy. Household estates around Leh—in surrounding villages such as Changspa, Sankar, Sabu, and Choglamsar—were converted into hotels, and households that previously took guests on an ad hoc basis became professionalized sections of the tourist industry. An important element of this expansion was the loss of domestic fields that previously supplied barley and peas to local homesteads. Household economies shifted increasingly to a cash basis, although the capacity to grow your own household barley in your own household fields and gift it as *tsampa* (its roast, ground form) remained a certain kind of status marker. Households as semi-autonomous farmsteads became part of the cash-linked hospitality industry, rendering cash—and not barley—as the principal signifier of household wealth.

In other words, while the shift from barley dough to cash speaks to their general indirect equivalence as tokens of wealth and therefore as carriers of demonic desire, this is specifically in a non-alienated sense: *tsampa* is the emergent wealth-object of the *subsistent* agricultural self; cash, by contrast, is the wealth-object of the *monetarized* guesthousing self.

The two are not, however, equivalent to one another and could not be readily exchanged: despite considerable demand from tourists, *tsampa* remains difficult to buy in Leh Bazaar and certainly not from locals, for whom even in 2012 it remained primarily a gift that one gave to a guest or brought as a contribution to a communal occasion. The type of offering, therefore, continues to carry with it the unalienated qualities of the giver in the form of the entire economic matrix within which their lives are embedded. As Parry notes of the general Maussian paradigm (particularly in its relation to *hau*, the Maori "spirit of the gift"):

> The general principle—of which this and the Maori *hau* are only two amongst a whole battery of illustrations—is the absence of any absolute disjunction between persons and things. It is because the thing contains the person that the donor retains a lien on what he has given away and we cannot therefore speak of an alienation of property; and it is because of this participation of the person in the object that the gift creates an enduring bond between persons.
>
> (Parry 1986, 457; see Mauss 1990 [1922], 16–17)

In seeking to square the circle of a gift that embodies the giver and yet does not involve reciprocity, Parry argues along with Raheja that the South Asian religious gift embodies not just the giver but, as we have seen above, the *inauspiciousness* of the giver. In Raheja's famous term, the gift has poison within it (Raheja 1988), and therefore the giver does not seek its burdensome return in any kind from the ritual recipient, whether Brahmin priest or Buddhist monk (Parry 1986). Certainly, this seems apposite when we look at the treatment of the dried *zan ril* in the New Year of households. But does the same logic apply when the *zan ril* are not left on a darkened crossroads for demons and animals to devour but handed over to the sangha?

Persons, Groups, and Actors

As discussed above, the interpretation of *dāna* as a form of exchange rests in large part on the notion that the sangha is a distinct social group from the laity. In Mauss's terms, this is a defining prerequisite of the concept of exchange—that it occurs between full legal entities or groups:

> First, it is not individuals but collectivities that impose obligations of exchange and contract upon each other. The contracting parties are legal

entities: clans, tribes, and families who confront and oppose one another either in groups who meet face to face in one spot, or through their chiefs, or in both these ways at once.

(Mauss 1990 [1922], 6)

Mauss's point here was historical: it is only in recent centuries that full legal personhood has become habitually associated with the individual per se; in legal antiquity, and outside modern Europe, legal and moral personhood was primarily associated with corporate groups (Mauss 1985). Parry puts this a little differently,[5] but the point is still there: before we can interpret *dāna* as "exchange," we must ask whether laity and sangha in Buddhist societies are indeed separate entities, groups, or persons in any economic, legal, or constitutional sense.

This would seem straightforward: Buddhist monks and nuns, after all, are *anāgarika*—"homeless ones" who, like the Buddha, have taken vows in order to leave behind household life. In Tibetan areas, however, the practice of this distinction varies dramatically. For example, as Silhé describes for Eastern Tibet (this volume), certain kinds of Tibetan sangha are *not* monastic but exist in self-replicating lineages and often quite self-sufficient communities: families and sometimes whole villages of religious specialists are called upon by outsiders for ritual services. This is hardly unique. However, entirely celibate monastic communities such as those of the Geluk school nonetheless dominate the religious landscape of Tibetan areas. Forbidden in principle from agricultural work as much as reproduction, monasteries and nunneries depend on surrounding lay communities to both provide for them economically and repopulate their ranks. In other words, it is precisely their *renunciation* of sexual reproduction and economic production that kept such institutions bound to lay communities.

Indeed, as I have argued in greater detail elsewhere, ordinary Buddhist monks and nuns actually remain members of their natal household estates, residing in monastic quarters that are economic extensions of those estates (Mills 2001, 61–81; see also Mills 2000, 2009). Like many Buddhist sangha members around the globe (and indeed the Buddha himself), their career of religious striving remains fenced around by their continuing, if transformed, relations with their families. Strenski famously described this as the "domestication of the sangha" from its original eremitic ideal (Strenski 1983), but this seems somewhat unfair. After all, the Buddhist presentation of the life of the Buddha Śākyamuni depicts him as renouncing family life but not ultimately as leaving his family: following his six years of spiritual striving and final enlightenment at Bodhgaya, he returns to teach the Buddhist dharma to his father Śuddhodana and the Abhidharma to his deceased mother Māyā in the Tāvatimsa heaven; his son Rāhula becomes the first novice monk of the Buddhist order and his wife Yaśodharā its first nun. This is not a departure from householding but a transformation of it.

If monastic communities are not wholly separate from laity as a group—indeed, are in almost all respects dependent upon them—then is *dāna* a form of exchange at all, rather than redistribution? Here, Carrier's more recent definition of exchange as "the transfer of things between social actors" (2012, 271) is helpful in unpacking the problem. Firstly, because it notes that, definitionally, exchange is a subset of the larger world of transfers—that is, those that occur *between* "social actors." And secondly, because his definition focuses on actors rather than predefined groups per se. But what is a social actor? Clearly it is not equitable simply with the human biological individual, since exchanges between commercial companies, nations, and caste groups are clearly "between social actors." Here instead, I will take the concept of the actor as secondary to that of action itself, defining a social actor as either *an individual or group across which a recognized social action is completed.*

In this sense, many transfers between individual persons are not exchanges between social actors (Testart 2013). For example: if while attending a Christian church service in Europe, a mother hands her infant daughter some money to put in the collection plate on their family's behalf, she has certainly *transferred* money to the child but we could hardly say that she had "engaged in exchange" with her, given her "a gift" or, indeed, "paid" her. In none of these cases would the mother expect reciprocity from her child for the action, and the child's actions are clearly "on behalf" of her larger household. Going one step further: when, in turn, the daughter puts the money on the collection plate, she has certainly engaged in a transfer, but has she engaged in an exchange? If the family are not members of that church congregation, then perhaps; but if they *are* regular members of the congregation, invested in its well-being, is such a gift really an exchange in which the gift is really alienated away from them? Indeed, at what point has the exchange happened? When it goes into the collection plate? When it is held up by the priest as an offering to God? Or when the priest subsequently puts it into the church bank account? If indeed the family's intention in offering the money was to support the priest's pastoral duties toward members of their own congregation, has it ever been either alienated or exchanged at all? Here, the boundaries of exchange, set up by Mauss and apotheosized by Levi-Strauss as the primal social act, begin to look rather chimeric and plastic to the specific intention behind the action.

Exchange versus Transfer in Collective Ritual Work

Here then, Buddhist *dāna* not appear as a form of exchange at all, but rather, as Jonutytė also argues, as "a social field with a variety of flows rather than static relations between two clearly separated groups of the sangha and the laity" (Jonutytė 2017 and this volume). For Jonutytė this creates a "pooling" of economic resources between laity and sangha; in what follows, I will argue that *dāna* transfers constitute less of a "pooling" and more of an intentional *trajectory* of shared, collective work, or, in the Ladakhi and Tibetan term, *las*.

While European thought habitually sees religious action as a qualitatively distinct category from secular work, labor, or economics, Tibetan societies such as Ladakh tend to regard the two as transformations of one another, as parallel and intertwined kinds of human action. Religious (and in particular, karmic) action has long been conceptualized as a corollary of agricultural labor, as *las gyu das*, "the accomplished fruit of action"—where *las* is both action and work, a term used in everyday parlance to speak of a job, correlated with *zhing las*, or "work in the fields" (Mills 2001, 73, 305). Like work, religious action can be either individual or communal, performed in isolation from others or in coordination. In coordinated forms, actors become bound together in the production of particular ends, whether it be harvesting the crops, building a house, or digging a water channel.

Similarly so with ritual action. There is a tendency among many Western commentators to assume karma is a wholly individual matter but, as I have explored in depth elsewhere (Mills 2015), Tibetan Buddhist notions of karmic process are *dominated* by powerful notions of shared karma (*chitun chi las*), mediated by acts of exchange, commensality, and inheritance. Such notions are mobilized at both the level of formal Buddhist philosophical and ethical literature, and of everyday monastic and lay practice. For key writers of the Tibetan Buddhist tradition, this dominant interpersonal flavor to karmic action derives from a conception of its *articulated* nature. Actions are seen as comprised of *sequentially related elements*: usually, an action's object, its intention, its execution, and its completion (see, e.g., Pabongka 1991, 443; Patrul 1998, 103–4; Tsong-kha-pa 2002, 218). All of this may exist within a single individual or be articulated across several, just as my mind's intention to write these words is being completed by my hands. Thus, the early twentieth-century Geluk incarnate Pabongka Rinpoché writes on the action of killing:

> Ordering someone else to do the killing is no different from doing it oneself. *A Treasury of Metaphysics* [by Vasabandhu] says: "It is all one for armies and so forth: all of them share equally in the deed."[6] That is, if eight people share in killing a sheep, each of them does not receive a *share* of the sin: each one receives the *full* sin of killing the sheep. When a general sends out many soldiers to the slaughter and a thousand men are killed, each soldier commits the sin of killing as many men as an individual soldier is capable of doing; *the general, however, gets the full sin of killing all one thousand men.* We may set a good example here in the Central Province, but everywhere in Tibet I believe ordained people are making others slaughter cattle for them, claiming, "These are our serfs."

But the slaughterer and the person who made him do it each commits the sin of taking a life. If the monk had done the killing with his own hands, only one person would have committed the sin.

(1991, 444; emphasis added)

In this way of looking at things, rituals that involve transfers between laity and the sangha are often not exchanges but forms of collective work or *las* that bind the two "groups" together as social actors within the intention and completion of a combined and collective action.

Such tensions between individualistic versus transactional interpretations of work are hardly new to anthropology. Since Louis Dumont's examination of the religious renouncer in Indian society in the 1960s (1980 [1966]), anthropological approaches to the person have been characterized by systematic criticism of the "Western individual" as a universal social category, a combination of "the capitalist notion of individual ownership, the Christian notion of the soul in an individual relationship with God, and the Western psychological value that every person has a 'core self'" (Hess 2006, 288). Assuming the individual to be the methodological baseline of all economic analysis has been critiqued in the Indian context since the writings of McKim Marriott (1976, 1990), and in the wider comparative field, Strathern's groundbreaking work on Melanesian society emphasized the impact of economic transfers on the ongoing formation of the "dividual"—that is, a field of unbounded persons whose identity is not fixed but depends on context and exchange practices (Busby 1997; Strathern 1986, 1992). Here, however, it is worth making a clear distinction between the notion of a "social actor" and Mauss's sense of the "category of the person" (Mauss 1985). When Pabongka Rinpoché speaks of a general ordering his soldiers, he is speaking of them as a military unit that acts as a single social actor, even though it may contain many persons.

In Leh Dosmoché, laity can be understood as bound to the sangha as a single social actor performing an act of karmic work and merit. In effect, to return to the indigenous metaphor, laity "sow" the sangha (as a ritual "field of merit") with offerings that are an extension of themselves, to produce the "fruit" of collective merit. This is not exchange, therefore, but *collective work*.

But in such collective work, who is the agent? Where does the *intention* lie? To continue with Pabongka Rinpoché's example, who is the general and who the foot soldier? Given the hierarchy of respect that attends upon the Buddhist sangha in Tibetan societies, it would be tempting—indeed, almost automatic—to assume that the principal agent of communal Buddhist rites is the sangha. Again, however, the Buddhist response to this, particularly from members of the sangha themselves, has been to reject the idea that the Buddhist sangha initiate religious action, but rather that it comes in response to requests from, and sponsorship by, the laity. The sangha, in this view, are passive recipients of whatever laity choose to give and the performers of whatever Buddhist rite laity demand. In other words, rather than simply supporting the sangha, Buddhist lay practitioners are engaging with the sangha as *extensions of their own moral and karmic action*, an act of collective ritual work, mediated by the redistribution of wealth *within* a single group, thus voiding the Maussian imperative for reciprocity.

The Return of the Gift: From Inauspicious to Auspicious

Above, we looked at Parry and Raheja's problem of the giving away of "the poisoned gift": the idea that in *dāna*, the gift's embodiment of the inauspiciousness of the donor means that there is no *wish* for reciprocity. Certainly, as with the *zan ril* in the household rites of New Year, the dough balls and money given at Dosmoché are seen as carrying the non-virtue and demons of the giver, and this as dangerously polluting, the reason why the *torma* and bowl are carried by local members of the untouchable castes. But ultimately, Parry's argument does not work for Dosmoché, precisely because what is given *is* returned—indeed, *it is forcibly claimed back*. Unlike the remains of the *gut'uk* stew in the household New Year, Dosmoché involves a return of the now *purified* offering—not to those who gave it but to their inheritors.

On the first days of Dosmoché, when the sangha are invoking the *choskyong* protector deities within the temples above the city, the main bazaar below is filled with young men: playing pool, gambling at dice tables, and walking arm-in-arm with their girlfriends—all surprising displays of immodesty by Ladakhi public standards. These young men are the *tashispa* ("auspicious ones"), destined to inherit the household estate and take it into the next generation. In much household ritual, they are a common focus of ritual protection, especially in their early years. But as they enter maturity, they are called upon to shoulder a growing number of ritual responsibilities regarding the future of the household, such as changing the contents of the household god shrine at new year, a shrine that both "holds" the god in place and marks the symbolic wealth of the household (Day 1989, 152; Mills 2001, 155).

It is these *tashispa* that overwhelmingly make up the final mock battle at the end of Dosmoché: after the various *torma* and *dos* have been consigned to the flames, they descend upon them in an almighty fight to get hold of the remains of the offerings, now purified as medicine and blessing. This mock battle is exclusively the prerogative of young *tashispa*, while their parents (who largely made the initial offerings) and their sisters look on in bemusement. Certainly, no member of the sangha, of whatever age or gender, becomes involved.

Conclusion

The dynamic here thus seems clear. The public rite of Dosmoché involves strong elements of indirect household inheritance through the medium of the sangha. The poisoned offering is given away by the older generation, to be reclaimed as medicine and blessing by the upcoming one. The sangha, by contrast, act as neither givers nor receivers of this redistributed symbolic gift *but transformers of it*. In doing so, they do not act as a separate or distinct legal group, but rather as peripheral members of their natal household, whose renunciation of its wealth and inheritance means they cannot receive it, let alone reciprocate it. They act as a nexus of redistributive transfers, not a recipient of exchange.

In such rites of expiation, the sangha are not Mauss's "distinct legal entity," and therefore not a subject of exchange. Nor are they, as is commonly assumed, the agential party (as it were, the general that orders the soldiers, in Pabongka's example), with the laity playing a supportive role in a ritual already decided upon and initiated by the sangha. Instead, the dynamic is in reality the other way around. If we view the individual lay participant, standing in the crowd at the side of the road as the procession goes past, and casting either their rupee note or their *zan ril* into the *drugchuma* bowl, the implication of the above is that this single act is the intentional *primum mobile* of the entire Dosmoché rite. Karma here is not understood to be a zero-sum game or a finite commodity to be moved around, but rather a single collective act multiplied among the many people that seek to participate within it. In such a context, rather than the laity being peripheral and merely supportive of the *sangha*'s actions, the sangha are the extension of the participatory agency of the laity that engage in Dosmoché. This is a view often reiterated by members of the monastic community themselves, for whom rituals are performed and teachings given because royal and lay sponsors ask for them, not because the sangha initiate them.

Leh Dosmoché is thus an example of transformative ritual labor: firstly, transforming participants' afflictive emotions into *zan ril* and cash, the embodied carriers of the demonic; secondly, ritually subjugating and purifying these through the evoked powers of Buddhist deities, transforming the burnt offerings into medicine and blessing; and thirdly, their vigorous reclamation by the young *tashispa*. Moments of transformative ritual labor are thus *connected* by transfers: but if anyone is the giver, it is the laity; and if anyone is the receiver, it is, again, the laity. Events such as Dosmoché thus involve a unification of laity and sangha within a single redistributive field of ritual action. Within this field, a social actor is not defined by a structurally preexisting social group or class but by *sharing in an agreed collective endeavor*—in this case, the ritual purification of a city and its wealth.

PART THREE

Managing Temples and Monasteries

CHAPTER SEVEN

Monks and the Morality of Exchange: Reflections on a Village Temple Case in Southwest China

Roger Casas

In 2012, while conducting fieldwork in southwest China for my PhD dissertation, I was invited by the Research Institute for Southwestern Frontier Research Centre for Ethnic Minorities (Yunnan University, Kunming) to give a talk about my work among Buddhist monastics in Sipsong Panna (Ch.: *Xishuangbanna*), a small prefecture in southern Yunnan Province. During the discussion, a Chinese academic in the audience asked about rumors concerning senior monks from that region allegedly benefiting from their position in order to build their own personal fortunes. I immediately thought of the many cases of embezzlement or inappropriate use of temple funds on the part of Thai monks coming regularly to light and provoking outraged reactions in the public media of that country by commentators questioning not only the behavior of the monastic community but also the overall commercialization of religion and the decay of morality in the kingdom, giving reasons to those who claim that ever since the time of the founder and the first orders, it has been all downhill for Buddhism.[1]

Responding to the question, however, I argued that, in my view, the southwest China context is very different from that of Thailand. To start with, the arrival of the Communist Party administration and, later on, of Chinese modernity and market economy into Sipsong Panna has long displaced and reoriented most symbolic and economic exchanges out of the temple and the village and into spaces outside these institutions. Although giving to the temple is still a fundamental feature of Buddhist practice in Sipsong Panna, the scale of donations is not large enough to allow for monks becoming rich through the misuse of money.

Apart from this, I would argue that other relevant factors limit what could be called the "freedom of economic action" of monastics in Sipsong Panna. A fundamental one, and the one this chapter mainly delves into, is that almost all monasteries in the region are located within villages and depend on villagers' donations for their sustenance. As a rule, local monks and novices ordain in the village they are born into, and, therefore, in spite of their a priori superior ritual status in relation to the laity, they belong to different hierarchies of age and prestige within the community, hierarchies in which they are potentially subordinated to other groups and individuals (Moerman 1966, 139). Monastics are therefore fundamentally subject to the demands and authority of lay villagers, and this implies a constant informal supervision and control of monks and novices' behavior on the part of the laity—including of course their *economic* behavior.[2]

In order to illustrate this idea, this chapter offers a case study of Sipsong Panna, a region in the south of Yunnan Province (southwest China) bordering Laos and Myanmar. The Tai-speaking population in Sipsong Panna is usually ascribed (by the Chinese state as well) to the so-called Theravāda or southern school of Buddhism, the dominant tradition in neighboring Thailand, Laos, and Myanmar. The interest of studying this site lies in the specificity of a context where traditional values are still widespread, while the demands placed on the individual (and especially on males) by the currently dominant "socialism with Chinese characteristics" are more intense than ever. In addition to this, the generally temporary nature of monastic ordination in Sipsong Panna (and the related fact that the large majority of monastics will eventually disrobe to become laymen and establish a household) offers an excellent opportunity to explore the "morality of exchange" and the tension between what Jonathan Parry and Maurice Bloch described as "two related but separate transactional orders: on the one hand transactions concerned with the reproduction of the long-term social and cosmic order; on the other, a 'sphere' of short-term transactions concerned with the arena of individual competition" (Parry and Bloch 1989, 24). I believe that notions such as "moral economy" or "morality of exchange" can still help give reason of ethnographically observed phenomena in so-called Buddhist contexts, under the condition that we avoid essentializing the dichotomy established (often by locals themselves) between a moral sphere of community and reciprocity, and an allegedly immoral one dominated by the notion of economic profit and driven by individual accumulation.[3]

The discussion starts with an introduction to the social and economic background of the Buddhist revival that took place in Sipsong Panna in the post-Maoist era. This is followed by an account of the management of rural temples (Tai: *wat*), for which I describe the economic routines of a single monastic community in an area next to the border with Shan State in Myanmar. The last part of the chapter focuses on the particular case of the abbot, the head monk of this particular monastic community,[4] to discuss how the demands of family and community concerning economic activities, and the expectations of the individual himself, may occasionally come into conflict. In spite of its focus on a very specific case, I argue that the tensions described in this chapter, as well as the conclusions drawn from the argument, can be applied not only to other temples in Sipsong Panna, but in other "Buddhist localities" as well.

Economic Development and Buddhism in Sipsong Panna

A multiethnic, historically semi-independent polity tributary to both Chinese and Burmese empires, Sipsong Panna became part of the contemporary project of the "Chinese Nation" only after the establishment of the People's Republic in 1949. In 1953 the region was integrated into national administrative structures as the Sipsong Panna Tai Autonomous Prefecture (Ch.: *Xishuangbanna Daizu Zizhizhou*). Together with several other groups in Yunnan Province, the Tai-speaking populations in Sipsong Panna, linguistically and culturally related to populations on the other side of the Myanmar and Lao borders, were then included within the "Dai" (Ch.: *Daizu*) category in the Chinese state ethnic classification system.[5]

After the stagnation created by the commune system and the political upheavals of the Maoist period, the economic development of Sipsong Panna gained momentum following the national-level economic and political reforms implemented in China at the end of the 1970s. In the last three to four decades, the exploitation of the area's cultural and natural resources has caused an acceleration in the processes of integration into national and regional economic circuits. At present, this small frontier prefecture (Ch.: *zhou*) is one of the fastest-developing areas in the economic quadrangle formed by China, Thailand, Laos, and Myanmar.[6]

Needless to say, these developments have provoked important social changes among the different populations in the region, for the most part and until very recently engaged in subsistence agricultural production together with petty trade. In the process of transforming traditional economies, the spread of a "socialism with Chinese characteristics" and of the state education system across the region is imposing contemporary national and ultimately global cultural standards and lifestyles, particularly those associated with consumerism and economic competition among individuals. In connection with this, the opening of the area to economic exploitation and the gradual improvement of infrastructure in Sipsong Panna have provoked, as in Tibet and other minority areas in China, the massive-scale migration of Han Chinese coming mainly from overpopulated areas in the East of the country.[7] Generally speaking, at present Han individuals control the region's economy as entrepreneurs and investors as well as intermediaries in the extraction and commercialization of local resources through their *guanxi*, relational business networks established and reproduced through a culturally specific economy of feasting and gift-giving (Osburg 2013). As members of most other "ethnic minorities" (Ch.: *shaoshu minzu*) in Sipsong Panna and elsewhere, the Tai Lue are at a disadvantage in terms of reaping the alleged benefits of development in a context where "ethnic peculiarities" (Ch.: *minzu tese*) may actually handicap their performance in the public education system. Ultimately, economic growth in Sipsong Panna has produced a socioeconomic distribution of groups according to ethnic lines. Even if the living standards of rural populations have significantly increased in the last decades, and many Tai Lue peasants have become actual *rentiers* living off their land without working it themselves, current socioeconomic configurations in Sipsong Panna threaten to perpetuate a situation of economic and cultural subordination for the *shaoshu minzu* (Sturgeon 2012).

These material and symbolic transformations have affected Buddhist practice among the Tai Lue.[8] Although part of the benefits brought by the rise in local living standards are re-invested in religious activities, including the material support of the sangha,[9] Buddhist monasticism is partly losing its traditional relevance in this new context, as alternative paths of social mobility, public education in particular, have opened for Tai Lue village boys in the reform period.[10] Importantly, the economic transformations succinctly described, and in particular the arrival in the area of the *laoban* (Ch.: "successful entrepreneur" or "boss") as a model of masculinity, have provoked a crisis of autochthonous models of manhood, symbolized by the Buddhist temple and by the discipline undergone by monastics in order to become "morally male tempered householders."[11] In spite of several successful examples of monks and former monks involved in commercial ventures in Sipsong Panna,[12] urban Tai Lue, and many among the rural population as well, have come to accept that monasticism and learning Tai language and script[13] may be a handicap in the development of their sons' careers, and that those boys enculturated in Chinese schools from an early age have more chances of progressing through the education system and being better positioned in the urban labor market. The ongoing, gradual but tangible decline in the number of ordinations can be understood as a sign of this process.[14]

While values related to farming and monastic masculinities are far from vanished, at present Sipsong Panna monks must deal with the requirements that the new economy places on them while continuing to be subject to traditional aspirations on the part of the rural communities most of them belong to. The next section explores the tension between these two sets of demands in the context of a village temple in southern Sipsong Panna, focusing on the case of its abbot and on his economic activities in particular. To what extent does a local "moral economy" set limits to the economic action of individual monks? How do Tai Lue monastics and those related to them negotiate the strains and contradictions that entail from the participation in profit-oriented business of men whose behavior is expected to be guided by selflessness and sacrifice for the community?

Managing Wat Ban Kao

Ban Kao[15] is located in Moeng Long, a large valley area around 50 kilometers to the south of Jinghong City, the administrative capital of the Sipsong Panna Prefecture. The village is an average-size settlement of about 150 households and slightly under 800 inhabitants, practically all of them, like the large majority of the Tai in Sipsong Panna, rural residents. This does not mean that these villagers are necessarily peasants, as important changes in the last few decades have transformed their lives, separating many from actual labor. Most significantly, while until 2010 most of the agricultural production in Ban Kao revolved around the cultivation of paddy, at that time most of the village land was rented out to outside investors and converted into banana plantations, in turn worked by impoverished Han migrants.[16] At the time of fieldwork, rubber was an important source of income for households in the area, as many families in the village possess variable amounts of hill land and rubber trees.[17] Tai villagers collected the rubber themselves, which was then sold to a small factory built just outside the village and part of a previously state-owned rubber farm (Ch.: *nongchang*) managed by Han Chinese. By 2017, however, the drop in the prices of rubber in the previous years had pushed many young males in Ban Kao to look for paid work in a sugar factory (Ch.: *tangchang*) located a few kilometers from the village.

When I first visited Ban Kao in 2004, the village *wat* was located in the outskirts of the settlement and surrounded by paddies. In 2005, the old structure was demolished and a new one built within the village itself. I was told that the relocation was carried out in order to make it more convenient for elderly villagers to reach the monastery, but the decision may be related to prospective changes in agricultural land use. Whatever the case, at that time, between six and eight novices (Tai: *pha*) and two fully ordained monks (Tai: *tu*) lived in the temple. Most of them gradually disrobed and were replaced by others, but no new collective ordinations have been celebrated since.[18]

As is the case with most Buddhist populations in Asia, in Ban Kao the village community sustains the monks and novices living in the monastery, providing them with food or cash to purchase it. Lay householders are also responsible for costs related to the maintenance of the temple.[19] I will now describe how this money is collected and distributed in order to meet these ends. Firstly, in order to fund the construction of a new temple, the reconstruction of an extant one, or the building of new structures within the monastery, extraordinary donations are arranged. For example, before the construction of the new Wat Ban Kao started in 2005, the temple organized an outdoor activity to collect money from villagers from this and other settlements. As in other similar ceremonies, during the activity the names of donors were read aloud by the monks through loudspeakers, and after the work was completed, they were further publicized by being inscribed on the wall of the main entrance to the *vihan* or ordination hall.[20]

Monastics obtain their "income" from regular festivals held at the monastery, as well as from private rituals conducted outside the temple for entire households or single individuals. Temple rituals are generally called in Tai *tan*, a derivation from the Pali word *dāna*, or "generosity" (see Benavides 2005; Sihlé 2017). The limited amounts of cash collected from occasional rituals are distributed by the abbot among temple dwellers and the *po chang* or lay specialist,[21] or any other ritual expert (usually an elderly man) who may have assisted the monks during the ceremony. The exception to this general model is the *tan tham*, the largest ritual of the year, in which villagers offer larger amounts of cash to the temple, through the purchasing of books to be read by monastics, as well as in the form of "money trees" made of banknotes and brought to the temple during the celebration of the ritual. Once the *tan tham* is over,[22] the money is taken off the money trees and counted by the temple novices, young monks, and the *kamakan* or lay committee (see below). According to the abbot of Wat Ban Kao, one fraction of the money goes to himself as leader of the monastic community; another goes to the junior monks (if any) and the novices; another part goes to "the Buddha," that is, to the temple itself, and a final portion, equivalent to the one received by each of the novices or the young monks, is given to the *po chang*. In general the money at disposal of temple dwellers is not very significant. As Tu Ho put it, the amount received by monastics in any given month through ordinary and extraordinary rituals and ceremonies ranges from only 100 or 200 (fifteen to twenty-five US dollars) to several thousand yuan, depending on the number of rituals conducted both within and outside the temple.

Apart from this money, at present the abbot of Wat Ban Kao receives a fixed monthly allowance of 1,200 yuan for the daily sustenance of monks and novices, most of which is employed in purchasing food. Although this is also brought to (or prepared in) the temple during *tan* festivals, and the alms round (Tai: *kum khao*) common in other Southeast Asian countries was also known in Sipsong Panna in the past, nowadays most of the food consumed by temple dwellers is purchased at the village market and prepared in the kitchen of the monastery by the novices themselves. The only remnant of the old ways is the morning offering made by elderly members of the community,[23] the *song sa khao*. After offering sticky rice and candles to the Buddha image on the main altar in the ordination or prayer hall (Tai: *vihan*), and to the different altars devoted to temple deities or *thevada* located within the temple, and once they have received the abbot's blessings,[24] the elders leave some rice and vegetables for the monk and novices as they return home.

It must be kept in mind that it is the whole village community, and not *only* the monks, who is responsible for the management of the temple, and that decisions regarding the running of the monastery (importantly, decisions concerning financial matters) are discussed and made by monastics and the laity, represented by the *kamakan* or temple lay committee (and, more informally, by all male elders). This committee usually has between two and four adult men. In the case of Wat Ban Kao, in 2017 the two members were relatively young former monks around fifty years old.[25]

Decisions concerning the temple include the use made of its grounds as recreational space. Particularly for men of all ages, the village temple is a place where it is possible to escape the demands of farming life and the household, to find "pleasure" (Tai: *tho, moun di*) and "fun" (Tai: *di eo, di lin*). During my fieldwork in Ban Kao it was common to find villagers in the temple during daytime, from teenagers playing games in their mobile phones or playing guitar with their monastic peers, to young and middle-age householders engaging in some or other remedy against boredom, such as card games or even cockfights (Tai: *to kai*).[26] Even if the abbot has a say in the management of all this nonreligious activity that takes place within temple boundaries (and concerning the participation of novices in particular), and as the chief monk of Wat Ban Kao always emphasized, temples belong to all villagers. The abbot is but a temporary occupant of a public office—there were others before and there will be more after him.[27]

The Vicissitudes of a Temple Abbot

The current abbot of Wat Ban Kao, Tu Ho, was born in 1982 and ordained as a novice in the early 1990s. According to the monk, who relied on his father's account of the story, when he was around eleven years old he decided to join several of his friends and ordain at the village temple.[28] At that time his parents had just established their own, independent household and were having trouble sustaining the several people living in it. Because of the significant expense that organizing an ordination ceremony represents, the boy's father tried hard to get him out of the idea. But the future monk was a headstrong kid and in the end he got his way.[29] His father was forced to sell the only tractor (Ch.: *tuolaji*) the family owned at the time in order to pay for the expenses related to the ceremony.

The initial refusal of Tu Ho's father to grant his son permission to ordain can be taken as a sign of the uncertainty informing monastic careers. Authors working on Theravāda Buddhism have usually focused on the social mobility that monastic education can provide, as a main motivation among those responsible for the ordination of a boy. In this sense, offering a son to the temple can be certainly interpreted as a kind of "investment." The ordination of a boy marks not only the beginning of a prospective prestige career within the village community for the individual but also a claim to prestige and status on the part of the whole family, as the symbolic gesture of "sacrificing" a child (most importantly, his labor) for the community reflects positively upon the position of his kin and affines.[30] Beyond "ideology of merit" explanations and notions of the karmic benefits acquired by those parents whose son is ordained,[31] it is clear that family prospects concerning status and economic benefits are important factors behind the ordination of a boy as novice.

In the case of Wat Ban Kao's abbot, the investment seems to have paid off, at least in terms of the status granted to him and his family in the village. Tu Ho does not only remain in the monkhood after thirty but maintains an excellent relation with the Ban Kao community and is well respected by the laity and other monks in other villages in Moeng Long and beyond. His monkly demeanor, his soft voice and gestures, is an important element in this,[32] although I believe that the most relevant factor is Tu Ho's ability at dealing with the expectations of different village groups. On one hand, the monk is always available to elderly villagers, offering not only his ritual expertise but also counseling and emotional support, always listening attentively and willing to engage in conversation with them on whatever mundane matters these elders may want to discuss; on the other, the abbot is also skilled at negotiating occasional, exacting demands on the part of his lay peers, who often invite him to participate in events of male commensality. This excellent reputation situates Tu Ho in a privileged position as a vector of resources for his family's household (more on this below).

Nevertheless, the benefit that ordaining a son may bring is not often realized. Most of those boys who ordain will disrobe at some point in their monastic career, more often than not before being fully ordained as monks or *tu* when they reach the age of twenty. Even if spending a few years in the sangha may bring prestige to the individual and his kin, ordaining involves risking or gambling on their reputation as well.[33] Building and maintaining this reputation certainly involve an intense and constant commitment, as well as a certain sacrifice. During my stays in Wat Ban Kao, Tu Ho left the temple at night only occasionally, usually to have dinner with some friend or other and always returning to his dormitory early in the evening. He would spend most of his nights in his room, watching Thai music videos and Chinese soap operas or listening to digitally recorded sermons by monks from Shan State (Myanmar), available at all times to the villagers who may need him. In present-day, fast-developing Sipsong Panna, not all young men nor their families are willing to accept this sacrifice nor the uncertainty of the outcome of the monastic experience—least of all at a moment when, as I have mentioned, becoming a monk may seriously curtail a young man's chances to acquire the necessary skills to make money.

The new demands imposed upon Tai householders by the new economy, in the form of children's school fees, household renovations, cars, and so on, are also likely to influence decisions on the part of monastics concerning their religious careers—Tu Ho is no exception to this. During my fieldwork, the abbot was often involved in money-making activities, complaining that he could not earn enough from villagers' donations.[34] As a solution to this problem, Tu Ho decided to produce house decorations in concrete (Tai: *dok*, "ornaments," literally "flowers"), to be sold to villagers in his own and other settlements. He had first done so after the new village monastery was built between 2005 and 2006, and what started as a hobby, awakened in him by another monk participating in the construction of Wat Ban Kao, ended up becoming a profitable activity, as the monk's fellow villagers asked him to produce decorations for them. According to Tu Ho himself, he had agreed to this only in order to help them save money, as bringing outside workers to do the job would be too expensive—in the end, they are all part of the same community or, as he put it, in the local language of kinship, "we are all brothers" (Tai: *pin pinong kan*).

The abbot was helped in this task by a divorced former novice from Ban Kao and a former monk from a nearby village who was responsible for finding new costumers and delivering the finished decorations to them, which involved frequently moving in and out of the temple and even the village, something the monk was not free to do. Tu Ho would design the decorative motifs himself, then use modeling clay and glass fiber to produce a mold based on the motif, and finally, often with the (unpaid) labour of the junior monk and the novices in the monastery, the concrete piece. The monk also produced Buddha images and animal figurines in plaster, which he later gilded with Thai-produced gold paint, and "sold" (Tai: *pucha*) to village residents so that they could in turn offer the figurines in temple festivals (Figure 7.1).[35] In spite of the debris and construction materials scattered around the back of the temple compound, apparently this activity did not bother other villagers. Some elders even helped the monk painting *dok* in exchange for cash. By 2013 Tu Ho and his partner had bought a small truck to transport the decorations, while the former novice just mentioned was helping them full-time.

In spite of his care, and of his good standing within the community, this occupation created some trouble for the abbot. One morning during the *tan tham* festival in August 2012, Tu Ho left the temple in order to help delivering the decorations he had produced for a household in another village. Later that day, and after returning to his monastery, the abbot told me he had heard that one of the village elders had made some unpleasant comments about him while he was absent. The criticism was apparently directed at the monk's work with *dok*, implying that if Tu Ho wanted to devote himself to this job, he should simply disrobe (Tai: *sik*). According to the abbot, the problem was not new and affected also the local *po chang*, the temple lay specialist, who had been unjustly chastised by the same elder

FIGURE 7.1 Between piety and business? Tu Ho working on his plaster Buddha images, 2012 (Photo: Roger Casas).

for occasionally not being able to participate in temple activities, of which, as mentioned, he was an essential part as mediator between the monks and the laity.

Tu Ho was in any case reluctant to concede that he was in the wrong. In fact, he made very clear he was not afraid of the elder and intended to confront him. As the monk himself anxiously put it, he also had a family with land and a house supporting him (Tai: *mi pinong, mi heun, mi na*). Furthermore, he threatened the lay committee with the possibility of leaving the village for some other temple, and even of disrobing altogether, but was ultimately dissuaded from doing so by the two members of the *kamakan*.

Later on, after the whole affair had simply died out, the monk admitted that the problem had not been so serious, even if being aware that someone was talking behind his back made him very uncomfortable. Among the Tai Lue, gossip (Tai: *kam cha*, literally "bad words") is a powerful and dangerous weapon, and the abbot feared that this issue could damage his reputation, in the sense that other villagers might come to agree that he was paying too much attention to his own business and withdrawing from his responsibilities toward them.

Indeed, at the time of his conflict with the elder, To Ho anxiously justified his own predicament in terms of the situation of his parents' household. Between 2011 and 2012, the abbot's family was replacing their old wooden house for a much larger construction in brick, concrete, and glass.[36] As was the case for other such projects in the village, the construction of a new house demanded a large expenditure on the part of the family, and, as he somehow continued to be a member of that household,[37] Tu Ho felt he had the obligation to help his parents and sibling—that was his main reason to produce *dok* for temples and households. He claimed that in order to support his family, he had even sold a second-hand car he owned. When, some time after this, I mentioned to him that he had continued selling *dok* after the reconstruction of his parents' household was completed, he referred, putting on a knowing smile, to the many different affairs he still had to think and take care of. In fact, although he did not say so explicitly, he might have been helping his family return a loan for the house.

Being a monk involves a constant negotiation concerning what is appropriate or not concerning the monk's (and his family's) interests while paying attention to the needs of the lay members of one's "parish." This is true of each and every monk in Sipsong Panna, while the fact that no written or unwritten rules regulate the daily minutiae of lay-monastic interaction (especially concerning economic affairs) means that this negotiation is always contingent on the conditions in that particular village community, down to the "personalities" of its monastic and lay members.

By 2013, after his parents' house had been already rebuilt, Tu Ho had bought a new car (apart from the small truck already mentioned). In relation to this purchase, when I asked him why he had bought the car with his own money, instead of allowing villagers to buy it for him (something monks in other villages do), the abbot replied that purchasing the vehicle with his own money gave him freedom. In this way, he could make use of the car without being exposed to the control and criticism of the villagers.

It is important to note that Tu Ho saw these activities not simply as contributing to his own or his family's welfare but also as part of his job as head of the temple. But caring about the improvement of the monastery as a space to be used by different groups could also be misunderstood. As an example of this, during a recent visit to Wat Kao, Tu Ho mentioned that it was him and the junior monk (who by 2017 had left to become the abbot in another village temple) who built most of the new *kuti* or monastic residence, where the abbot hosts visitors from within and outside the village, using their own labor as well as money from their own pockets. According to the monk, not everyone in the village understood that these projects were not aimed at improving the quality of life of monastics but the temple itself.

Whatever the case, at the moment of writing this, Tu Ho only produces *dok* and figurines occasionally, as he and his former partner have parted ways. It seems as if the business was going a little too well, and there was too much money coming in. At that moment, Tu Ho decided to quit, because, as he stated, a monk "shouldn't be doing this kind of thing." Nevertheless, and further illustrating the ambivalence of the relation of monks to remunerated work, in 2016 the abbot was responsible for building the village entrance archway, designing the monument and working in its construction. Tu Ho himself proposed the deal to the village head, in order to save the community some money. Once again, bringing workers from outside the village would have been much more costly, so this was a win-win situation for both the abbot and the villagers.[38] He was helped in this task by the young divorcee who helped him producing *dok* in the past. According to Tu Ho, they received the considerable amount of 10,000 yuan (around 1,500 US dollars) each for the job. As he himself admitted, "today you need to make money; if you don't have money, you can't do anything."

Conclusion

The political, social, and economic transformations that have mutated China into a world superpower have created in Sipsong Panna a very different context in relation to that in which Tai Lue boys and young men ordained only a few decades ago. Tai Lue monastics, and particularly those who will disrobe and become householders "when the time comes" (Tai: *vilaa hot liao*), must now navigate the demands brought upon them by a market economy "with Chinese characteristics"—even if they are not expected to become affluent *laoban*, they must nevertheless be able to make money. At the same time, during the time they spend in the monastery, these men are also subject to the sometimes conflicting requirements of the communities to which they belong, requirements which often set limits to that performance.

Seen in this way, the contemporary context of Sipsong Panna may seem determined by what Parry and Bloch deemed as the "morality of exchange" (1989). Tai Lue monks must balance their own, short-term goals of economic gain and individual prosperity, with those long-term on the part of the lay community, allegedly invested in the continuity of the monastic community as worthy ritual experts capable of giving villagers the opportunity to gain merit.

However, the actual situation might be a little more complicated. First of all, as this chapter shows, the very idea of money and economic gain as a "tainting" endeavor that may put at risk the ritual purity of monastics must be qualified. In spite of what the "Theravāda canon" may say concerning the handling of money by monks (see Benavides 2005, 83), specialists such as Jeffrey Samuels have demonstrated that it is factors other than canonical norms—factors "determined by time, region, and context—that influence and even determine people's conceptions of monastic purity" (2010, 29). Monks in Sipsong Panna have long been familiar with money. Nevertheless, money-making and the individual accumulation of capital are not necessarily fundamental concerns for these men. Monastics often opt to keep away from such affairs, which may hinder their own, morally oriented projects of self-making. In the case of Tu Ho, the monk's main worry was the welfare of the temple and its dwellers, a goal for which he sometimes had to confront lay villagers head-on. In relation to this, he was very aware of how his own interests and those of his family might come into conflict with his job as head of the monastic community.

Indeed, in rural Sipsong Panna, family interests are predominant, and, to the extent that the individual's economic activities are often aimed at the prosperity of the household, it can be argued that the household, and not the individual, is the institution defined by the agonistic sphere of short-term interests. This competition among households, arguably exacerbated in the contemporary context, risks at all times invading the village temple. I have seen more than one case in which intra-village strife among families has forced a monk to disrobe or to leave. As for those individual goals of self-transformation intrinsic to the monastic experience, Tu Ho's case is a good example of the difficulties of balancing honest intentions to be a good monk and become a "morally male tempered householder," worthy of his fellow villagers' respect upon disrobing (Keyes 1986), with demands to perform successfully in the new economy, demands that have increased exponentially since the 1980s. In this sense, the tensions and frustrations described in this chapter shape the experiences of many other young and middle-aged monks in present-day Sipsong Panna. Expectedly, it is those individual, modest projects of self-making on the part of monks that have nowadays become most vulnerable and fragile, and men often find themselves forced to abandon them under pressure from their families, the village community, or from their own lack of motivation in a context in which the monastic experience as such has lost most of the value it held in the not-so-distant past. As for Tu Ho, for the moment he has managed to keep his own monastic project alive. Nevertheless, in the contingent and ever-shifting world of the Chinese frontier, even the most immediate future is impossible to predict.

CHAPTER EIGHT

Wealthy Mendicants: The Balancing Act of Sri Lankan Forest Monks

Prabhath Sirisena

Venerable Megha smiles and asks, "Do you see the snake?"

We are at the dining hall (dāna sālā),[1] where the community gathers for the daily meal. It is located where the village meets the forest: the gravel road ends here, and the narrow, meandering paths through the forest begin. It is not rare to see wild animals appear near the dining hall, seemingly to catch a glimpse of the wider world outside. But I don't see the snake.

Venerable Megha is smiling. In his hand he holds a hundred-rupee note.

The rift between the teachings contained in Buddhist texts and how Buddhists practice their religion is the subject of both academic and popular debate. The early Buddhist texts espouse a way of life that values—and demands—renunciation, simplicity, and diligent practice in solitude (Holt 1981; Wijayaratna 1990). Schopen (1997, 4), however, observes there to be "no actual evidence that the textual ideal was ever fully or even partially implemented in actual practice." Historiography of Buddhism rarely finds an audience among the practitioners of the religion, particularly the most committed of them: the monastics. Driven by the faith in the teachings and happily oblivious to academic skepticism, some of them actually try to practice what the texts say. The past century has seen such attempts in the Theravāda tradition in both Thailand (Tiyavanich 1997) and Sri Lanka (Carrithers 1983).

While the fundamental problem of suffering (*dukkha*) and the solution declared by the Buddha are supposed to be universal, modern societies seem to share little with the social, cultural, and economic contexts of the middle Ganges Valley of the fifth century BC where the teachings were first delivered. Modern monastic practitioners face the challenge of adhering to the Vinaya rules established "for the excellence and comfort of the order" and "for supporting the training"[2] in a dramatically transformed world that has also affected how Buddhism is conceived.[3]

This chapter explores how a reform movement that has looked to the ancient past through the Buddhist texts for its way of practice has nonetheless managed to thrive in the present by being inventive in financial management. This careful balancing act between the supposedly authentic practice of monks and the financial stability of monasteries has become particularly important today for ensuring the long-term survival and growth of monastic communities that cultivate a way of life that is dramatically, and increasingly, different from lay society.

In this study I will focus on one of the largest forest monasteries in Sri Lanka, which provides residence to more than a hundred monks of various nationalities. It promotes *Theravāda* textual orthodoxy and places a strong emphasis on meditation and solitary practice. The monastery draws lavish support from both Sri Lankan and international Buddhist laity, often exceeding the needs of the resident sangha. Carefully designed processes allow this sangha to manage the monastic funds while staying within the Vinaya boundaries that they purport to follow, which prohibit them from accepting or handling money. What roles do monks and lay Buddhists play in these processes, and how do they come to assume those roles? How do the monastics navigate the relationship between the faith they inspire and the resulting "gains, offerings and fame" which the *Theravāda* teachings proclaim to be "a bitter, harsh impediment" to enlightenment?[4] These are some of the questions I will attempt to answer.

Autoethnography was imposed on this study by the natural course of events: in December 2007, I left home with the intention of becoming a forest monk. After a few months spent as an *anagārika* (a candidate for ordination), in March 2008 I received the "going forth" (*pabbajjā*) in the forest tradition, and a year later, higher ordination (*upasampadā*). It was a lifelong commitment: I believed that I would remain a forest monk for the rest of my days. And yet, few people manage to endure the difficult life in the forest sangha. Unfortunately, I was not one of them. I returned to lay life in October 2011, with the blessings of my teachers and monastic companions. Nonetheless, the years spent as a forest monk was a time full of "epiphanies" (Denzin 2014, 28), a significantly transformative period that changed the trajectory of my life. I continue to stay in contact with my forest monastic friends and maintain a close affinity with the monastic organization as a lay supporter.

Each individual brings some skills obtained in lay life into their monastic life. Most of these fall into the category of "hindrances to practice" in sangha parlance. My grasp of English and information technology—rare, and rarely useful, skills in the sangha—proved to be hindrances that eventually offered me unique insights into the administrative processes of a large forest monastery: knowledge that is hardly obtainable by a young monk, let alone a layperson or an "outsider." Thus, this study draws heavily on my personal experiences and memories from those monastic days, and these personal accounts have been augmented by discussions with forest monks who were my contemporaries, now senior monks who are either solitary practitioners or abbots of their own monasteries.

There is a clear advantage in using the autoethnographic approach in a study that involves the forest sangha. It is a closed community, both physically and socially; forest monasteries have defined visiting hours and often also designated visitation areas. Forest monks have limited contact with outsiders, not just laypeople but also Buddhist monastics of other traditions. Socializing (saṅgaṇikārāmatā) and idle talk (bhassārāmatā) are not encouraged,[5] and monks are expected to observe mindfulness in their daily activities when they are not engaged in sitting meditation. The teachings encourage solitude (viveka), and the Vinaya has many rules that circumscribe the relationships the sangha may have with laity. For many monks, the only time they meet others is during the daily meal, and the only laypeople they come into contact are those who work or stay at the monastery.

Even Carrithers, who spent several years on his anthropological study of Sri Lankan forest monks, has had difficulties crossing this boundary:

> When I visited hermitages in widely separated parts of the island to discuss the saṃsthāva and its history with its members, I met strikingly similar treatment: I was received courteously, as at other hermitages, my questions were answered thoroughly, even enthusiastically, but when it came time for the monk to go about his duties, he would say firmly something like, "I have work to do now," and I would have to rise and leave.
>
> (Carrithers 1983, 201)

Autoethnography affords us a way to obtain unrestricted access to this elusive community and confront "the tension between insider and outsider perspectives, between social practice and social constraint" (Reed-Danahay 2009, 32).

Forest Monks of Sri Lanka

*"When I was a young monk, I didn't know places like these even existed,"
says Venerable Ananda. Before re-ordaining in the forest tradition, he
had been a* thera—*a senior monk of more than ten years—in a different
tradition, and it shows: he is knowledgeable about the doctrine, and has
a natural calmness that suggest years spent in robes.*

*"You hadn't heard of forest monks?" I'm surprised that any Buddhist—
let alone a monk—would not know about our tradition.*

*"Not really, I didn't know what that actually meant. I remember once
when we were cleaning the temple grounds and mowing the grass, I said
to a friend: did you know that, in the ancient past, monks would not
damage even a single leaf of a tree?"*

"So for you, the Vinaya was mostly the stuff of legend?"

*"Yes, and I thought that all places were like our temple. That's why I
always say, regardless of whatever problems there might be, this is still a
special place."*

*The monastery is indeed a special place. It has ancient roots: where the
current stupa stands, there are ruins of an ancient stupa complex dating
back two millennia. It is large, spreading over an entire mountain range,
some of it dense forest, some being reforested, some grassland. It is home
to about one hundred monks.*

*The monastery is silent. Meditation is the focus here. In the three large
meditation halls, where group sittings and silent retreats are conducted,
and in the solitude of their own huts, monks try to follow those ancient
instructions: "A monk, having gone to the forest, to the foot of a tree or
to an empty hut, sits down with his legs crossed, sets his body erect and
his mindfulness alert."*[6]

The contemporary Sri Lankan forest monastic tradition is a modern
phenomenon. Despite the long history of Buddhism in Sri Lanka, the forest
sangha of today is mainly the result of reform movements that emerged only
about a century ago. Founded by the charismatic senior monk Kaḍavädduvē
Jinavaṃsa in 1951, *Śrī Kalyāṇī Yogāśrama Saṃsthā*[7] (hereafter referred to as
the *Saṃsthā*) has now emerged to be the the de facto forest monastic organization
in the country. There are a handful of other groups and monasteries that
purport a forest monastic lifestyle, but none of them have seen the growth
or stability of the *Saṃsthā*—so much so that the forest sangha is almost
synonymous with it.

The *Saṃsthā* has about 150 monasteries spread around the country and
a community of more than 1,500 monks. The monasteries of the *Saṃsthā*
vary in size, from small residences in urban areas to forests spanning
thousands of acres. In a forest monastery, each monk[8] has his own dwelling,
which is small, not more than a few square meters, and can be a cave,

wattle-and-daub hut, wooden shack, or, most commonly, a brick-and-mortar hut. The largest building in a monastery is often the dining hall, which also acts as a communal gathering place. The larger monasteries have a *sīmā*, a building where acts of monastic discipline (*vinayakamma*), such as the biweekly recitation of the monastic rules (*pātimokkha*), take place. All but the smallest and the remotest monasteries will also have a stupa and a Bodhi tree.

Forest monks live simple lives. They do not have the burden of social obligations toward the laity like the "village-dwelling" (*gāmavāsī*) monks. Depending on the focus of the monastery, the monks will spend the majority

FIGURE 8.1 A Buddhist monk in a Sri Lankan forest monastery, walking from his hut to the meditation hall, 2009 (Photo: Nanditha Sirisena, with permission).

of their time studying or meditating, mostly in the solitude of their huts. There is very little supervision: monks are responsible for their own practice. When outside their monasteries, forest monks are easily recognized by their outward appearance: they wear the robe covering both shoulders, their robes are made of cotton cloth and are of a duller and darker hue than those of village monks, they carry their bowl with them, and often walk barefoot. A *Saṃsthā* monk might also carry a white umbrella made of palm leaf (Sinhala: *Gotu atta*), a unique instrument not seen in other traditions. Most of them—and exceptions are rare—will carry themselves in a calm and polite yet aloof manner (Figure 8.1).

This way of life emerged as a result of *Saṃsthā* founders attempting to reconstruct Buddhist monasticism based on the texts. Thus, which texts they consider to be authoritative has important implications on how they practice. The official position of the *Saṃsthā* is that the Pali Tipiṭaka in its entirety—including all books of the Abhidhamma piṭaka and all books of the Khuddaka Nikāya—and the Pali commentaries are the teachings of the Buddha (*Buddhavacana*) or awakened disciples (*sāvakabhāsita*). The *Saṃsthā* adheres to a strict commentarial interpretation of the *Theravāda* Vinaya, evidently the strictest among all Sri Lankan sects. In this approach to evaluating the texts, the *Saṃsthā* is not very different from the mainstream monastic community in Sri Lanka. They are, however, unique in trying to actually put those teachings into practice. This has important implications on how forest monks of the *Saṃsthā* relate to money and property.

Monks and Money

We watch as Venerable Megha hands over the hundred-rupee note he picked up in the monastery grounds to Mr. Jayadewa, the fatherly monastery attendant.

"I'm a worrier monk," *says Venerable Tissa. He is from the UK.*

The metaphor of the warrior appears in many Suttas, where the monks are admonished to fight Māra *the evil one, the personification of mental defilements and death.*

"No, not warrior, W-O-R-R-I-E-R."

Recently ordained forest monks are often worried about breaking the Vinaya. The Pātimokkha, *with its two hundred and twenty rules—not to mention the thousands of procedural rules in the* Khandhaka—*is a big step from the ten rules of a novice. It usually takes a few months for a monk to settle into this new way of life. Some monks like Venerable Tissa are troubled by doubts even after years spent in the sangha.*

"There's no harm in touching money. The Vinaya explicitly says that we can pick up money or valuables left behind by lay people and place them in a safe place for them to collect." *I remind him of the relevant monastic rule.*[9]

"Yes, but I don't trust my own mind. What if I accept the money in my mind while holding it? I prefer to not take any chances."

As an object of veneration, the sangha exists both on a conceptual level—as one of the three jewels (*tiratana*) of the religion—and a physical level, as contemporary communities of monks. Sri Lankans tend to "respect the institution of the Sangha, rather than each and every monk" (Bartholomeusz 1994, 246). As Seneviratne (1999, 278) notes, lay Buddhists are capable of being extremely critical of monks even while overtly respecting them:

> This critique is expressed in the saying that the Buddhists worship the robe and not the wearer. Sociologically, this is not so trivial as it sounds. It encapsulates and expresses the entire problem of the Sangha of today … for it points to the gap between the ideal and reality. That is, the morality of the Sangha is an ideal to be talked about, but not practiced.

The forest monk, with his strict adherence to Vinaya, cuts a striking figure in this context: an embodiment of the ideal. For Buddhists, "living the life of the monk just as the Vinaya prescribes it is very close, as close as it is possible to get, to acting out in daily life the spiritual goal of attaining *Nibbāna*" (Gombrich 2006, 89). The more virtuous a monk is, the better a "field of merit" (*puññakkhetta*) he is supposed to make (Gombrich 1971, 325; Spiro 1982, 109)—a belief rooted in the teachings themselves.[10]

Thus, many donors consider it more advantageous to direct their offerings at forest monks than village monks (Bartholomeusz 1994, 246). However, it is important to note that this is not a mere "crass calculus of merits and demerits" (Strenski 1983, 474). There is a significant emotional factor in the merit-making activities of Buddhist laity: *puñña* (a meritorious act), for most of them, is that which makes them happy (Samuels 2008). If the heart is not elated and faith (*saddhā*) is not roused when making an offering, they consider the merit to be less or even nullified. And few images elate the hearts and arouse the faith of lay Buddhists than that of a forest monk.

The story of how the ascetic dedication and strict Vinaya adherence of forest monks draws lavish support from lay Buddhists is one that dates back to the earliest monastic settlements in Sri Lanka (Coningham 1995). Gombrich (1971, 325) notes how a donor who wished to donate a meal to the forest monastery at Salgala had to book a year in advance. In many well-known forest monasteries in Sri Lanka today, including the one where I resided, it is no longer possible to book such a donation at all: every day of the year has been booked by groups of donors who have made annual pilgrimages out of the practice. Prospective donors on waiting lists are known to plead with those who already have a booking to let them participate in making offerings.

Donations are not limited to food: significant amounts of other goods such as robes, bowls, food, medicine, and stationery are offered to forest monks—commonly referred to as "allowable requisites" (*kappiyabhaṇḍa*)—as well as financial donations to the monasteries. The largest and best-known forest monasteries in Sri Lanka receive millions of rupees (hundreds of thousands of dollars) every year in donations from both local and foreign supporters.

In most other monastic organizations and temples in Sri Lanka, the monks are directly in charge of the money, either personally or through a "donor council" (*dāyaka sabhā*) of laypeople that is usually under the guidance of the abbot. The bank accounts will be operated by the monks themselves. However, the *Theravāda* Vinaya is quite clear about money and money substitutes like gold and silver (*jātarūparajata*): "If a monk accepts money, or has someone accept it in his stead, or consents to have it deposited for him, he commits an offense of expiation involving forfeiture."[11] The Vinaya definition of *jātarūparajata* extends to "whatever is used" in commerce,[12] so it includes modern inventions like paper money and credit cards (Von Hinüber 1995). The next two *Nissaggiya Pācittiya* rules in the *Pātimokkha* forbid monks from engaging in any form of buying, selling, or bartering, regardless of whether it involves money (Thanissaro 2013, 225).

The issue of money and money substitutes is a fundamental one in Buddhist monasticism: all extant Vinaya texts contain the rule against accepting *jātarūparajata*, and all the background stories, although they vary between the traditions, presuppose "the existence of some proscription against the possession of gold and silver" (Juo-Hsueh 2008). This attitude toward money is clearly evident in the Sutras too.[13] Accepting money was one of the ten illicit practices—and arguably the most important one (Poussin 1976, 52)—that was rejected at the second council.[14]

Thus, it is natural that in their reconstruction of monasticism following the *Theravāda* commentarial tradition, the *Saṃsthā* instituted a strict policy of their monks not accepting or handling money. This immediately distinguished them from other monks and continues to be a key characteristic of the forest monastic identity.

Money is required—and made abundantly available by generous donors—for setting up, maintaining, and developing forest monasteries and communities. The processes that have been set up to enable forest monks to manage the money that they do not own are subtle and inventive. It takes an intelligent and experienced monk, and a compliant and informed group of lay supporters, to make these processes work.

The Abbot and the Council of Donors

As charismatic as he is, Venerable Vimala Thera does not immediately strike one as the abbot of the monastery. There are several monks who are much senior to him. However, here in this most important place—one of the largest, most respected meditation monasteries in the country—he wields authority.

His small office is in the administrative building next to the dining hall, which also houses the library, the storeroom, the medicine store as well as a dormitory for the sick monks. Located right next to the monastery gates, this is the interface between the forest and the village, the monks and the laity.

The office is sparse. It has a desk and a chair, a cupboard for documents and keys, and a simple bed. Venerable Vimala sleeps in the office on most nights. His assigned dwelling is a cave in the forest, where he resides occasionally.

Every monk in the monastery has some communal duties assigned to them, and mine are the roles of the assistant librarian and some sort of communications assistant to Venerable Vimala, to help him manage monastery emails and official documents. Thus, I get to see the abbot more often than most monks in the monastery, particularly in his administrative capacity.

This is an important distinction, for Venerable Vimala is also the main meditation teacher here: Apart from the few monks who are senior to him, every single member of this community including myself has received meditation instructions from Venerable Vimala at some point, and many continue to do so. He is known as an insightful teacher who is creative with meditation, not always following the standard method of the Saṃsthā, *open to borrowing from other traditions and on occasion, even suggesting new techniques drawn from his own experience.*

Venerable Vimala is sitting on the ground, outside the office building, as he usually does in the mornings. I greet him, placing my palms together. He smiles and nods his head.

"There is an email to reply. We have to thank the person, and tell them that we will organize a paritta *chanting[15] as they wish."*

I step into the room, sit on the only chair, and boot up the office computer. The email is from one of the biggest donors of the monastery.

Dear Bhante Vimala,

Greetings from Singapore! I hope Bhante is in good health, and the venerables are practicing in harmony.

I wish to offer Bhante allowable requisites to the value of $50,000. If Bhante and the venerables at the monastery need any allowable requisites, please request them from your kappiya[16] Mr. Godage.

Bhante, my company will be opening a new office on the 15th of next month. Could Bhante and the sangha kindly chant paritta for me, my family and my company on that day? Thank you very much!

The *Saṃsthā* does not have abbots or "head monks" in the sense of a "controlling *Viharadhipati*" as defined in the Buddhist Temporalities Ordinance of Sri Lanka (Act 19 of 1931), who manages the property and finances of the monastery. However, at any monastery, there will be one monk—usually the most senior—who acts as the leader of the monastery sangha and takes over the administrative responsibilities: a *vihārādhipati* for legal purposes. All finances, on the other hand, are managed by the *dāyaka sabhā* of the monastery, a council of lay supporters formally registered with the Ministry of Buddhist Affairs. The council officials are "elected" annually. In practice, they are appointed uncontested almost always. The abbot will act as the chief advisor (Sinhala: *pradhāna anuśāsaka*).

The abbot has great authority and influence over the council, more so than any other monk. Though all funds and financial management are entirely in the hands of the council, it is very rare for a council member to oppose, challenge, or question a decision of the abbot, put forth as a "suggestion" to be enacted by them. This authority originates from two sources: the natural deference laypeople have for monks—especially forest monks—and the personal charisma of the abbot. The conviction that the abbot is acting within the confines of the Vinaya makes this easier for the council, as they do not have to act as judges of morality: a burden that sometimes befalls the lay supporters of other temples (Schonthal 2016).

The donations to the monastery are made in several ways. "Allowable requisites" can be donated directly, either to individual monks or to the sangha in general. Every daily donor group and most visitors to the monastery make such donations. After the daily meal, a group of monks conduct a Vinaya ritual to make the offers made to the sangha distributable to individual monks, so that they are not at risk of breaking the Vinaya rule which states that a monk may not knowingly divert to himself gains that had been allocated to the sangha.[17] Thereafter, these goods end up in the monastery storeroom and are distributed upon request by the monk in charge (*bhāṇḍāgarika*) (Silk 2008, 160), who has been informally appointed by the abbot. Monks enter their requests in a book kept in the dining hall. These are worded with respect and humility: "May the venerable see it fit to offer me a toothbrush," "May there be batteries (size AA) for my torch," "Venerable sir, much merit for providing me with a notebook (single ruled, 160 pages or more)." The *bhāṇḍāgarika* monk fulfills these requests on a daily basis.

Monetary donations are received by the council mainly in the form of direct deposits to bank accounts, the details of which are shared with prospective donors upon request and when they express a wish to donate. It is also possible to make monetary donations to the monastery at a council office located outside the monastery boundary, in the same building where the daily meal preparations happen. An official of the council or a monastery attendant will be present to accept the donations and offer receipts. After taking care of immediate cash requirements of the monastery, the remaining funds are deposited in one of the bank accounts of the council. Some donors prefer to leave money—up to a hundred dollars—with attendants who live in the monastery, so that they may use it for the immediate needs of the monks.

However, some of the less knowledgeable donors express their wish to donate directly to monks, often to the abbot. The guideline followed in such instances is *Nissaggiya Pācittiya* 10,[18] the longest rule in the *Pātimokkha*. While it refers to a monetary donation for a robe, it is applied as a template for the protocol to follow when dealing with all money offers regardless of the intended purpose. The commentarial discussions of this rule are extensive and elaborate. The gist is that when money is offered for a certain purpose—as long as it is allowable for monks—the donor should be told that monks do not accept money; if the discerning donor then asks for a steward or attendant—not what to do with the money, nor to whom the money should be given—the monk should point out a suitable person; then the donor may leave the money with that person and inform the monk. However, these situations are handled in a simpler way in the *Saṃsthā*.

When a lay supporter expresses their wish to make a donation, either explicitly stating that this will be a monetary donation or implying it, the monk will simply reply, "you should talk to this person," referring to either a council official or a monastery attendant, without alluding to the donation in any way, as if it were a different discussion altogether. If they continue to talk about the donation because they fail to grasp what was being hinted at, the monk's replies would remain polite yet repetitive: "please talk to Mr. so-and-so." If an attendant is nearby, the monk may call him and say to the attendant, "you should talk to this lay supporter," referring to the donor and leave the conversation. It is then up to the attendant to inform the donor about the intricacies involved in financial donations, so that they can make their offering in a manner that is in accordance with the Vinaya.

The largest donations are usually made by affluent Sri Lankan and foreign donors, who are often better informed about the processes to follow. They will collaborate with someone from the council and transfer the funds, and then inform the abbot via email. Occasionally, though, there are lay supporters who express their wish to donate via email sent directly to the monastery address. In such instances, their email is forwarded to a council official, who initiates a conversation excluding the monks. The prospective donor may also receive a reply from the monastery pointing to an online guide that explains the correct procedure.

The abbot is the only monk who is directly kept informed of the funds in all the council accounts. The monastic sangha, on the other hand, seems to be perfectly happy to be oblivious to it. Reflecting their general attitude toward money, monks have rarely shown any interest in getting to know these figures. When it comes to utilizing these funds, *Nissaggiya Pācittiya* 10 again acts as the guide. The monk may prompt and remind the steward two or three times to use the funds for the intended purpose and may stand in silence four, five, or six times; if the steward fails to deliver, the monk is to refrain from making any further requests. Furthermore, the monk may also inform the donor that their donation has not been used for its intended purpose. If the use of the funds is obtained through more requests than allowed, it is to be forfeited, and the monk should make a confession. Here, too, the practice in the *Saṃsthā* is simpler, owing to the strong relationship between the abbot and the laypeople involved.

The abbot personally oversees the construction work and other projects—such as installing a new Buddha statue or funding work at another monastery—that require large amounts of funds. These initiatives are planned by the abbot, sometimes with the assistance of other monks, sometimes consulting lay supporters who have expertise in relevant fields, and then passed over to the council. The council acts as a facilitator, not as a controller: once the decision has been made by the abbot, they will fund its execution without question. And here too, other monks are quite content to not get involved unless asked: I met only three other monks who took any initiative on construction work. Interestingly, two of them have now become abbots of their own monasteries.

When monks need something that requires monastery funds to be utilized—for example, to travel outside the monastery for a medical appointment—they will inform the abbot. Depending on the required amount, the abbot will then instruct a monastery attendant or a council official to assist the monk. These lay supporters are efficient: a monk never has to go to the extent of having to make silent prompts as mentioned in the Vinaya rule. Usually one request is all it takes and rarely a second reminder.

Monks seldom make any direct requests from council officials or monastery attendants, unless the request requires only an insignificant amount of money or it is for something already kept in stock, such as monastic furniture. These requests are fulfilled without delay. If a monk does request something that requires a substantial amount of money, the lay supporter will usually ask the monk to talk to the abbot. For their personal needs—for example, to obtain a book that is not available in the monastery library—the monks are more likely to contact their personal supporters first: usually family members or friends and donors who have explicitly invited them to make such requests.

Officials and Monastery Attendants

"I arrived here together with Bhante Vimala fifteen years ago. We built this place together," says Jayadewa Mahattayā—Mr. Jayadewa. He is a gentle, friendly, soft-spoken man, sixty years old, and estranged from his family. He lives in a small room on the ground floor of the two-storied dining hall, always at hand to attend to the needs of the monks. And just like the monks, Jayadewa has few possessions.

"Did you come here planning to ordain?" I ask him.

"Yes, that was my intention, but I had to take care of the monks. Life was very difficult back then. We had no facilities. We built it all slowly. I think I'm too old to ordain now."

Dressed in a white shirt and sarong, Jayadewa is a fatherly presence in the monastery, always by the side of monks in monastic activities. He has known most monks since they were laypeople who visited this place hoping to ordain. Trusted by both monks and lay supporters, he is often the first person to advise donors on Vinaya requirements, and to direct them to the relevant donor council officials when they offer to make donations.

The council officials and monastery attendants play critical roles in ensuring the donations are handled properly, managing the finances of the monastery and putting the funds to use in ways that allow the monks to adhere to the Vinaya rules. Without their knowledge of the Vinaya and supportive attitude, it would not be possible for the monastery to function properly.

The council members are a diverse group. The majority of them are people from the local community. Because most forest monasteries are located in remote areas, they are often villagers with low income. They are the lay supporters who are most likely to be present at the monastery, work in the council office, volunteer their time for monastery projects, and assist monks in person. Since the monasteries draw support from all over the country, the local communities are not burdened by obligations to financially support the sangha. The "outside" supporters, likely from the burgeoning urban middle class, form a smaller yet influential part of the council. And then there are the largest donors, who are not members of the council: they rarely visit the monastery but wield more influence over monastic activities than any other lay supporter. They single-handedly sponsor large projects in the monastery, such as the construction of a new meditation hall, and are relied upon by the monastic community for bigger undertakings, such as supporting monks in their pilgrimages and visits to other countries.

Mr. Jayadewa is one of the three full-time monastery attendants. They are people who have voluntarily dedicated their life to serving in the monastery. They do not draw a salary, but their needs are taken care of by the donor council. In Vinaya terms these monastery attendants play the role of *ārāmika*:

> The hierarchical position of an *ārāmika* is between a novice and a lay follower. He may carry out physical or manual work (clearing caves or rock overhangs). He has some authority with respect to the organization of the monastery (he is asked for permission to leave [in a monk's case] or enter [in a nun's case] a monastery if no monk and no novice is present), or he acts as the personal attendant of a monk (*veyyāvaccakāra*).
> (Kieffer-Pülz 2007, 17)

The monastery also has a steady stream of temporary attendants, in the form of *anagārikas*—people who have left their homes to stay at the monastery and are awaiting ordination—and lay Buddhists who stay at the monastery as meditation retreatants. The former group follows the same ten precepts as novice monks (*sāmaṇera*), so they are unable to handle money. The latter also have to follow the ten precepts while they are at the monastery: they have to hand over all money to the donor council office, to be picked up again when they leave.

Meditation retreatants at the monastery do not enjoy the privileges or freedom offered at private, lay or secular retreats: they should be ready to serve monks when necessary. They may be requested, by a meditation teacher or a monastery attendant, to switch to five precepts and assist monks with money matters, particularly as travel companions who will pay for transport and any other needed services, using the funds issued by the donor council. With more than a hundred monks and only three full-time monastery attendants, their services are required quite often. The retreatants are usually happy to oblige, but they also have the freedom to decline, and some do.

Reciprocity

Carrithers notes how, from the early days of the *Saṃsthā*, one of the constant problems was the "expectations and generosity of lay supporters" (1983, 260). Participating in merit-making ceremonies (Sinhala: *pinkam*) like all-night *paritta* chanting, which are "often expensive, lengthy, and busy affairs, quite at odds with the meditative ideal" (1983, 260), is traditionally one of the chief services of monks, which the *Saṃsthā* has attempted to avoid:

> In view of their experience with the village Sangha, whose status is legitimated in the village by performance of *pinkam*, lay supporters naturally expect the same services from meditating monks. The *saṃsthāva* has dealt with this problem in a variety of ways. The most drastic is to abandon a hermitage altogether. I know of at least five instances in which they have done so.
>
> (ibid., 261)

Thus, the monastery, through the council, has made it very clear to its supporters that they will not be taking part in any *pinkam*. The monks have unabashedly embraced the "selfish" epithet sometimes attributed to them (Silber 1981).

However, on full moon days (Sinhala: *Poya*) of May and June—the most important ones to Sri Lankan Buddhists, the first being *Vesak*, which celebrates the birth, awakening, and the final cessation of the Buddha, and the second being *Poson*, when Buddhism is said to have been introduced to the country—the monastery opens up its gates to the public, and the villagers join the monks in making offerings to the Buddha (*Buddha-pūjā*). The largest ceremony, however, happens on the *Kaṭhina* Day, when monks end their annual rains retreat (*vassa*): thousands of people visit the monastery to make offerings.

Compromises, however, have been made for the benefit of the largest of donors. Once or twice a year, there might be a *paritta* chanting organized on a full moon day. The main purpose is to bless the monastics and help them progress in their practice. A secondary purpose is to bless this or that donor and their family, and to wish them prosperity. It is a private affair of monks; there are no laypeople attending except those who are resident at the monastery at the time. The next day, the large donor is informed that they have been blessed.

But offering blessings and being a field of merit are not the only ways the monastery benefits the laity. Sometimes, the material donations made to the monastery find their way back to laypeople as well.

The storeroom in the monastery is always filled to capacity: there are far too many books, pens, pencils, torches, bars of soap, toothbrushes than needed by the sangha even for years, and more keep coming every day. But according to the Vinaya, these can only be distributed among the monks and *ārāmikas*. As Seneviratne (1999, 320) notes, it is "part of the complex of the basic and unquestionable cultural assumptions of Sinhala Buddhism that the monks, despite their vast properties, should not be a source of economic benefit to the laity ... The return gift to the laity was non-material." Monastic property is deemed "taboo for the laity."

This leads to another arrangement of the monastery: every once in a while, the excess items from the storeroom are carefully categorized and packed into labeled boxes, and donated to the nuns of a local temple, who then donate them in turn to orphanages, elderly homes, and temples that are in need. The robes and bowls, packed as the popular "eight requisites" (Sinhala: *aṭa pirikara*)—which are fit only for ceremonial purposes and not actual use—are also donated to the monks of local temples that are experiencing financial difficulties. These, however, are more likely to eventually find their way back to various shops that sell Buddhist items. The Vinaya rules are broken, but technically not by the forest monks, and it is done for the benefit of those who are really in need.

The Mendicants

The gong from the dāna sālā *echoes through the mountains. It is dawn, and the "right time" has begun. I pick up the bowl and start the trek down the mountain to the dining hall.*

My friend Venerable Gavesaka is already there when I arrive. Most forest monks are gaunt creatures, but he looks thinner than most of us. Subsisting on a single meal obtained from piṇḍapāta—*the daily alms round—could have that effect on a monk on the long term.*

"What route are you taking today?" he asks.

The group of monks who go on piṇḍapāta have prepared a simple map of the villages surrounding the monastery, with numbered paths. The map is accompanied by a chart where we note down which path will be used by each of us on that day. This is to make sure that each path is taken by only one monk, so that the villagers would not be burdened by having to donate more than once a day.

"I'm thinking of taking 3. Where are you going?" I ask him.

"21."

Every numbered path is several kilometers long, but my friend has an affinity for the particularly long ones, where the "begging" begins quite far from the monastery. They often take him several hours of walking. What motivates him is not wanderlust: he wants to make sure that those villagers are not denied the opportunity to donate food to a mendicant monk.

Gavesaka leaves for his long piṇḍapāta round while I rearrange the robe to step out of the monastery. The intricate "outside" style covers both shoulders, and from the neck down to the shins, while still offering plenty of convenience and control. The monk in me appreciates its simple effectiveness; the Buddhist in me just likes how it looks. I know that this is a sight that inspires.

Every single day I step out of the monastery for piṇḍapāta, I am surprised by the evocative power of the sight I conjure, and I understand that this is not a personal accomplishment: I am merely playing a role in an ancient play, my appearance a canvas onto which the faithful project their devotion, like I myself used to even as a child. The villagers, too, never fail to surprise me with their generosity: by their ability to give so much, while having so little.

Yet some memories are stronger than others:

A woman with her two children, in front of their mud hut, with its thatched roof of coconut leaves. Their worn clothes, their bare feet. A bar of soap in her hand—her only offering, for they have no food. My initial rejection, for we are only to accept food, and her tears. A bar of soap in my bowl.

A group of small children, led by their elder sister, in front of their wooden shack of a home. A bowl of rice and several dishes of vegetables, placed respectfully on a small table. Each child, taking his or her turn, offering food. My attempt to accept only one spoonful of each dish, so that there is enough left for them. My failed attempt, for they insist on putting it all in my bowl.

An old man, emerging slowly from his little mud hut—a dwelling smaller and more decrepit than most in the monastery. His bent back, trembling limbs, his unstable gait. A cardboard box in his hands. Two biscuits, placed respectfully in my bowl. The old man, on his knees, venerating the mendicant.

Piṇḍapāta is one of the many ways in which the monks voluntarily strive toward the ascetic ideal, to simplify their lives, to have few desires (*appicchatā*), and to be contented with little (*santuṭṭhitā*), qualities the teachings encourage them to cultivate and declare to be of great benefit.[19] The lavish support from donors, on the other hand, if not handled properly, can become a great obstacle.[20] The more committed the monks are to asceticism, the stronger the support from the laity: a paradox the monks of the *Saṃsthā* are well aware of and seek to negotiate intelligently.

Due to his position as a leader of the sangha, as a meditation teacher sought after by monks and laity, and as the chief administrator of a large monastery, this risk is perhaps most imminent to the abbot. Thus, his worn robes, simple office, cave dwelling, and meager possessions. Though he has a busy schedule and rarely goes on *piṇḍapāta*, he leaves his bowl open in the *dāna sālā*, to be filled by whatever that the *piṇḍapāta* monks can share, which would then be his daily meal. And, like the abbots before him, his adherence to the Vinaya leaves us with another paradox: a powerful man in control of wealth that is far beyond what is ever achievable for the vast majority of Sri Lankans and yet a poor man, a mendicant, a forest monk who has robes and a bowl as his only possessions.

Abbreviations

References to Pali texts are to the section and sutta number, and the volume and page number of the editions of the Pali Text Society (PTS).

AN Aṅguttaranikāya
MN Majjhimanikāya
SN Saṃyuttanikāya
Vin Vinaya Piṭaka

CHAPTER NINE

Monastic Business Expansion in Post-Mao Tibet: Risk, Trust, and Perception

Jane Caple

Samten, a senior monk at a large scholastic center in northeast Tibet, was discussing the fixing of prices for butter lamps in monastic assembly halls and temples.[1] Although not a major source of monastic income, the money generated through the provision of these lamps, as well as cash left as offerings, goes toward the upkeep of these monastic buildings. Samten felt that fixing prices made things simple and convenient (*tapdé* [stabs bde])[2] but was critical of the high amount charged in some monasteries, arguing that butter lamps should be sold at cost price: "If it costs ten *yuan* to make, then the price should be ten *yuan*." If they are expensive, he argued, there is a risk that some people might think that monks are being deceitful (*gokor* [mgo bskor]):

> There are different kinds of people. Some might be happy to pay 100 but others will not trust monks [*yichegyu maré akhutso* (yid ches rgyu ma red a khu tsho)]. [They will think] monks are taking a lot of money for the butter lamps, doing business and deceiving people—oh, then the monastery is meaningless [*gyumtsen mégi* (rgyu mtshan med gi)].

Samten was not against the idea of monasteries "doing business" and generating profit per se. Monasteries are *obligated* to make profits in order to maintain the capital of perpetual endowments—a mechanism of monastic financing that Gregory Schopen (2004, 81) traces back to the first century CE and the emergence of fully institutionalized, permanent, landed monasteries.[3] Moreover, as this chapter will discuss, monastic business has become an increasingly important strand of financing for many Tibetan Buddhist monasteries over the past ten to fifteen years. This has been a development that Samten has, in broad terms, advocated for as a way for monasteries to distance themselves from other morally problematic forms of financing. However, he was deeply concerned about how monastic engagement in market-type exchanges might be perceived by the public.

The need to generate income while maintaining generalized trust or belief (*yiché* [yid ches]) and faith (*depa* [dad pa]) in the sangha is certainly not a new problematic for monastic leaders attempting to carve out a "moral" economy for their monasteries (see, e.g., Jansen 2018; Wood 2013). However, Samten's comments reflect not only ideas about the proper conduct of monks but also a more general ambivalence—felt by both monks and laypeople—toward the idea of profit and its generation. Accelerated state-led development, particularly since the turn of the millennium, has brought about rapid social and economic change, and with it increasing wealth, inequalities, and a sense of risk and uncertainty in society and everyday life. This chapter examines monastic business as a modality of financing in these wider contexts. It starts by providing an outline of the history of contemporary Tibetan monastic business development and its relationship to other monastic economic modalities, including gifts and remunerations for religious services. It then goes on to discuss the intersection between monastic business expansion and perceptions that the pursuit of wealth and power—and more generally self-interest—is taking precedence over erudition and virtuous action, including faith. Although monks and monastic businesses are implicated in this perceived rise of economic-mindedness, the sense of risk and uncertainty that it has produced simultaneously positions them as a trustworthy "moral other." Embedded in the broader context of the monastic economy, monastic business transactions have the potential to exceed the sphere of the market. Finally, the chapter returns to the issue of public perception and the questions this raises about moral agency as well as the divergent epistemological foundations upon which etic and emic categorizations of economic modalities are based. The chapter draws on fieldwork conducted over a total of two years between 2008 and 2015 in Geluk monasteries and Tibetan communities on the northeastern edge of the Tibetan Plateau (in Amdo/Qinghai).[4] Data were gathered at large scholastic centers such as Rongwo and Ditsa in Repgong[5] and Western Bayen, housing upward of 700 and 400 monks, respectively, as of 2015, as well as at smaller practice centers and branch monasteries more focused on ritual, housing 25–150 monks; and during time spent in both urban and rural (mostly farming) households in Repgong and the provincial capital, Xining.

Monastic Business as a Modality of Lay-Monastic Transfer

As examined in detail elsewhere (Caple 2019), the development of profit-making enterprises has become an increasingly important strand of monastic financing for Geluk monasteries in northeast Tibet, reflecting a more general pattern in other Tibetan areas. This has been the result of both pragmatic and ethical imperatives for monasteries to secure a sustainable economic base—imperatives centered on the relationship between monasteries and their patron communities. The revival of Geluk monasteries in the early 1980s involved a resurgence of historical relationships between particular reincarnate lamas, monasteries, and communities, even though monasteries had lost their claims to the lands and people historically under their jurisdiction.[6] This resurgence first presented itself in the spontaneous outpouring of donations as monasteries started to reopen in the early 1980s and was more firmly reinstitutionalized as they reestablished offices responsible for collecting alms from their patron communities. However, monasteries have more recently sought to reduce and ultimately eradicate their reliance on institutionalized alms collection, instead collecting contributions toward capital funds and investing these funds in profit-making enterprises, including moneylending, shops, medical clinics, and the manufacture of religious products.[7] Referred to as "the path to self-sufficiency," monks consider this the key shift in monastic financing during the post-Mao period. Although converging with state policy, this "new" form of monastic financing is based on historical precedent (e.g., the loaning on interest of monastic capital and engagement in trade) and also takes inspiration from the economic activities of Geluk monasteries rebuilt in exile in India. Moreover, monks themselves advocated for reform. In addition to the practical difficulties monastic officials faced fund-raising in the same communities each year, organized alms collection was seen to place a burden on the public and carried connotations of coercion or tax-like obligation. It was also too easily associated with the disreputable practices of dishonest or fake monks, an issue to which I will return. Unlike the Buryat lama profiled by Jonutytė (this volume), who also did not collect donations on moral grounds, monastic leaders in northeast Tibet have not eschewed lay sponsorship.[8] Rather, the idea is that monasteries should be able to rely on their own funds if no one volunteers to sponsor a particular event or one of the daily teas during a dharma session. These "communal teas" (*mangja* [mang ja]) are meals of varying levels of modesty, from bread and tea to noodles or rice and vegetables (all the monasteries I visited had stopped serving meat). Monks receive them one to three times daily during dharma sessions and other regular religious events, and they constitute the main collective monastic expense.

The extent and contribution of business to central monastic economies varies. Sponsorship from laypeople remains a major source of funding, some of it direct and some channeled through those reincarnate lamas and monks who redistribute wealth received from their patrons. It has increased in parallel with growing wealth and political uncertainties, as well as the extension of patronage networks in the Sinophone world (see Caple 2015; Smyer Yü 2012). According to a steward at a highly reputed scholastic monastery housing roughly 400 monks (Ditsa), during his term of office (2011–13) the monastery was meeting just over half (*c*. 270,000 yuan) of its total annual costs (*c*. 480,000 yuan) through its businesses; the rest was met by regular and occasional sponsors (Caple 2019, 49). By 2014, a senior monk reported a surplus of roughly 200,000 yuan, distributed among the monks to encourage them to stay in the monastery by obviating their need to go out to generate income (ibid., 50, 106). He attributed this to the success of their commercial ventures, particularly the manufacture and sale of religious products (although an increase in sponsorship might also have played a role: new relationships with Chinese patrons had been formed in the preceding years). Other scholastic centers, including Rongwo and Gartsé monasteries, had also developed a portfolio of monastic enterprises, as had some branch monasteries and practice centers (for further details, see ibid., 41–51). Others remained more heavily reliant on their reincarnate lamas and, in practice, at least some stewards still needed to actively solicit donations through their personal networks (see ibid., 46–7, for an example).

In his discussion of the Buddhist gift, Sihlé (2015, 253) has argued for the importance of making an analytical "distinction between 'gifts' strictly speaking and patterns of transfers that are more akin to an exchange or transaction, such as the provision of ritual services and their remuneration." When monks draw a distinction between events funded by the monastery and through sponsorship, the latter can encompass both modalities. Geluk monks perform rituals for the dead and merit-accumulation, and more pragmatically oriented rituals for health, prosperity, and success. Like the non-monastic religious specialists Sihlé discusses in this volume, monks perform household rituals (*drongchok* [grong chog]) in the community; this is an important source of livelihood for many of them.[9] However, people can also request services at monasteries, performed in the assembly hall when the monks gather. Each monk will receive a share of all remunerations (as well as donations) given that day. Remunerations can range from very modest to significant sums, the amount as well as services requested scrupulously recorded by a monastic official. For example, a friend with health problems gave 200 yuan (*c*. US$30) when she requested services at a scholastic center with roughly 700 monks. A batch of receipts I viewed in 2012 at another scholastic center with over 400 monks recorded lower sums, such as ten yuan for services for a student who had an exam or twenty yuan for services for a woman who was pregnant. Yet, at the same monastery, roughly sixty households had spent many times this amount sponsoring communal teas that year at an average cost of 1,500–2,000 yuan depending on the relative modesty of the meal, added to which might be cash disbursements (*gyé* ['gyed]) for each monk. Some involved requests for services, such as prayers and offerings for the deceased on a death anniversary, and were therefore strictly remunerations; if a sponsor requests services, this implies a mutual obligation that is absent when someone funds a tea simply in order to respect and support the monks and accumulate merit (i.e., as a gift proper). However, the relative proportion of teas funded through these two modalities was not clear and, more generally in the context of discussions about monastic financing, did not seem to matter to my interlocutors. Either way, they were funded directly by sponsors, rather than by the monastery.[10]

My research suggests that in the Geluk context the key operative distinction when it comes to religious giving is that between voluntarily made transfers (including donations and remunerations for religious services) and those which are solicited or, in the case of donations, even coerced (Caple 2015, 2017). The transfer of wealth to monks as religious service providers has, as Sihlé (2015) argues, a much stronger reciprocal element than gifts proper, even if it differs in some respects from market exchange. However, in the contemporary Geluk monastic context at least, the distinction between different kinds of religious services seems to have greater significance than the distinction between gift and remuneration. While rites for the dead are unequivocally viewed as a key monastic role, some monks and laypeople feel that Geluk monks should not be spending time—and generating income from—performing rituals oriented toward more pragmatic concerns, such as success in business. The latter is more likely to be associated with economic-mindedness—a trope to which I will return. There is particular ambivalence toward monks going out to perform household rituals (see also Sihlé, this volume) but also some toward monks spending too much time performing ritual services in monasteries. However, as evident in the moral logics behind the expansion of monastic business, active collection or solicitation of donations can also be problematic.

Developed as a mechanism of financing to obviate the need to actively collect donations, monastic business represents a modality of transfer explicitly oriented toward the generation of profit. Both gifts and remunerations position the laity as patrons to monks as a field of merit and power, and the ethics and efficacy of both gifts and remunerations are dependent on faith.[11] By contrast, monastic business transactions would seem to operate according to the logic of market exchange, the relationship between the parties being that of consumers and producers/sellers. As this chapter goes on to discuss, the idea of the monk as a particular kind of moral subject means that monastic engagement in the burgeoning cash-based market economy can be delicate to negotiate, but also creates the potential for it to exceed market logics.

Authenticity, Profit, and Deception

During a visit to northeast Tibet in 2013, a conversation with two young men about monastic business development turned to issues of authenticity and trust. It is better to be discriminating these days, argued Norbu, a self-educated businessman, because it is no longer possible to know that someone is a "real (*ngoma* [ngo ma]) monk" simply because he is wearing monastic robes. The notion that a monk is "real" can be literal: Has the man wearing robes taken the vow of renunciation or is he a layman in monks' clothes? However, it can also have a broader meaning: Is the man wearing robes the kind of moral subject that a monk should be? This was evident when Dorje, a teacher, directly followed Norbu's comment with a comparison of the conduct of temple caretakers at two monasteries: Rongwo Monastery, his regional Geluk monastic seat, and Kumbum—a major monastic center, pilgrimage destination, and tourist attraction located near the provincial capital. Referring to the offering lamps sold in assembly halls and temples, he claimed:

> At Rongwo Monastery, you know that the butter lamp will be burnt completely, whereas at Kumbum the temple caretaker will put it out, top it up and resell it. If you go there once or twice you will not see this, but after a time you realize. It is not good—it is like cheating. I never offer lamps or give money there, just do circumambulation and prostrations.

There are many stories circulating about monks and lamas who are "fake" (*dzünma* [rdzun ma]) and/or who deceive people, for example collecting donations under false pretenses, embezzling funds intended for monastic projects, and providing religious services which they are not qualified to perform (see also Makley 2007, 266; Smyer Yü 2012, 99–125). More generally, there is a perception among both laypeople and monks that many monks (and lamas) "these days" are more focused on chasing money than on studying and practicing, and that monasteries are placing too much emphasis on external development and wealth creation, to the detriment of monastic discipline and education. As Klepeis (this volume) shows in her study of Ganden Sumtsenling in Shangri-La and its "bad" monks, mass state-sponsored tourism at Tibetan Buddhist monasteries in China can generate particular suspicion of monastics, both politically and morally. In northeast Tibet, Kumbum Monastery—a major tourist destination—acts as the archetype of perceived monastic moral decline (Caple 2019, 86–92). It retains its importance as a pilgrimage destination as the birthplace of Tsongkhapa (1357–1419), whose works inspired the formation of the Geluk tradition, but in the eyes of many Tibetans has become like a park or museum, stripped of its meaning as a monastery. Such stories and perceptions are not exclusive to Tibetan Buddhism. Crackdowns on fake or profiteering monks in China—including temple closures—have been reported in the global media (e.g., BBC 2014; Florcruz 2013),[12] as have corruption scandals involving monastic leaders (e.g., Shi 2017). The academic literature refers to complaints about "fake" monks at Theravāda Buddhist and Daoist temples (Borchert 2005, 103; Fielder 2019, 88; Svensson 2010, 226), and "fake monks who work nine to five" at Chan monasteries (Nichols 2015, 412). A perceived lack of authenticity and purity in contemporary Chinese Buddhism has been one of the reasons why some Chinese Buddhists have turned to Tibetan Buddhism (Jones 2011, 548–9; see also Caple 2015; Smyer Yü 2012).

Monks in the part of northeast Tibet where I work are acutely aware of—and participate in—the circulation of cautionary tales about "fake" monks or the economic-mindedness of particular monasteries.[13] Concerns over maintaining the faith and trust of the laity and bolstering their own monasteries' reputations by distancing themselves from the practices of disreputable monks provided a key impetus for the expansion of monastic businesses. Some monasteries—like Ditsa mentioned above—have channeled profits from these businesses into disbursements for their monks with the aim of reducing their need to go out to generate income. However, such concerns also make monastic participation in the burgeoning market economy delicate to negotiate. As in postsocialist societies in Eastern Europe, Russia, and Central Asia (see, e.g., Humphrey and Mandel 2002), people in China are still coming to terms with a normative shift away from the collectivism of the Maoist period. Tibetans are also experiencing tensions between "development" and market rationality, and deeply ingrained values and sensibilities shaped by understandings of Buddhist values and Tibetan identity. Ambivalence toward the idea of profit voiced by Samten at the start of this chapter—the notion that buying something for two yuan and selling it on for three is a form of "deception"—is not only problematic for monks. At least some people who make offerings and request rituals for success in future business ventures will also make donations to offset the negative results of past profits. An economically minded, profit-oriented "other" is often counterposed to a moral (religious/faithful) "us." Depending on the context this "other" might be "the Chinese," Muslims, officials or entrepreneurs as a class (counterposed to ordinary folk), the people of a neighboring village—or, as we have seen, the monks of Kumbum. Although people generally aspire to greater prosperity, increasing wealth and inequalities are associated with competitiveness, dishonesty, and deception, as well as community breakdown (see also Makley 2014). Added to this is political uncertainty, which has intensified since protests in 2008 and the subsequent wave of self-immolations, and an awareness that "development" is a "legitimising narrative for state power" (Yeh 2013, 175)—as well as a legitimizing narrative for state appropriation of resources (Makley 2018, 25). There is ambivalence toward the morality of officials and their enrichment through, as Makley (2007, 127) puts it, "the expropriation of the ordinary folks that had begun in 1958." Such doubt now extends to emerging entrepreneurial elites, (usually) men who gain status through their success, wealth, and influence but might be disapproved of or at least morally and/or politically suspect (see also Jinba 2014).[14] Among some of my interlocutors (monastic and lay), it also extends to wealthy monasteries and monks.

As in premodern Tibet, a moral distinction is drawn between business conducted by monks for the collective (i.e., for the sangha), which is considered appropriate, and that which is conducted for personal profit. The problematic here is therefore somewhat different to that of monks "chasing" or embezzling money for personal enrichment as discussed by Klepeis (this volume)—although there is a risk that business conducted for the collective might be conflated with such conduct. In the scenario outlined by Samten, he emphasized that the caretaker does not keep the profits from inflated prices for butter lamps for himself. He wants to make more money for the monastery. "These days it can be like this," Samten claimed:

> After one year the caretaker will change and they will announce to the monastery how much money they made. ... Then the caretakers are in competition. For example, if the previous caretaker provided 100,000 *yuan*, then I want to give 200,000. ... Then they need to try to find a way to make money. Then the price will go up. Usually it is ten yuan for one lamp, then the next caretaker [will charge] twenty.

Although this was a hypothetical scenario, it reflects a genuine tension felt by at least some monks involved in businesses on behalf of their monasteries— particularly those who work in shops since this involves them in everyday face-to-face commercial transactions and, depending on the customers, negotiation of prices. Some of the monastic shopkeepers and managers with whom I have spoken expressed uneasiness about their work, partly because it takes them away from their studies and practice, but also because of the association of making profit with deception. At the same time, they clearly felt under pressure to do a good job in their service to the monastery and to make a healthy profit—at least as much as, if not more, than their predecessors.

Monks holding key monastic offices (e.g., steward or manager) must provide an accounting of income and expenditure to the assembly of monks at the end of the year and/or their term of office, swearing they have not used any income for personal purposes, only to cover necessary expenses. This ritual of verification works to enforce monastic discipline— as one monk remarked, if he swears in the assembly hall, he "cannot take the money." Yet, the public nature of this accounting to the community also places pressure on officials to excel in their work for the community. Moreover, in many cases, each monk will get a share of excess (in some cases all) profits. One shopkeeper openly admitted that it was a "very hard job" that no one wanted to do, not only because of the work involved but also because of the pressure to generate income. In his case, the profits would be distributed among the monks at the end of his term of office. If he did not make much money, he felt that other monks would think that he had not worked hard enough. Despite his efforts, he was doubtful as to his prospects. Alluding but not openly referring to a series of self-immolations in Repgong in 2012, he said that the shop had made a lot of money the previous year because people wanted to make many offerings and therefore bought lots of butter. However, this year it was going to be difficult, particularly since the price of caterpillar fungus (*ophiocordyceps sinensis*), a major source of cash income in the area, had gone down. This meant that people had less disposable income.[15]

In Chinese Buddhist monasteries, it seems to be common to find lay attendants looking after temples and involved in monastic administration and finance (see, e.g., Carter 2017). Although ultimate financial authority rests with their abbots, Theravāda monasteries in Thailand, Burma, and Sri Lanka also rely to varying degrees on lay workers/attendants or nuns (who are unable to receive full ordination) to handle money (see, e.g., Bunnag 1973, 129–35; Kawanami 1990, 24–5; Horstmann, this volume). Prabhath Sirisena (this volume) argues that in Sri Lanka the forest monk tradition goes furthest, with all finances managed by an organization of lay supporters under the supervision of the abbot. However, in the Geluk monasteries of Repgong and Western Bayen, monastic "work," including that related to finance, is mostly carried out by monks, reflecting a broader pattern in Geluk monasteries elsewhere (e.g., Mills 2001) as well as historically. Monks are expected to take their turn in providing service to their monasteries, including by working as temple caretakers and stewards or managers responsible for generating income and managing the finances for monastic activities (donations and businesses), and at the most senior level, on the monastery's management committee which oversees financial as well as religious and political affairs. Visiting a historically famous monastery to the north of the provincial capital to make offerings for a person recently deceased, the Tibetan friend accompanying me was shocked to find a male lay attendant in the assembly hall and a female lay attendant in one of the temples—and no visible presence of monks. Similarly, the presence of lay attendants in temples has been an element in some of the critiques I have heard leveled at Kumbum. Handling transactions with visitors who wish to light butter lamps is only a minor part of the role of a temple caretaker, which also includes looking after the monastery's shrines and inner objects and making daily offerings. In the Tibetan context, it is seen as a monastic role. The explicitly Buddhist space and context perhaps explains why Samten felt that butter lamps should be sold at cost price, even though he was in favor of monasteries developing other kinds of profit-making enterprise to generate income.[16]

When it comes to the day-to-day running of explicitly profit-oriented commercial enterprises such as shops, particularly those located outside monasteries, there is greater ambivalence and debate. There seems to be no question that monks should be in control of monastic finance, but even those who strongly agree with monasteries becoming more self-sufficient can be uneasy about monks themselves engaging in everyday commercial transactions (see also Caple 2019, 99–105). Unlike the job of caretaker, the day-to-day work of a shopkeeper is viewed as secular, and monks worry about the impact it might have on the minds and conduct of monk workers, the ultimate risk being that they will disrobe. Others, including Samten, also feel that it presents the wrong image to a public already perceived to be questioning the value (*rintang* [rin thang]) of monks. Since they are established with the explicit purpose of generating income, it would make no sense to argue that monastic businesses such as shops make no profit, as Samten argued in the case of butter lamps in temples. Instead, some monks believe that it would be better to either lease them or hire lay workers for public-facing roles—Gartsé Monastery in Repgong has already opted for this latter option (see Caple 2019, 48). Such arguments are based on the idea that monks should (ideally) be—and be seen to be—a particular kind of moral subject. Yet, as we will see, this same idea also serves to validate monastic business and take it beyond the sphere of the market.

Risk, Trust, and Altruism

Issues of trust and authenticity centered on notions of the real (*ngoma*) and the fake (*dzünma*) extend far beyond lay-monastic interactions. Scandals about adulterated, poor quality, and "fake" food and medicines serve as some of the most extreme examples of immoral profiteering and moral crisis in contemporary China. As Yan Yunxiang (2012, 717) argues, the idea that people will knowingly produce products harmful to others for the sake of making profits has led to an erosion of social trust and a "deeply felt sense of insecurity." It represents the epitome of the trope that "these days" there are "all kinds of people," a sense that is intensified by the distanciation of the production and circulation of goods from tangible social and geographical relations, as well as generalized distrust in government institutions introduced to ensure and strengthen product safety (Wang et al. 2015). Although state-led marketization of local economies and a perceived shift in societal values have fed into contemporary perceptions of monastic moral decline, the risk and uncertainty involved in everyday market transactions simultaneously position monks and monastic businesses as a trustworthy moral "other."

Farming and herding communities in northeast Tibet have been undergoing a transition from a subsistence to a cash-based economy and integration into national and global markets. Increased mobility, diversification of household income, and changing consumer tastes, as well as rapid urbanization and the sale of animals and land, mean that in both rural and urban contexts people are becoming increasingly reliant on the market and mass-produced products. Some households—even whole villages—in Repgong no longer produce what I have heard referred to as "real" butter, milk, yogurt, and grain, in other words that which they make themselves. They therefore face uncertainty and risk in terms of both the fairness of everyday commercial transactions (are they being cheated over prices?) and the authenticity and safety of the products they buy and consume. Food scandals are a topic of everyday conversation in both rural and urban households, circulating through sensationalized television reports, social media, and word of mouth. The most globally prominent of these was the adulteration of infant milk formula with melamine in 2008, but there have been many other cases since, including mass-produced vacuum-packed spicy snacks that were reported to have made children ill, prompting a short-lived campaign in northeast Tibet to buy up and burn these products. Concerns about the authenticity of products extend beyond food and medicine to religious goods such as butter and incense, their quality or purity having implications for their efficacy as offerings. A retired official with whom I was discussing food quality and safety, for example, expressed distrust of mass-produced butter for offerings. He referred to a brand commonly sold in local shops that is processed and packaged in Guangzhou in southeast China, but authenticated with a quality assurance stamp from one of the main Geluk seats, Drepung Monastery:

> I doubt the monastery knows where it has been produced. It is better not to use this kind of butter for offerings. Water is fine. The butter on the market is made in inner China and it may not be pure because it may be extracted from wood or waste. Whatever it is, purity and faith are the key.

Just as one cannot know whether a monk is real or fake just by his robes, it is impossible to assess the authenticity and purity of mass-produced products through their packaging. Mass manufacturers are perceived to "only think about making profits" (as the retired official put it) and will employ deception in order to make and sell their goods.

Monastery businesses—or at least the businesses of some monasteries—seem to provide a degree of security for contemporary Tibetan consumers in the context of these wider uncertainties. Shops located in urban centers, as well as in some villages, have signage marking them out as monastery-owned shops but are otherwise similar in appearance and layout to other Tibetan general stores. There are certain products that monastery shops should not sell, including meat, animal skins, alcohol, and cigarettes. However, all such shops stock snacks, drinks, and sweets, as well as religious products, such as offering scarves and treasure vases, which are stacked on higher shelves. The rest of the stock is determined by their location and customer base, for example, whether they are located inside monasteries and largely cater to

FIGURE 9.1 Monastery wholesale shop with signboard outside advertising a store that sells milk products from the local highlands, with the tagline "*Dri* [female yaks] of natural medicinal grasslands/The essence of pure (*lhad med*) milk," Repgong, 2012 (Photo: Jane Caple).

monks or are in town, catering to Tibetans from nearby villages and those coming into town from further afield to purchase goods (particularly in the lead-up to the New Year) (Figure 9.1). In some cases, some of the religious products on sale, such as incense, longevity pills, and treasure vases, are produced by the monastery. This is an area of monastic business with relatively high profit margins—in 2009, one monastic leader reported an investment of 20,000 yuan with a return at the end of the year of 60,000, far more than the monastery had previously made from moneylending (Caple 2019, 50).

People can be confident that religious products and medicines manufactured in local monasteries by their monks and sold in their shops are "real." An elderly monk doctor, for example, said that business at his monastery medical clinic was good because people know that monks are not only concerned with making money. It is not the same, he argued, if a clinic is leased out to a private medical practitioner who uses only the "name" of the monastery. He told me that his high success rate in curing patients had bolstered the clinic's reputation. This was achieved through his efforts to ensure that the substances he sourced to make the medicines were of high quality, as well as the fact that, as a monastery clinic, they were blessed by lamas and monks.[17] However, other goods sold in monastery shops are purchased from larger wholesale outlets and therefore packaged milk, butter, snacks, and other foodstuffs are of the same brands as those found in other local shops. Even so, the fact that these are *monastery* shops seems to give people confidence that they will not be cheated as they might be in another store and that they will be sold high-quality products rather than "fakes"—particularly if the shops are run by monks. This has led some of my monastic interlocutors to make an explicitly moral argument for monks themselves to run monastic businesses, despite concerns about the ethics of this. Working for the collective good of their monastery rather than for personal gain, monks' motivation and moral qualities (their minds) are—ideally at least—perceived to be different from those of laypeople who are primarily interested in making a profit for themselves. Monks understand their responsibility to their community and the negative karmic consequences of embezzling monastery funds—and as we have seen, they have to account to the rest of the monastic community.

In his study of the Tibetan medicine industry, Martin Saxer (2013, 217) argues that "the need to be economically successful while meeting Tibetan expectations of morality requires profit to be counterbalanced by altruism in one form or another." In the case of the medicine industry, this might be the foundation of a clinic or hospital or some other form of social engagement, whereby the company takes on the role of a sponsor. According to Saxer (2013, 226), this locates "the industry in the moral realm of Tibetan Buddhism," which is central to the perceived "quality and efficacy of a treatment." Such a counterbalance of motivations can be seen as a "natural" quality of monastic business—at least in the case of those monasteries with good reputations. This seems to be why monastery-produced religious products and medicines, as well as monastic businesses more generally, can be more trusted, as well as more valued than other private enterprises and products. In their conversations with me, monastic leaders emphasized the altruistic as well as profit-oriented motivations of their enterprise development. For example, senior monks from Ditsa, a highly reputed scholastic monastery that has expanded its business activities considerably, even since 2008, were keen to emphasize that they did not make much profit from their medical clinic because they sold the medicine at a low price. One also explained that they used the monastery truck to go to the provincial capital to buy food and other supplies for local people during the New Year. They sold these goods on at wholesale prices, even though this undermined the profitability of their own shops. They care about helping people, he said, not just about making profit.

Moreover, whatever profit these businesses do make is used to serve and support the sangha. This further separates them from ordinary commercial enterprises. As one businessman put it, he would not only choose to use a monastery shop because he trusted it, but also because it was like an indirect donation: "In a way it's not like business because the profit will go to the monastery." I had first heard this logic expressed in 2009 in relation to moneylending: a temple caretaker claimed that people borrowed money from his monastery because of financial hardship, but also because the interest went toward taking care of the monastery. A couple of months later, when visiting a different monastery with a Tibetan colleague, our monastic host made a similar comment: local laypeople do not have much money to give, he said, but when they borrow money, the interest goes to the monastery. My colleague, a former monk, interjected (in English): "It's kind of like an offering." I was reminded of this interpretation on subsequent occasions when people talked about using monastery shops. Some people, it seems, will go out of their way to do this, while for others it is an assumed "good" even if, in practice, they opt to shop elsewhere for reasons of convenience or price.[18] This is somewhat similar to me, as a British consumer, knowing that I should buy clothes from a charity shop for ethical reasons. It is environmentally friendly, making a modest contribution toward sustainability; and the profits are used for the good, supporting the activities of whichever charity runs the shop. I "know" that buying clothes in one of these shops is the "right" thing to do—even if, in practice, I often end up buying mass-produced clothes online through Amazon for the sake of convenience. There can also be a strong personal and affective relationship between the consumer and the business: it is not just any Tibetan monastery they are supporting through their patronage, it is "their" local monastery—even if this kind of patronage is conceptually distinct from "Buddhist" patronage (i.e., the gift). Monks at Ditsa, which has shops, a restaurant, and other services inside the monastery, are supposed to use these businesses rather than those in the adjacent village. Although they do not always comply, the idea is that wealth will circulate within the monastic community (Caple 2019, 103).[19] The point is that commercial transactions in a monastery shop have the potential to exceed the logics of a market exchange—even those involving the purchase of nonreligious products such as drinks and snacks.

Trust, Faith, and Perception

The discussion thus far shows that what places a particular transaction in the moral realm of Tibetan Buddhism is not only the conduct and (ultimately) altruistic intentions of the monastery and individual monks running the businesses but also how the transaction is perceived and experienced by the public.[20] This raises some interesting questions about moral agency, as we will see if we return briefly to the risks of monastic engagement in market-type exchanges—and more general critiques of the economic-mindedness of contemporary monks and monasteries.

Samten's concern about butter lamp prices was rooted in the notion that there are "different kinds of people," some of whom would not trust monks who charged high prices. This echoes the trope employed by Norbu above: since these days there are all kinds of people, one cannot necessarily trust a monk to be "real." However, Samten was using the notion with reference to the wider public: the people interacting with the temple caretaker in his hypothetical scenario. How might they perceive and thus assess the significance and implications of high prices for butter lamps? Some people might pay 100 yuan without question, but others might be distrustful. As such, there seems to be two levels to his critique. Firstly, he alludes to a moral problem among monastics. In the scenario he outlined they are not inflating prices for personal financial gain, but they are doing so through competitiveness—an unwholesome mode of action also critiqued in local moral discourse about contemporary practices of conspicuous religious giving (see Caple 2017). However, I suspect that he was also getting at the problem of faith and its unsteadiness or lack in contemporary society—a trope central to perceptions of a societal shift in values and the rise of a "spirit of calculation" (Bourdieu 2001 [1998], 105).

The risk, Samten said, was that people *who did not understand* would, from the actions of one caretaker, lose trust in monks and question the purpose or meaning of monasteries. As I comprehend it, understanding in the sense implied by Samten is intimately related to moral (virtuous) action, which includes respecting, trusting, and having faith in the sangha.[21] An educated person might be able to talk about how and why one should respect monks, but to truly understand would imply that I *do* (i.e., perform and generate) respect, for example, by standing up in the presence of a monk. To understand is not simply to have conscious knowledge of Buddhist principles or the workings of karma and merit. It is also related to disposition. This is true both in a Bourdieusian sense of habitus, which is inculcated through socialization and action, and in the sense of karmic imprints—the traces of past actions and connections from previous lives. Thus, one senior monk, arguing against the idea proposed by some of my interlocutors that uneducated ordinary folk have blind faith, said that a person who has never read books and studied might have understanding and therefore faith and trust through their karmic imprints and connections. They might even have stronger faith, he argued, than monks who study and have knowledge about the dharma. To possess faith implies a particular way of knowing, perceiving, relating to, and acting in the world. In his work on the economy of symbolic goods, Bourdieu (2001 [1998], 92–122) distinguishes between an "objective" economic truth of practice and "subjective" lived truth, the latter shaped by "the categories of perception and appreciation at play in the field" and involving misrecognition of the former. However, for Samten, the reduction of the monastic-lay relationship to the economic dimension of a single transaction is itself a form of misrecognition.

The relationship between trust, faith, and perception was more explicit in a debate between Norbu and Dorje. As described above, Norbu, a self-educated businessman, felt that it was probably better for people to be discriminating because of the prevalence of fake monks "these days." However, before this he had intimated that a generalized lack of respect for monks was itself a moral problem. He and Dorje were disagreeing about whether or not monks should be engaging in business. Referring to the distinction in monastic regulations between those doing business for the monastery and those making money for themselves, Norbu argued that since "most are working for the monastery, there is no problem." The response from Dorje echoed the concerns of monastics like Samten: "But before, people would automatically respect monks—oh it's a monk!," he said, miming the act of standing. "Then they see them working in the shop and their status goes down." For Norbu, however, this was a problem with "the people," not the monks, indicative of social change and shifting values. It was a question of faith: "Before, people had faith … now they also think about power and money." Diminishing respect for monks was not because they were working in shops but because "the categories of perception and appreciation at play in the field" (Bourdieu 2001 [1998], 112) were changing. Faith was being superseded by a spirit of calculation, leading people to privilege relationships with political leaders and businessmen, thus placing them "higher" than monks.

Concluding Remarks

Northeast Tibetan monastic business expansion over the past ten to fifteen years has occurred in the context of accelerated state-led development and a sense of increased risk and uncertainty in society and everyday life. As we have seen, monks and monastic business have been implicated in perceptions of the increased dominance of economic-mindedness, but they have been simultaneously positioned as a trustworthy moral other. Monastic business transactions are clearly a modality of transfer distinct from gifts and remunerations. Some people might go out of their way to use a monastery shop, but nobody has suggested to me that they would pay more for the products they buy there. To the contrary, some of my interlocutors have implied that if the prices are high they may choose to go elsewhere. Even if people view the patronage of monastic businesses as a kind of giving, we cannot really call the money that they give to monasteries a "gift" in the Buddhist sense. It is certainly not marked publicly as such; the customer's name will not appear on a list of the monastery's donors nor be read out in the assembly hall. Similarly, the dynamics of the purchase of specifically religious goods, whether these are butter lamps in a temple or religious products for sale in a monastery shop, are different from those of the remuneration of monastics for the provision of religious services. The sale of religious products involves a clear and explicit exchange of cash for commodities—and in many cases prices are fixed (although customers might try to haggle). Any question of efficacy relates to the products—and by extension the monastery and/or lamas who made and/or blessed them— rather than to the monastic worker who is selling them (unless he is a doctor who makes his own medicines). By contrast, as Sihlé (2015, 356) argues, not only is there ideologically no fixed price for religious services (even if in practice there is a going rate), the "social identities of participants" and moral qualities of individual specialist(s) can matter—although monks are remunerated for their services, not the results (Caple 2015, 467). Finally, in the case of household rituals, remuneration is only one element in a repertoire of ritual etiquette through which householders "do" faith and respect, considered like the gift proper to be virtuous action (ibid., 467–8). This is absent in transfers involving the purchase of religious products, even though a lay patron might interact with a monastic shopkeeper or temple caretaker with greater deference than a lay shopkeeper.

Nevertheless, as long as businesses run by monks are for the benefit of the sangha, market transactions can still be located in the moral realm of Tibetan Buddhism and remain embedded in the broader moral-economic framework of the monastic economy. A transaction in a monastery shop is part of a cycle of transfers oriented toward the maintenance and reproduction of the sangha—and thus also its role in society as a field of merit, power, and (ideally) moral distinction. At the level of the local and particular, it is an exchange often conditioned by a much longer relationship of patronage between particular communities and households and "their" monasteries and monastic communities, which also encompasses other modalities of transfer, including those of gifts, remunerations, and obligations. It can therefore be experienced and perceived as something that exceeds a commercial transaction. There is no euphemization or misrecognition: the monastery is running a "shop" which is named and presented as such. Purchasing something in that shop, whether a can of drink or an offering scarf, is clearly—objectively—a market exchange of cash for commodities. From a Bourdieusian perspective, it is through the subjective "lived truth of practices" (Bourdieu 2001 [1998], 114) that it has the potential to exceed this economic dimension, becoming something more than it "objectively" is. Borrowing from Testart's analysis of "gift" exchanges between friends (2001, 742, cited in Sihlé 2015, 356), we could argue that the parties are thus "given a larger role" than they have, the "reality of exchange" disappearing behind—or in this case, more accurately exceeded by—"the fiction of a [*quasi*-]gift." However, we should keep in mind that this privileges a particular ("scientific") regime of knowledge over other ways of seeing and understanding the world. Samten and Norbu might perhaps argue that to reduce lay-monastic transfers to their economic dimensions is to subjugate the "objective reality" that our actions unfold within a moral universe ordered by the workings of karma and merit—in other words, it is to misrecognize the objective truth of practice (i.e., karma; Tib.: *las*) as a moral force. Inverting Testart's logic, might economistic readings of lay-monastic transfers represent (for them) the disappearance of their reality behind the fiction of "the market"?

PART FOUR

Capitalism, Decline, and Rebirth

CHAPTER TEN

Regeneration and the Age of Decline: Purification and Rebirth in Mongolian Buddhist Economies

Saskia Abrahms-Kavunenko

Following the end of the socialist period in Mongolia, the promise of regeneration and purification constitutes an important economic component of rebuilding, revitalizing, and maintaining Buddhist institutions. In economic terms, the financial consequences of seeking renewal, purification, and rebirth at temples constitute a significant portion of temple incomes. For international donors, the opportunity to contribute to the revitalization of Buddhist institutions in a democratic Asian nation with a strong historical connection to Tibet has become a major incentive—with some millenarian implications.

Existing in dynamic tension with the possibilities of purification and rejuvenation are concerns about degeneration. When I first carried out fieldwork in Ulaanbaatar from 2009 to 2010 at dharma centers[1] and local temples, I was surprised to find that in spite of Buddhism's relatively recent revitalization, both the laity and the Buddhist sangha discussed Buddhism as though it were in a state of decline. There are a number of factors that influence this sense of deterioration. Firstly, many of the old lamas who reinhabited and built temples in the 1990s have died. Around half of the temples that they initially built have shut down, representing a significant contraction of the initial revitalization (Teleki 2009). Secondly, the transition to capitalism has added to suspicions surrounding the motivations of religious specialists. Thirdly, transnational Buddhist organizations have specific ambitions for how religious rejuvenation should unfold in Mongolia, and the activities of the Mongolian sangha do not always fit with these ideals.

As well as ushering in new freedoms, such as the freedom to practice religion, the end of socialism has brought with it new economic instabilities and growing inequalities. Ulaanbaatar has experienced a widening gap between the rich and the poor over the last three decades. This increase in economic inequality has been accompanied by a deterioration of the city's air quality, an increase in noise pollution, rising ambient stresses, and misgivings about crime. The Buddhist sangha, who themselves are connected to the ordinary concerns of making money and supporting a family, are entangled in the prevailing disquietudes of the postsocialist capital. Indeed, as this chapter will argue, the ways that religious specialists are remunerated for their work are particularly sensitive to the uneasiness surrounding certain livelihoods in the capital.

Transnational Buddhist organizations and global Buddhist figures, such as the Fourteenth Dalai Lama, inform expectations about how the Mongolian sangha should conduct themselves and what their obligations to the broader community are. Many Mongols report that some members of the Buddhist sangha are not true (*ünen*) lamas and some of these concerns reflect critiques from global Buddhist organizations. Yet, the presence of translocal Buddhist networks and their efforts to help renew Buddhism in Mongolia also imbue local Buddhist institutions with a sense of importance. Commentaries about degeneration dialogue with the possibilities of purification and rejuvenation which, given the current political situation in Tibet, sometimes contain within them the perceived millenarian potential for an epochal Buddhist rebirth in Mongolia.

Regeneration

On a cool autumn evening in September 2015, as the air in Ulaanbaatar is starting to thicken with the acrid-smelling smog that characterizes the long cold winter, I, along with a close friend and my husband, depart on the overnight train heading to the Energy Centre (*Energiin Töv*) in the Gobi Desert. The Energy Centre is a major pilgrimage site where pilgrims travel to refresh (*sergeekh*) their vital energies, or *khiimori* (literally, windhorse). Some travel to the Energy Centre out of curiosity (like our agnostic Mongolian companion) or because they have heard of the Centre's curative properties. Students visit before important exams, to reenergize and better their chances of receiving good grades. At the Energy Centre and related sites of pilgrimage, we participate in activities to imbibe good energy, to purify negative elements, and to be reborn.

Just before 4:30 a.m., we awake in the four-person sleeper carriage and ready ourselves to disembark the train. As the train comes to a halt, we climb down the rickety metal steps onto the small concrete platform of Sainshand Station and are met by local drivers waiting to transport pilgrims to the site. With our newly found driver Enkhamar, a robust man in his late forties, we set off, driving in the dark early morning toward the spot where Danzanravjaa is said to have left his energy. Danzanravjaa (1803–57), the fifth reincarnation of the Noyon Khutagt lineage, was born during the Qing Empire to a poor Mongolian family in the Gobi Desert. He is known for being an egalitarian lama and is well loved by Mongols as an antihero to the Qing Empire's Gelugpa orthodoxy. His play *The Life Story of the Moon Cuckoo (Saran Khökhöö Namtar)* is one of Mongolia's best known. As well as being an influential playwright, he was considered to be a powerful healer. The Energy Centre is believed to be the site where he left his healing energy for those in need of its restorative properties.

Unlike many of Mongolia's Buddhist treasures, most of the artifacts connected to Danzanravjaa miraculously survived the socialist purges in the early twentieth century. When it was clear that Danzanravjaa's temple Khamarin Khiid was going to be ransacked, Lama Tuduv, the curator responsible for his possessions, meticulously packed them and hid dozens of crates in the desert. Two months later, soldiers arrived to destroy the monastery, seize its contents, and arrest the resident lamas. Lama Tuduv hid with his sister and survived the violent purges of the late 1930s that claimed the lives of over 36,000 people, half of whom were lamas (Kaplonski 2012). In the decades that followed, Lama Tuduv taught his grandson Altangerel the whereabouts and the contents of the crates (Kohn 2006, 9–10). In 1991, a few months after Lama Tuduv's death, his grandson began to dig up the hidden crates. Due to the dry conditions in the desert, the artifacts were well preserved. Most are now housed at the Danzanravjaa Museum in Sainshand. A number of boxes still remain hidden in the Gobi, as there are concerns about the safety of the artifacts against theft, fire, and improper storage (Kohn 2006).

The Energy Centre is a popular pilgrimage site. We, along with the other pilgrims who have traveled to the Gobi by overnight train, are taken in the early morning to a small *ger* camp[2] to rest. At 6:30 a.m., Enkhamar returns and we drive to a rocky hill rise facing east, which is a-topped with two breast-shaped *stūpa* (Sans) that are covered with dried milk and connected to one another by a plank wrapped in sky-blue prayer scarves (*khadag*). Enkhamar instructs the women in our small group to offer milk to the domes and recite the mantra "*om maritze man sohar.*" Our friend and I follow the other female pilgrims, circumambulating the *stūpa* three times, making oblations of milk and reciting the mantra of Marici, a female emanation of enlightenment who rides a wild boar. This mantra, we are told by our driver, connects one to the energies of the light and the sun, and clears obstacles.

Our oblations of milk at the site reference the purity and strength of the maternal bond and are thought to purify (*ariulakh*)[3] impurities, removing obstacles (Thrift 2014). Offering milk to the cardinal directions, often in the form of the first cup of milk tea, is a daily practice carried out by many Mongolian women, both in the countryside and in the city, and this practice initiates many ritual activities. As the sun begins to rise, we rejoin the men and, with around seventy other pilgrims, turn east, holding our palms up to face the sun and inhale its energy, light, and purification.[4]

Enkhamar tells us that we are lucky that rain has fallen just a few days before, so the air, which can be enshrouded in dust at this time of year, is unusually clear. The increasing severity of dust storms in the Gobi is linked to the disruption of sand due to mining activities and these have become emblematic of a murky present through which it is difficult to see clearly (Abrahms-Kavunenko 2019; Jackson 2015; see also Højer and Pedersen 2008). We arrive at the Energy Centre, which is a patch of earth where the sandy earth changes to a dark red, a notable shift from the dull brown, in light and dark-colored hues that characterizes the surrounding landscape. The sands of the Energy Centre are half-enclosed by a porous mandala, shaped out of large and small white *stūpa* (Figure 10.1). Like pilgrims who follow one another or the advice of a knowledgeable friend or relative (Abrahms-Kavunenko 2012; Humphrey 1997), we mimic the other pilgrims, feeding pigeons and walking to the left, circumambulating the inside of the mandala in a clockwise direction. On a patch of red sand to the west we sit, facing the rising sun. Others sit with us to soak in the dawn and the good energy. We continue our circumambulation, bathing ourselves in smoke from the burning incense for purification and pausing to sing a song in reverence of Danzanravjaa.

FIGURE 10.1 Pilgrims at the Energy Centre bask in the sunrise, 2015 (Photo: Saskia Abrahms-Kavunenko).

A short trip away, the next spot on the pilgrimage route are the meditation caves, built during Danzanravjaa's lifetime. Though most of the 108 caves have long since disintegrated in the rocky red desert sand, we ascend on a crumbling path from the bottom of the small valley to visit what remains. Here Enkhamar points out the famous sakura tree, a gift from Dazanravjaa's Japanese student. It is such a miracle the tree grows in the desert at all that it attracts many pilgrims in the otherwise windy, inhospitable Mongolian spring, who come to see it blossom. As we continue up the valley we peer into the remaining caves. Some have offerings of closed sacred vases (*bumba*)[5] that are shoved into the cracks of their ceilings. In another the floor is wet from recent oblations of vodka. The final cave toward the top of the valley has two openings around the width of a human being. Enkhamar explains that if we crawl through these gaps we will cleanse our bad karma. Even if we don't realize it, for example if we accidentally kill a fly, he tells us, we are making bad karma. Our group of three all squeeze through, crawling with some difficulty on our hands and knees and laughing with relief as we complete the awkward task. Having been reborn we are ready to continue to the next spot on the pilgrimage route.

Changing Buddhist Economies

By the turn of the twentieth century, Buddhist institutions in Mongolia had amassed large quantities of wealth through land, labor, and material objects. Monasteries were among the few permanent buildings in the country and had, over many centuries, settled in important locations for communication and trade (Moses 1977). High lamas owned vast estates and herds. The Eighth Javzandamba, as the most important lama in the country, possessed the largest estate. As well his extensive landholdings, he had around 90,000 disciples/serfs (*shavi*), many of whom worked herding the estate's cattle. This number was drawn from a total population of around 647,504 people recorded in the 1918 census (Even 2011, 628). Although the Javzandamba had considerable power in the country, Buddhist monasteries were decentralized, with no single organization having complete authority. Serving under various secular nobles and the religious elite, the labor of nomadic herders was organized within feudal hierarchies (Kaplonski 2014). Supplementing the monasteries' extensive treasuries of living wealth, the laity paid tribute to temples through the gifts donated during festivals and by sending family members to join the monasteries.

Toward the end of Mongolia's suzerainty in the Qing Empire, around 17 percent of the national herd was owned by temples (Kaplonski 2014, 17). Most Mongols had a lama in the family. After the socialist government came to power in 1921, the considerable influence of Buddhist institutions had become known as the "lama question/problem" (*lamiin asuudal*). In the 1920s, the socialist government began to attempt to wrest power from the religious and aristocratic elites. The government's initial attacks on Buddhist monasteries were (mostly) non-violent, focusing primarily on depriving temples of their wealth (Kaplonski 2014). In the early 1930s, the government attempted to indoctrinate poor lamas into class-consciousness and created economic incentives to entice them away from the temples. The government created a steep tax rate targeting high lamas which rose rapidly throughout the 1930s (Bawden 1968, 361). In the late 1930s, the government's attacks became violent and thousands of lamas, along with ethnic minorities, aristocrats, and other political opponents, were murdered (Kaplonski 2014).

In the early twentieth century the capital city's landscape was dominated by the two main temples, Gandantegchenliin Khiid (Gandan) in the west, housing a large statue of a standing Avalokiteśvara (*Janraisig*), the Buddha of compassion, and Züün Khüree Dashchoilin Khiid (Dashchoilin) in the east, housing a grand statue of Maitreya (*Maidar*). Around these extensive monastic complexes and bureaucratic and aristocratic residences, foreigners and merchants settled to carry out trade to the north of the Tuul River. This landscape changed considerably during the socialist period, as major landmarks, city parks, new administrative and cultural buildings, apartment blocks, and grid roads were built in the newly named Ulaanbaatar (meaning "red hero"). The temple of Gandan was allowed to remain as a demonstration of the state's religious tolerance (Kaplonski 2004). The roof of its highest temple dwarfed most of the nearby buildings in the city. The colorfully painted dome-shaped structures that make up the temple of Dashchoilin Khiid were used for housing a circus, and many smaller temples were contracted or destroyed (Majer and Teleki 2018).

In Ulaanbaatar today, visits to Buddhist temples occur sporadically. Most laypeople,[6] Buddhists and non-Buddhists alike, told me that they attend temples during specific festivals or when they are experiencing difficulties in their lives. Most Mongols go at least once a year during the Lunar New Year (Tsagaan Sar) festivities. Very few of my interlocutors, excepting those who attend educational classes at dharma centers, make regular visits (Abrahms-Kavunenko 2012, 2019). During visits at temples most people circumambulate sacred objects, feed the birds nearby, touch certain sacred objects, and spin prayer wheels. Many pay to seek advice from lamas and purchase prayers to be read for themselves and their families. As these sources of income tend to be irregular, this has created funding shortages for some temples, which can no longer rely upon the living wealth of the land and bonded labor or the regular patronage of a pious population. When I asked lamas about finances, all told me that it was difficult to maintain temples without the consistent support of a committed lay population. The lack of regular donations, I was told, makes it difficult for individual lamas to continue their religious vocation and creates challenges for temples wanting to educate lamas and to support them financially, either through housing or regular salaries. As Munkhbaatar, a lama responsible for multiple administrative roles at Gandan, told me:

> We have 800 monks at Gandan monastery. It is the center of Mongolian Buddhism. Only 300 monks get a so-called salary. It is not a proper salary. Because a proper salary, a minimum salary level, is 190,000. This [minimum salary] was declared by the state so that you can pay social insurance and health insurance. Below that there is no social insurance. When you get older then you don't receive a pension. Most of the monks receive below 190,000 [a month].

When I questioned him further, asking how lamas could survive on such an income, he replied that most lamas were supported by their extended family. 190,000 a month (around US$95 in mid-2016) is a very low salary. A reasonable wage at this time was around 600,000 *tögrög* a month and even on this wage it may be difficult to buy important durable items, such as shoes.

Due to personal choices, local economic constraints, limited temple housing, and historical precedents, most of the Mongolian sangha are not fully ordained and live, as most other Mongols do, in apartments, houses, or *ger*, with their wives and/or relatives. The practice of living within the walls of monasteries has not been continued on a large scale. There are few temples that have quarters for resident lamas and those that do, such as Betüv Khiid, the Sakya Pandita Dharma Chakra Monastery, and the Idgaachoinzinlin Datsan at Gandan, tend to be for young lamas in training, with limited space for older lamas. The Foundation for the Preservation of the Mahayana Tradition's (FPMT) Dara Ekh Khiid has space for resident nuns to the east of the city, but the numbers of this project's residential nuns have dwindled for a variety of reasons.

While most Mongols that I spoke to (especially those who infrequently attended temples) are not aware of the prescriptions of the Vinaya, most distinguished between true (*ünen*) and authentic (*jinkhene*) lamas and those that are not. Some laypeople and lamas told me that being a married lama was part of a local tradition, with some lamas recalling the presocialist period when it was a common practice for lamas to have wives and children (Jadamba and Schittich 2010; Kaplonski 2014). Although married lamas are the norm, most are fairly coy about the subject, indicating that it is an open secret rather than a completely accepted practice as it is in Japan (Covell 2005; see also Humphrey and Ujeed 2013 regarding Inner Mongolia). One lama from Gandan explained to me that he had been married but had found that the financial stress of co-supporting a wife and child (it would be unusual for his wife to not have a job), at contemporary levels of consumption, placed too much pressure on his vocation and this was the reason he decided to get a divorce.

As public religious practices and temples were oppressed during socialism, Buddhist institutions lost possession of their estates and no longer received regular donations from the laity. The postsocialist "sangha economies" in Mongolia now depend upon remuneration from laypeople for rituals, irregular local donations, and funding from transnational Buddhist networks. The ideal of the non-reciprocated gift (Laidlaw 2000; Parry 1986) is not an important aspect of giving money to religious specialists in Mongolia. Most urban Mongols expect ritual efficacy, the building of statues, or the material improvement of temples when they make donations (Abrahms-Kavunenko 2015b). Among my interlocutors who irregularly attend temples and regularly visit dharma centers, making merit is not associated with donations to temples. Instead, most donations are given to temples with a sense of reciprocity (Abrahms-Kavunenko 2015b; Sihlé 2015). However, this kind of remuneration is discussed and thought about differently than payments for other services, such as paying for a meal in a restaurant. Many of my interlocutors specifically complained that all too often payments for rituals too closely resembled paying for something in a shop. Unlike other kinds of more mundane transactions, most people told me that it was important that the lamas they saw were well-educated, moral, and/or motivated to help others.

Capitalism and Degeneration

The postsocialist period has seen a dramatic rise in social inequalities. Poverty rates rose from 0 percent in 1990 to 24 percent in 1994 (Sneath 2002, 193). Following the economy's devastating decline in the 1990s, the Mongolian economy experienced a growth spurt in the early 2010s, such as in 2011, when, fueled by a mining boom, it grew by 17.5 percent (Chuluundorj and Danzanbaljir 2014, 276). Although the expansion of the economy improved the material wealth of some, the UNDP estimates that, following the boom, one in five Mongols were still living below the poverty line in 2014 (UNDP 2016). By 2014, largely due to changes in the global economy, Mongolia was back in a state of economic crisis, this time with considerable amounts of international debt (Bonilla 2016). Over the last few decades, Ulaanbaatar has grown with new apartment blocks and shopping malls being built in old socialist planned parks (Kaplonski 2004). *Ger* neighborhoods[7] now expand the city to the north, west, and east, comprising around 83 percent of Ulaanbaatar's settled areas (World Bank 2015, 1). While in the presocialist period temples dominated the landscape, urban temples now struggle for visibility amid the rising skyline. Before 1990, Ulaanbaatar's population was below 600,000 people. At present it is home to more than 1.38 million people, almost half of the national population.

Accompanying rising social inequalities, concerns about dubious moral imperatives have become commonplace in Ulaanbaatar. As Sneath writes, in the postsocialist period, gifts, such as a bottle of vodka to a school teacher, which were formerly seen as part of normal patterns of exchange, have become mired in anxieties about corruption (2006). During my fieldwork, particularly in 2015 and 2016 when the economy was grinding to a formidable halt, friends frequently expressed concerns about embezzlement. Some explained to me how they had to make extra payments for services at hospitals to doctors and nurses, while others reported high-level corruption, describing in detail specific cases of large amounts of development money meant for health, aid, or infrastructural projects going missing.

In an economy where mining is the dominant source of the country's income, corruption is not the only way that one can experience ill effects from earning money. Unsettling the ground is seen by many as morally dubious (Delaplace 2010; High and Schlesinger 2010). Among artisanal miners in Mongolia, High noticed that money made directly from mining has a different "regime of value" (Appadurai 1988) and is worth less when it is used to buy products from the local store near the mine site (High 2013b). As artisanal miners make money from directly harming the land, they try to avoid purchases that could reify the contaminated ways in which the money has been made. Transforming the negative spiritual value of this money into investments, such as a herding animal, could multiply the negative effects and pass it on the rest of the herd, resulting in exponentially bad results (High 2013).

Just as mining is thought by some to benefit from the misfortunes of local spirits and the environment, professions which benefit from the misfortune of other humans are negatively viewed. In Højer's research in Ulaanbaatar, he found that pawnshops were believed by many of the employees to be places of spiritual danger. Pawnshops contain objects which have been removed from the owner out of desperation for money, rather than being willingly parted with. As a consequence, the unwillingly estranged objects could potentially be enshrouded in bad energy (*muu energi*), carrying this negativity into the shop (Højer 2012).

Payments to Buddhist lamas take on a different kind of quality. Although trading ritual efficacy for monetary remuneration is the most common way that laypeople interact with Buddhist economies, because of the nature of the transaction, there are appropriate and inappropriate ways for religious specialists to make money. Religious specialists, just like workers at pawnshops, make their living from people who have problems in their lives. Because of this, as in Parry's account of *dan* in India (1986), donations to religious specialists can produce pollution if the ritual specialist does not have the right motivation. In Mongolia, in order for the gift not to produce bad results for religious specialists and nullify the positive effects for the donor, lamas and other religious specialists must have nonmonetary motivations (see also Buyandelger 2013). As a lama who worked in an important administrative position at a temple, and who himself did not follow the Vinaya, told me:

When you share the benefits meant for the ... fully ordained lamas, you end up creating bad karma. It is actually wrong to be respected and receive offerings like they do. You might have been observing that Mongolian lamas look like they are suffering from the effect of undue privilege, aren't they? They are really fat, suffering from sickness inside. They are psychologically affected as well. That means that karma is at work: they are suffering from the results of unearned benefits.

Unlike payments to other service industries, donations to temples are moralized. In many of the temples in Ulaanbaatar, rituals and prayers are purchased at a small booth or shop serviced by laypeople or Buddhist lamas. A receipt is printed and the prayers are read the following morning. Some temples have lists that detail the prices of prayers and these lists are frequently criticized. While lamas explained to me that the price lists were to provide accountability for donations, for many they were evidence that, as capitalism has become a part of daily life, religious specialists were now motivated by monetary concerns rather than helping those in need. As a friend, Enkhtur, explained in 2015:

> I feel bad when at Gandan they ask you for 1,000 [around 50 US cents]. I feel bad because it's supposed to be a religious thing and you shouldn't have a price on things. When I go to Bakula Rinpoche [at Betüv Khiid] and Dashchoilin they don't ask how much you give. So I feel better. At least, you know, they are not after money.

Although I suspect that these price lists have existed since the Democratic Revolution, if not before when Gandan had to pay taxes on lay donations,[8] they were frequently discussed as evidence of the deterioration of Mongolian Buddhism.

Most people told me that they visited temples based on the advice of family members or friends. While a couple of people insisted that true lamas were celibate, the more common measures of trustworthiness or authenticity were being well-educated, morally upstanding, and motivated by the wish to help others. As one friend who identified as a Christian explained to me about her visits to a lama from the Övs Province where she was born:

> Oyuka: We have known him for a long time, he started a little bit smaller ... He had his own place, small but close to his home and everyone goes there to wait for him. Some people even go there at six o'clock in the morning ... Because it's really busy. A lot of people go there and queue.
> Saskia: Is it expensive to go there?
> Oyuka: No ... it's a donation. If people want to give 1,000 or 5,000 [around US$0.50 and 2.50, respectively], he doesn't care. Because we believe in him and he tells exactly what happens, that's why people like to give more.

Saskia: What is the money going towards?
Oyuka: It's to appreciate what he does ... I get a benefit from that.
   After that I feel much better and I think that things are going well.
   I mean after I meet him and he says "OK, these things happened to
   you and because of this, now you have this problem." Or "your job
   will be fine, don't worry" and "now you know some problems will be
   there but it's just normal things, so don't worry and your health will
   be fine this year ..." He helps with things like that.

Oyuka's family trusts this lama because he is from Övs and because he
doesn't specify the donation that he expects, indicating that he is not
motivated by remuneration. Giving money to him feels like a good thing
because he is perceived to be capable and motivated by the strong intention
to help her family. Lama Otgonbaatar who runs the new Sakya temple in the
east of the city told me that in his experience most Mongolian donors would
visit a temple for a number of years before they felt that they could trust
the institution and, only after this, would they give a donation. Most local
donors, he told me, liked to see their donations instantiated in a material
item, such as a completed statue or shrine. While his temple, which quite
unusually has living quarters for resident lamas, receives generous donations
from individual foreign donors for the day-to-day running of the temple,
because of the inconsistencies of local donations, the temple has decided
to construct a car park underneath the building to fund its electricity and
heating costs.

   In spite of an uneasiness about whom to trust, laypeople overwhelmingly
told me that they feel refreshed and reenergized after visits to temples. Some
described how the sutra readings they had received from a particularly
good lama had cured them or unburdened them of a particular anxiety or
difficulty. Others were vaguer about the results, comparing ritual efficacy
with getting an insurance policy, something that might just protect them in
case of an emergency. Still others told me that prayers would only work if
you believed in them, which in some cases would underline the importance
of the relationship between the lama and the recipient of the prayers.

   Rather than being anti-generative of religious practices, uncertainties
about the motivations or authenticity of religious specialists cause people to
seek out multiple religious specialists, thus multiplying religious economies in
the capital (see also Abrahms-Kavunenko 2015a). People tend to seek ritual
efficacy from a wide range of public religious specialists when they have
a problem, Buddhists and non-Buddhists alike. Many of my interlocutors
told me that their infrequent visits to religious specialists in times of need
involved a variety of religious traditions. For instance, after the death of a
middle-class friend's relative, several family members sought out different
lamas to see if the death had occurred at the right time and how the family
member should be buried. She also sought the advice of the family shaman
(shamans are not usually consulted about death) to test which of the lamas
was, as she said, "telling the truth." Others told me that when they had a

problem, such as an illness in the family, they would visit various kinds of soothsayers, shamans, Buddhists and attend Christian services. Concerns about moral decline compel, rather than discourage, people to seek out ritual efficacy for rejuvenation and purification.

Buddhist Eschatologies and Transnational Economies

According to many of my lay and monastic interlocutors, the initial period of the revitalization of Buddhism was optimistic. During this time old lamas who had been practicing before the socialist period, some of them in secret, put on traditional Mongolian robes and began to practice in public (Majer 2009). These householder lamas were considered by many to represent unbroken lineages of Mongolian Buddhism, with knowledge of secret and powerful rituals. During this period treasures, such as Danzanravjaa's artifacts, were made public and people could once again visit pilgrimage sites openly. The 1990s were the first time when young men and a few young women left for India to study the dharma, hopeful of the new Buddhist revitalization. Some people were approached by old lamas who visited households, looking for promising young candidates who would make suitable lamas. Lama Otgonbaatar told me that he was chosen by the newly reopened Erdene Zuu[9] because of his academic achievements at the local school. A friend, Lama Zorigt, explained to me that in 1997 when he was eleven years old, lamas from the Lam Rim temple to the south of Gandan came to his grandmother's house, asking if there was a child in the family who was born in the year of the tiger, an auspicious year for a religious vocation. Because of this visitation and the encouragement of his pious grandmother, he traveled to India to study Buddhism.

During the 1990s and early 2000s, the first temples and dharma centers were revitalized and built. In this period Betüv Khiid, a temple to the southeast of Gandan which focuses on formally educating young lamas, was constructed. The temple was constructed by Bakula Rinpoche, India's ambassador to Mongolia, in an area of the city notorious for its crime. The temple's placement, according to a friend who worked at it, was intended to bring light and rejuvenation to a dark area of the city. Other temples and centers were started with international funding including those supported by the FPMT, such as the Idgaachoinzinlin Datsan at Gandan, the Dara Ekh Khiid nunnery, and Shredrup Ling, a dharma center in the center of the city. At dharma centers, classes were offered to laypeople, and centers such as Jampa Ling and Shredrup Ling also placed an emphasis on charity and community education.

The importance of transnational funding in the building of new dharma centers and temples, along with the restoration of old temples, such as Dashchoilin, has meant that global Buddhist reform ideas have influenced local understandings. On the one hand, dharma centers with their interest in revitalizing Mongolian Buddhism, indicate to Mongols that their country is a powerful site for Buddhist rejuvenation. On the other, transnational organizations tend to have particular ideas about how Buddhism should be practiced, emphasizing lay education and the importance of the Vinaya. Their concerns about local lamas not being celibate and the public discouragement of married lamas by figures such as the Dalai Lama encourage local ideas that the Mongolian sangha is in a state of decline. Additionally, there is now a sense that the sangha ought not be a burden on the laity (see also Caple 2010 regarding the Tibetan Buddhist revival in China) and should be involved in charitable activities for the benefit of laypeople. These ideas have been heavily influenced by the presence of Christian organizations' missionary charities in the country (see Abrahms-Kavunenko 2012, 2019). Local temples and dharma centers do make efforts to carry out charitable works but these are often constrained by financial limitations, which do not seem to limit the activities of Christian missionary organizations, who often collect a tithe from their congregation, to the same extent (Wallace 2015).

For Mongols, narratives about degeneration are linked to new economic imperatives embedded within capitalism, environmental destruction, the severing of religious lineages during the socialist period, the lure of modern life, and a lack of education. For the Tibetan diaspora with whom many Mongols study in India, ideas of degeneration are linked to monetary incentives and capitalism, tensions between being "authentically" Tibetan and the attraction of consumer lifestyles, and the Mongolian sangha's inability to replicate Tibetan monasticism (Ahmed 2006; Prost 2006). In both, concerns about the economic imperatives of global capitalism and the need for Buddhist institutions and religious specialists to support themselves without regular donations, landholdings, and tax revenues are present. Rather than generating good karma, for many contemporary Western and Asian supporters, donations to Buddhist institutions are connected to narratives of regeneration and the idea that Buddhist mystical traditions will enlighten a troubled world (Campergue 2015). Economic support is often given to charismatic Tibetan high lamas in diaspora, meaning that these figures become nodes in transnational economic networks that connect foreign donors to India and Buddhist institutions elsewhere.

Situated within a global network of Buddhist philanthropy, ideas of rebirth and revitalization are reflected and refracted in the funding of the postsocialist rebuilding of Mongolian Buddhism. Transnational organizations tend to be optimistic about the promise of Mongolia as a place of rejuvenation but pessimistic about the activities of married (and predominantly Gelugpa) lamas. The presence of international organizations and visits from high lamas, along with a number of controversial visits from the Dalai Lama, have caused some Mongols to discuss whether the next

Dalai Lama will be reborn in Mongolia. While some people I spoke to were excited by this prospect, not everyone is happy about this idea. A few middle-class aquaintances complained to me that the rebirth of Dalai Lama, if it happened in Mongolia, would damage Mongolia's relationship with China and therefore Mongolia's economic future. The rebirth of the yet publicly unidentified (but found) Javzandamba reincarnation and the accompanying announcement confirming his rebirth by the Dalai Lama have caused its own forms of political controversy both internally and internationally (see Jadamba 2018).

Narratives of decline in many ways reflect broader global Buddhist narratives about degeneration in both the past and the present. The idea of decline has been present in many Buddhist societies. The Buddha Maitreya is foretold to emerge when the world has forgotten the Buddhist teachings. Ladwig argues that Buddhist eschatologies tend to emphasize the regenerative aspects that follow from degeneration (2014), but there is a feeling in Mongolia that the decline of the dharma may not need to be complete for a millenarian-style restoration to occur. As Lama Otgonbaatar told me in 2016:

> The Buddha himself said that his teachings will spread in the North. It seems that that time has arrived. The Dalai Lama, the Sakya Lama, all are saying that they have lost their freedom in Tibet. If India befriends China they will be finished. The Tibetans in the West will lose their cultural identity. Therefore, only Mongols are destined to inherit this wonderful tradition … That means for Mongolian lamas the time of great historic responsibility has arrived … In Southern India, there are 500 Mongolian lamas studying. We have a great hope for those lamas. The next year we will have the very first Geshe. We don't need temples for pujas, we need dormitories at Gandan in order to receive these wonderful practitioners. We are supposed to provide their housing and monastic living conditions.

Other lamas and laypeople explained to me that there were prophecies that Mongolia was to be the lamp (denlüü) of global Buddhism in the future. Mongolia, I was told, was the perfect place for Buddhist revitalization as it was an Asian country and therefore, unlike Buddhism in the west, had a cultural milieu suited to Buddhism. Some Mongols explained to me that the spirits embedded in the Mongolian landscape had powerful energetic properties beneficial for the growth of Buddhism.

The optimism surrounding the renewal of Buddhism in Mongolia is shared by many Mongols and is instantiated in two separate large Maitreya statue projects in and near Ulaanbaatar that symbolize the reignition of the lamp of Buddhism after socialism. Both are large depictions of the artworks of the First Javzandamba. At the time of this writing, the statue of a seated Maitreya at Dashchoilin Khiid has been completed and consecrated, referencing the presocialist history of the temple. The construction of another colossal statue of a standing Maitreya has begun to the south of Ulaanbaatar (its face and feet were completed at the time of writing). The statue will be 54 meters tall, supported by a 108-meter tall *stūpa*, an engineering necessity on the windswept Mongolian steppe. Next to it, an eco-city is planned that will house thousands of lay Buddhists and monastics, complete with a meditation hall and a new temple for the Dalai Lama. As discussed by Tsultemin, depictions of Maitreya have been linked historically to state-making activities and the assertion of Gelugpa dominance in Mongolia (2015). When depicted as a standing bodhisattva, Maitreya appears as a Chakravartin,[10] instantiating both state and Buddhist power in the region (Tsultemin 2015). A couple of friends told me of rumors that large numbers of the Tibetan diaspora living in India would come and resettle in the city. When I asked Buddhist lamas about the project in 2016, most replied diplomatically that they supported any project that helped to remind laypeople of the importance of Buddhism. This project, if it really intends to house the Dalai Lama, would be highly controversial due to a range of complex geopolitical issues, most notably the strain on the relationship with China (see Abrahms-Kavunenko 2019; Jadamba 2018).

The construction of colossal Buddhist statues in the past and the present has been tied to local and translocal issues surrounding the state and the sangha (Smith 2018; Tsultemin 2015). The new Maitreya statues are being constructed with reference to the recent rebuilding of an Avalokiteśvara statue in the large temple to the north of Gandan in 1997. When I first arrived in Mongolia and expressed an interest in Buddhism to a new friend, she showed me this statue, and even though she was fairly cynical about Buddhist institutions as a whole, she explained that it was rebuilt with the love of the Mongolian people in a time when there was very little money in the country. The original depiction of the bodhisattva had been built from 1911 to 1913, just after Mongolia proclaimed its independence from the Qing Empire. The statue remained until the late 1930s when it was destroyed during the socialist purges. Its restoration links Mongolia's independence from the USSR with the previous declarations of independence from the Manchu Dynasty and the connection of Buddhism with both (Vanchikova 2014). In the same way, the Maitreya statues, along with symbolizing the lamp of Buddhism being ignited in the north, navigate state power and geopolitics.

Conclusion

Just as one would travel overnight to the desert to refresh one's energies, to rejuvenate, and to be reborn, the rebirth of Maitreya offers a symbolic presence of the possibilities of a new era with all of its eschatological (and perhaps geopolitical) implications. It is precisely because of the sense of degeneration that rebirth is not only considered possible but necessary in the present era. Mongolian Buddhist narratives of decline fit well into broader narratives that are present in the city, in both broadly moral and Buddhist framings. The idea of a strong, independent Buddhist country (with mountains and yaks) in northern Asia inspires donations from foreign donors, the presence of transnational Buddhist organizations, and funding for Mongols to study overseas. Yet the presence of these transnational organizations with their "reform" ideas about moral conduct, monasticism, and lay practice themselves add to the growing sense among urbanites that Buddhism in Mongolia is in decline.

This dynamic tension connects and creates blockages in transnational and local Buddhist economies and discourses with broader economic flows. Ideas about preservation, illumination, and reinvigoration coincide with feelings of degeneration and decay that have accompanied Ulaanbaatar's transition to capitalism. Since 1990, the changing city has instantiated feelings of hope and disillusionment, as new building projects and shiny malls accompany the pressingly obvious decay of the socialist buildings and the city's infrastructure. In a city with chronically poor air throughout the winter months, the nation's fortunes rise and fall unpredictably. Gifts to lamas and other kinds of transactions are imbued with feelings of uncertainty.

In this context, Buddhist doctrine and cultural forms contain within them a rich metaphorical lexicon describing both decline and regeneration, and the possibilities for rebirth in deterioration. For Mongolia's sangha, metaphors of decline, obscuration, and degeneration dynamically interplay with hopes for purification, regeneration, and ultimately, rebirth and enlightenment. These narratives condition how local temples can connect to transnational funding and whether they will continue to benefit from local support.

CHAPTER ELEVEN

Saintly Entrepreneurialism and Political Aspirations of Theravadin Saints in Mainland Southeast Asia

Alexander Horstmann

Since the 1990s, the Thai-speaking region in Lanna (Northern Thailand) and around the Mekong River, comprising Northern Thailand, the Shan State in Myanmar, northwest Laos, and southwest China, has experienced an unprecedented boom of Buddhism (Cohen 2001), following a time of persecution of Buddhist monks and destruction of temples in Communist China, Laos, and Cambodia in the 1970s (Davis 2005). The Southeast Asian Massif in mainland Southeast Asia and southwest China extends from the Himalayan Plateau and has been discussed as "Zomia," a society made up from different highland groups who—according to James C. Scott—have been marginalized by the states and do not have a world religion (Scott 2009). This hypothesis has been criticized, as Buddhism has a long tradition among highlanders, especially among the Shan, the Thai Lue and Thai Kuen, the Palaung, and the Karen. Also, the Hui are Chinese Muslims, and many of the highlanders, as the Kachin and Chin, follow Christian traditions. The relative marginalization can also be contested, and the entanglements of Buddhist monks in educational and pilgrimage networks are one aspect of the highlanders' cosmopolitanism, not of their marginality (cf. Michaud 2010).[1]

This is especially applicable for the former Tai kingdoms, which included Sipsongpanna (Xishuangbanna) in southwest China, Shan State in Myanmar, and Muang Sing in northern Laos that share the same Theravāda Buddhist traditions. The rising charismatic monks who were widely revered as "saints" were said to possess special abilities and miraculous powers that were grounded in the millenarian beliefs of the future Buddha, Ariya Metteyya, who would liberate the peasants from exploitation and suffering and bring economic prosperity and fertility.

Current saints also are often regarded as reincarnations of Khruba Sriwichai (1878–1931) who was widely revered for his genuine compassion and his contribution to sasana. While Scott has emphasized the millenarian tradition of ethnic highlanders and interpreted it in his concept of Zomia's state evasion and resistance of highlanders to the state, the contemporary saints are connected with the national sangha and have extensive networks with the highest echelons of society, including very wealthy elements of the military and business elites.

I would argue that the new generation of charismatic monks were constituting a new phenomenon of what I would call "wealthy ascetics," in the sense that they combine symbols and signs of prosperity religion and concerns for economic development with the ascetic discipline of the forest hermit. I suggest that the wealthy ascetics manage to exploit existing beliefs and projections in a savior saint and his miraculous powers acquired through ascetic practices and meditative discipline, but they are not the traditional monks but personify a new type of saint. These wealthy ascetics are widely known among the Tai-speaking ethnic groups as *khruba* (venerated teacher). *Khruba* monks hold different forms of legitimizing authority and power. The title of *khruba* is an unofficial honorary status that is bestowed on the monk by his followers. But there is also a special honorary appointment ceremony as *khruba*, carried out by the Thai Kuen or Thai Yai (Shan) monks in Kengtung, Mong Yawng, and Tachilek, Shan State, Myanmar (and requiring a lay sponsor), following long recognition of the saintly qualities of a monk. Third, there is the possibility of official ranks and royal titles under the Thai sangha as monastery abbots (*phrakhru*). So, there are different possibilities of recognition and pathways to *khruba* status, with interesting opportunities of self-appointment and appointment by officeholders. Kengtung, Mong Yawng, and Tachilek are the places where Thai Kuen and Thai Yai monks give a special status to the *khruba* position, but it is also clear that the entitlement to *khruba* shifted from seniority to economic success. Most *khruba* of the new generation of *khruba* monks thus emerge from Northern Thailand for the simple reason that wealthy urban Thai patrons from the business and military elite are among the strongest financial sponsors.

Working among the Karens in Northern Thailand and Eastern Myanmar, Hayami also finds a growing class gap between the devotees, with the powerful elites of business tycoons and military generals sponsoring the ceremonies, while the villagers and labor migrants provide voluntary labor (2017). Hayami explains the classical pattern as follows: the master wanders along Buddha's path, following his intuition, "sits down heavily" (*nang nak*), and meditates. The villagers come and greet the monk, paying their respect and their faith (*sattha*). *Baramee* translated as charisma then emerges from the faith (*sattha*) to the meditating monk (*nang nak*). In the classical pattern, the attraction to the saint is based on the millenarian expectations of the villagers and the asceticism of the monk who serves as an example of purity to the laity.

Following Pisith Nasee (2018) and Amporn Jirattikorn (2016), I argue that the traditional concept of millenarian Buddhism and the patterns of exchange as explained by Hayami do not fully capture the changes that occurred in the culture of capitalism-consumerism and the proliferation of a new generation of *khruba* whom—for reasons of convenience—we may call modern or *Neo-khruba*. As Pisith explains, *khruba* operate in a contested space: *khruba* is a political arena, "in which certain groups compete for the construction of the meaning of being *khruba*" (2018, 9). Conservative monks argue that the prosperity-oriented practices of modern *khruba* have deviated from the role model of the "real-good *khruba*" and have removed the *khruba* from the conduct (*vinaya*) and Buddhist doctrine. The modern group of *khruba* have a more flexible way of adapting to the new conditions of capitalism-consumerism and to the expectations of the followers. By designing luxurious temples (and focusing on specific temples), organizing of grand temple events (with a popular TV moderator), inventing new rituals, and creating objects of worship for sale, the modern *khruba* have actively adapted and molded Buddhist practices to respond to the expectations of their new clientele. By combining traditional practices and modern elements of prosperity religion, the modern *khruba* turn to existing cultural repertoires and beliefs, but invent new elements to communicate them better to the new urban middle class, such as the regular retreat, the marketing of the amulets, and the choice of the temple's interior, such as the Buddha images, the demons, and the guardians. The temple becomes a fantasy and modern theme park, where grand things are happening. *Khruba* Ariyachart was presented with a prize from Mae Fa Luang University in Chiang Rai Province, Northern Thailand, for bringing so many tourists from as far as China, Hong Kong, and Taiwan to his temple. Money generally replaces voluntary labor (mostly vanishing in capitalism) and other donations, becoming the dominant exchange medium. The money from the donations is kept on the temple's account and managed by a committee of trusted and mostly influential followers of the monk and is exempted from tax. Khruba Ariyachart receives substantial donations from banks and companies on occasion of important ceremonies (such as the *Kathin* ceremony) which he sometimes reciprocates with investments into public buildings.

Let us look at the new ritual and practice of Khruba Ariyachart as an example for illustration. I visited Khruba Ariyachart with my research assistant for his birthday ceremony and his appointment to high official in the Thai sangha and was delighted to be presented with the biography that has been published on that occasion. Ariyachart was famous for his practice of retreat (*nirothakam*). The retreat is based on a mulberry paper booklet believed to be written by the holy Khruba Sriwichai as a primary source for the practice.

The site for the retreat—created especially for this occasion—was a small makeshift shelter made of bamboo and hay. Khruba Ariyachart sat in the hole in the mediation posture. He was not allowed to stand, eat, urinate, or defecate. Khruba Ariyachart has to hold the retreat on a regular basis to demonstrate his determination for Buddhism and willingness to purify, and his obedience to the ascetic practices associated with the *thudong* forest monk tradition (Phisit 2018, 19).

His amulets are repositories of his power and are bestsellers. Before being packaged, these amulets are submerged in a full alms bowl of herbal oil and blessed. A miniature statue of Mae Nang Kwak, the woman of a thousand scales of gold, representing fertility and eternal wealth, created after Ariyachart's imagination, is also a bestseller, sold at the shop of his luxurious monastery. Ariyachart uses TV, YouTube channels, and printed materials to communicate information on the objects and their efficacy as well as sharing magical-supernatural stories from amulet holders (Pisith 2018, 20–3).

The devotees are happy to contribute and to reinforce their relationship to the saint. It is a win-win situation in which the saint provides the poor with new fields of merit-making, while the rich provide the saint with the means to build new monasteries. Followers ally with the saint for different reasons and motivations. The poor hope to become rich, the middle class is attracted by mouth-to-mouth propaganda or images in the social media, and the wealthy hope to gain in prestige. Following their intuition or a revelation in a dream, the charismatic *khrubas* invest into religious structures—looking into the reconstruction of sacred sites or the renovation of monasteries built by Sriwichai. Some of them also invest into a school, a police station, a hospital, and into better roads, but to a lesser degree. It seems that the asceticism of the monk is so powerful because it provides the precise inverse of his capitalist donors—and is thus a source of capital.

Exploring the rising popularity of relatively young saints, their rise to the apex of charisma, and why followers are so eager to donate lavishly to the saints, I argue that the *ton bun* contribute to their charisma by building strong cults focusing on their personalities as prosperity monks who provide the laity with generous gifts in the form of relics, monasteries, and pagodas, in reciprocity for their donation and support. I offer a theoretical discussion of redistribution, followed by ethnographic vignettes that illustrate the individualized styles of selected monks from the current top tier of *khruba*. I thereby provide insights into the dynamics of the monks' economic and political entanglements, their relationship to an increasingly diverse and transnational community of believers, and into their ethics of redistribution. Gifts to the laity are also significant in the Buryat case (see Jonutytè) but the context of the Mekong region is one of economic growth and generous donations to the popular and charismatic *khruba*. In a sense, the *khruba* offers an example for the imagination of moral leadership in a world perceived as confusing and complex. He stands for the rebuilding of a transnational and missionary "Buddha-land," one that nostalgically recalls the Tai Buddhist kingdoms in which the king and the Buddhist monk used to be brothers.

The Politics of Redistribution among Buddhist Saints

The emergence of diversified devotional communities centered on the current family of famous holy men of Lanna is a new phenomenon connected to processes of nation-building, urban elite patronage, the presence of the holy men in cyberspace, and the expansion of capitalist markets and neoliberalism. In her essay on the Karen (self-proclaimed) saint U Tuzana, Kwanchewan adopts the framework of assemblages from Deleuze and Guattari (1987), in which the components have a certain autonomy from the whole and also possess diverse motivations and expectations. Karen followers of Karen *khruba* (following the discipline of a utopian moral community) include Karen migrant workers and Thai billionaires (Kwanchewan 2017, 149).

The funds circulating in the temple economies of the living saints enable them to build hundreds of monasteries, ordination halls, and pagodas and to renovate and upgrade old places of Buddhist worship and pilgrimage. Doing so, they contribute to the vitality of Theravāda Buddhism in various ways. In Buddhist revivalism, moral regeneration and the construction and repair of "sacred things" are intertwined. Through the repair and construction of monastic structures, the saint is involved in nothing minor than the restoration of Buddhist society from "the age of Ariya Maitreya, based on Buddhist morality and Buddhist instruction through Buddhist sermons" (Cohen 2001, 143). The saints regard the monasteries, pagodas, and Buddha images as gifts to the laity and in particular to needy ethnic highland communities. One of the saints Khruba Boonchum, more than any other monk, is widely regarded as a god-savior and reincarnated Buddha by the Shan and has become a missionary in his own right, contributing religious buildings to the non-Buddhist Lahu and Wa. The new monasteries, embodying the saint's image, are regarded as a form of a highly elevated and civilized Buddhism.

The new monasteries have something of a spectacular consumption of festivities or religious tourism, celebrating the veneration of the new saints who find themselves on the apex of Buddhism, contributing to its greatness (Pisith 2018). The new monastery for Boonchum in Tachilek is fully gold-plated and decorated with the finest arts and gigantic Buddha images. Theravāda Buddhism has become commodified, with the different *khruba* competing for visibility and fame. With some rising entrepreneurs and business tycoons at the top of Boonchum's and Saengla's patronage networks, Theravāda Buddhism in the *khruba* version has strong elements of prosperity religion. The fame of the *khruba* is further increased by the presentation of the ceremonies in print, CDs, Facebook groups, or on Twitter.

Buddhism becomes, in the words of Amporn Jirattikorn, a floating signifier "which makes it possible for a religious figure to be consumed, reconstructed and re-defined" (Amporn 2016). Referring to Appadurai's work on "imagination," Amporn argues that the consumption of the *khruba*'s image "says much about the world we live, a world in which media produce images and imagination in the sacred realm." The *khruba* has set a new dynamic in motion in which different participants participate in very different ways. I think that the Lanna saints are undergoing a transformation, similar to the northeastern forest monks in the past. From modest beginnings, they have become superstars of the Buddhist public sphere (Taylor 1993).

For Japan, Rambelli argues that objects and *stūpa*, as representation of doctrines and ideas, have played an essential role in Buddhist transformations while affecting the nature of Buddhism itself (Rambelli 2007, 259). In the case of Buddhist sacred objects, relations between an object and its users, producers, and the actual processes involved tend to be emphasized, displayed, and sacralized. Rambelli's perspective is very creative and has the additional advantage of overcoming some instrumentalist Marxist assumptions on the modes of production. With Rambelli, we can say that Buddhist buildings in Thailand—*stūpa* (in Thai: *that*), ordination halls (*viharn*), and pagodas (*chedi*)—are devoted to Buddha and, housing the Buddha image, in a way, embody the Buddha himself. Religious labor devoted to the construction of these edifices is embedded in elaborate Buddhist ritual. Thus, objects and *stūpa* have played an essential role in Buddhist transformations but tend to widen the class divide, rather than diminishing it.

The current trend of the personality cult revolving around charismatic monks is modeled after the template of Khruba Sriwichai and the nostalgic longing for and revitalization of his aura and contribution to Theravāda Buddhism in Northern Thailand. Sriwichai also combined outer-worldly qualities of the forest monk and this-worldly concerns for economic development. Widely renowned for his super-miraculous powers, Sriwichai enjoyed huge popular support and was able to mobilize capital and peasant labor for meritorious religious buildings, temples, ordination halls, and pagodas. Bowie explains that Sriwichai was rightly seen as a central figure of resistance to Siamese oppression and domination in Northern Thailand and that the population, stricken by devastating epidemics and the fear of military conscription, projected its hope on the charismatic monk as a leader for mobilizing discontent with the Siamese assault on local cultural traditions and on the Lanna sangha in particular (Bowie 2014). Dissatisfied with an increasingly unpopular state sangha, and thirsty for new spirituality, the urban middle class in Chiang Mai turned toward a new generation of charismatic monks, teachers, and religious leaders.

By exchanging objects (spiritual capital) with merit (spiritual cash) (Rambelli 2007), by providing fields of merit, and by drawing faith, the saint produces religion (Hayami 2017) and positions himself in the religious field. To keep his reputation of a wealthy ascetic, the *khruba* monk has to balance carefully between loyalties to different elites and populations. Since there is constant gossip about corruption and immoral practices, imaging the saint as a pure and authentic ascetic is key to the monk's moral integrity. In a time, where the saint enjoys high popularity, Thai national elites tend to endorse the saints and push to harness his potentially subversive millenarian Buddhism to a conservative national agenda. In this way, the state supports charismatic monks who can be incorporated into existing structures of religious organization and governance while disciplining or marginalizing monks who opt out of dominating power structures.

While the saints operate in the same field of Buddhist merit-making, they also develop different styles. In ethnographic case studies of different saints, the communication with different class segments in public rituals is crucial. In theory, the saint's sermon encompasses everybody into a system of mass-mediatized symbolic kinship, but in practice he may privilege some and leave out others.

How Charisma Works: Marketing the Saints and Emerging Patronage

The saint possesses miraculous powers, capable of learning the Buddhist scriptures from young age, producing food from nowhere, designing beautiful temple architecture, and contributing to the building and renovation of religious structures from early age. Charisma is something like the social capital of the saint. Naturally, his charisma is enhanced by eloquent preaching, humor, empathy, and by the aura of deep meditation practices and mindfulness.

To understand how charisma works in enhancing the visibility of the *khruba*, it is wise to take a step back and reflect about the transformation of religion, the new role Buddhism plays in society, and the creation of value in the spiritual economy. For this, a material approach, focusing how people "make religion happen" and how religion plays "a part in their world-making" (Meyer 2012, 9), is needed. To make sense of our world, we have to understand how culture is mediated. Not only is religion itself mediated by new media technologies, religion also mediates and communicates meanings and experiences. Concentrating on the material manifestations of religion in the world enables us—as Meyer explains (2012, 7)—"to study religion through the vector of practices, concrete acts that involve people, their bodies, things, pictures, texts and other media through which religion becomes tangible present." Religion becomes concrete and is negotiated through people, their practices, and use of objects. With Meyer, I am interested in exploring the workings of religion, globalization, and media in the public sphere. In her more recent work, Meyer shows how religious films and images create sensational effects on the side of the audiences and move their senses. This can be directly applied to the *khruba* where social media create similar emotional effects and allow fans to constantly follow the ritual calendar of the monk, participate in his merit-making, and "like" his activities in Facebook. But the mediation of the saint's charisma culminates in public rituals, especially personalized birthday ceremonies, which are now firmly integrated into the lifecycle of Buddhist public ritual. The monastery of the saint becomes a pilgrimage center, and some of the pilgrims have taken weeks and substantial resources to make it to the ceremony. They all try to be in close proximity to the saint and are more than re-compensated by the saint's presence after many hours of waiting in the sun. When the saint is preaching in the ordination hall, he integrates everybody into his imagined community, and this image of uniformity is further enhanced by the special clothes, amulets, bracelets, and headwear that devotees don for the purpose of the festival. No moment is more symbolic than the moment the *khruba* is lifted up in his palanquin, wearing a crown that symbolizes sacred kingship and leadership, to be carried by the crowds in a formal procession to the ordination hall. There are video CDs and tapes of his preaching and his ritual activities on sale. Important are the religious structures as a material manifestation of the saint's acumen. The Buddha images and amulets become duplicates of the Buddha, especially after they are ritually awakened.

Things indeed circulate in the spiritual economy. This is the case for sacred objects like amulets that are believed to give special powers for protection or the fulfillment of desires and ventures. Images of the saint are ubiquitous, easily accessible on Facebook, Twitter, cellphone, and the new middle class comes from Bangkok and Chiang Mai to take pictures of the saint and keep them as souvenirs. Let us have a closer look at the divergent styles and imaging campaigns of the most popular *khruba*. The vignettes are based on my participant observation in various birthday ceremonies and other occasions.

The Father Figure: Khruba Saengla of Wat Sai Muang, Tachilek

The father figure of all three *khruba* monks introduced is Khruba Saengla based in the monastery of Wat Sai Muang, Tachilek, a border town located on the Thai-Myanmar border in Shan State. He is eighty-eight years old and the gray eminence for a new generation of relatively young saints. Saengla hails from Sipsongpanna in Yunnan, southwest China, but had to escape to Shan State during the Cultural Revolution. He holds priestly appointments in the Shan and Myanmar sangha. He has supporters among Shan business elites and Myanmar generals and used to be close to the Shan drug lord and secession leader Khun Sa and the Chinese Guomintang battalion retreating to Mae Fa Luang, Northern Thailand, after the Second World War. Saengla is reputed to have contributed greatly to the development of Tachilek, building temples, schools, and hospitals. Outside of Tachilek, on a hilltop and with a view of Mae Sai on the Thai side, the wealthy urban patron and chairman of the temple committee of Wat Sai Muang was building a luxurious temple, envisioned as a pilgrimage center and tourist attraction. His birthday ceremony included a governmental delegation from the Thai border town of Mae Sai, devotees from Tachilek and from the wider region, and a delegation of Tai Lue from Sipsongpanna, the supreme patriarch of Kengtung (Chiang Tung), and a big delegation of the Thai sangha from Chiang Mai. More than any other monk, Khruba Saengla is recognized as a spiritual leader and has established extensive patronage networks with the sangha in Thailand, Myanmar, and southwest China as well as with influential and wealthy patrons. His public ceremony included a worship ceremony in traditional Yuan style including Yuan ritual elements on the first day and a more formal Thai-style ceremony on the second day, presided by the supreme patriarch and attended by a Thai delegation of prominent monks. The celebration of Saengla's birthday on the first day included the appointment of the much younger Khruba Jao Theaung of Chiang Mai (Northern Thailand).

Khruba Boonchum Captivates the Masses

More than any other monk, Khruba Boonchum's preaching and charisma captivates the masses. Boonchum's image is omnipresent in all parts of the Mekong region, and he attracts thousands of followers to his sermons in Thailand, Myanmar, and Xishuangbanna. This saint is widely known as an ascetic monk who has mastered meditation practice in perfection. Among all contemporary *khruba* monks, Boonchum is known as the greatest who has achieved nirvana in his lifetime. Boonchum provides communities of different origin and even different faith with the possibility of identification and worship. Among his close acquaintances of the Shan community in Myanmar, he is worshiped as a bodhisattva (living Buddha), and many of his followers among the Palaung, Wa, and Lahu see him as a Buddhist god-king or prophet. While Boonchum does not seem to handle any money by himself, he has accomplished many building projects, accumulating great merit in the minds of his followers by modernizing old reliquaries, reconstructing old ordination halls, and renovating numerous temples and *stūpa*. Boonchum has constantly wandered to Buddhist sites in the Mekong region as well as in the Himalayas, in a way creating a cosmological map of monastic networks and Buddha images. He has been responsible for the mobilization of funds for the reconstruction of the *viharn* at Wat Bandai near his birthplace in Mae Chan, Chiang Rai, from early age when he was still a novice. Thai military and business elites have built the Doi Wiang Kaeo foundation for Boonchum, located near Chiang Saen on a huge plot of land, and have endowed it with a well-filled bank account. The park area is deserted most of the year and gets crowded only for the birthday ceremony of Khruba Boonchum. Boonchum prefers to stay in Shan State where he has built the monastery Wat Dornruang in Muang Pong, Myanmar, one hour by speedboat from Chiang Saen. The birthday ceremony was held there from January 1, culminating with rituals on January 4 and 6 while the birthday ceremony at Doi Wiang Kaeo, on the Thai side, was held on January 6–8. Both ceremonies attracted communities and followers in the hundreds, but the composition of the community of followers diverged in both places. Wat Dornruang was exclusively Khruba Boonchum's homebase and the followers were dressed in traditional costumes, expressing that they are servants of Khruba Boonchum, as the representative of the future Buddha, as well as loyal followers. The appointed servants of Boonchum were entitled to wear a crown, with the name and date of birth written on it by the *khruba*. Different Palaung communities identified Boonchum as bodhisattva, the Buddha. Whole Palaung communities have resettled in Muang Pong, cultivating rice on the *khruba*'s land, while Tai Lue, Lahu, and Wa had traveled weeks to participate in the birthday ritual. Several wealthy businesspeople from Shan State were also among the closest servants of Boonchum and actively supported his projects of renovating relics, Buddhist caves, and monasteries. In Thailand, on the contrary, the Thai military elite and their families dominated the ceremony and approached the saint to greet him personally and to take close-up photographs. Images of the Thai King abounded, and members of the royal family sent messengers to salute and to donate generously. Members of the Thai middle class were also flocking to Wiang Kaeo, taking their photographs but leaving early on the last day.

The Smart Saint: Khuba Ariyachart and His National Faith Community

On the last day of his birthday ceremony in January 2017, Khuba Ariyachart was carried in a procession around his monastery holding 100, 500, and 1,000 baht money notes, blessing the money notes by touching his forehead and spreading the money into the excited crowd. This incident demonstrates the charismatic monk Ariyachart's fascination with money. His numerous followers have bestowed the honorary title of khruba on him. Khruba Ariyachart, called by his followers Khuba Keng (meaning smart, able, intelligent), is only thirty-seven years old, good-looking, and exceptionally intelligent and eloquent, and is the abbot of Wat Sang Kaew Photiyan in Mae Suai, Chiang Rai Province. The huge, colorful monastery displays three gigantic statues of the most famous Buddhist saints of Northern, Central, and Southern Thailand and many more Buddha images, snakes, dragons, and demons and thus places Ariyachart in a genealogical order to the great saints of the past.

I take Ariyachart and his redistribution of money to reflect on the branding and concerted PR-campaign of a monk to become a star in the lifeworld of a Buddhist space that is designed to attract flowers and money and to create a space of religious performance in which the spiritual power of the monk is highlighted. During major festivities, money trees were placed in front of Keng's ordination hall, each of them worth 100,000 baht. For the important Kathin ceremony, *khruba* Keng cashed in the substantial sum of sixteen million baht. He did not hide his success, announcing it even proudly by loudspeaker.

His followers comprising wealthy urban elites, businesspeople, bureaucrats, intellectuals, and members of the royal family see him as authentic: they believe that he used his funds to contribute to the good of society. And indeed, he does: in the colorful book that one of his followers, a media mogul, has produced, Keng outlines meticulously the sums he spent for the building of different monasteries. Khuba Ariyachart has a special ability that sets him apart from hundreds of other monks: he is seen not only as spiritually powerful but also as learned. At the young age of thirty-six, he has been awarded the title of Jao Khun in the official Thai sangha, surpassing nine steps of studying and exams.

The Meditator: Khruba Boonchum and His Transnational Faith Community

While Khruba Boonchum enjoys a large multi-faith following, and while he has supplied communities with so many new monasteries, his building projects have become an integral part of the economy, adding to its growth and prosperity. It is difficult to say if the donations are reciprocated and how they are redistributed by the *khrubas*. Many people benefit from the patronage of the saints simply by being elected among the closest servants, and some have made speedy careers as entrepreneurs in the service of the saint, benefitting from the building projects and being associated with his fame. Khruba Boonchum is presiding over a project of rebuilding the Land of the Buddha in postmodern forms in the big cultural landscape of mainland Southeast Asia.

Beginning at Wat Dornruang in 1986, Khruba Boonchum has built a very sophisticated entourage, with many hundred disciples who are called "servants of the Buddha." The majority are Shan and wear elegant traditional Shan costumes. They come from different walks of life, including rural community leaders as well as wealthy entrepreneurs and businesspeople. They act as bodyguards of the saint during rituals and are always in standby to help in public works and rituals. They are entitled to wear a crown, with their name and date of birth inscribed. Different highland communities can be identified by the colors of their traditional clothes: during the rituals, the status and origin of communities are thus easily identified. There is a sea of blue, red, and green. There are Palaung communities from the mountains in Northern Shan State, affected by the violence and unable to make ends meet, who moved to Muang Pong to cultivate wet rice. While they still do not have enough rice to eat, they are available for public works and understand themselves as loyal subjects of the saint.

Everybody is involved in symbolically and materially sanctifying the charisma and reputation of the saint: the laborers who are employed as servants of the Buddha, the peasants who till the land, the driver, the military general who kneels in front of the saint during a ritual, and the businessman who has the honor to sponsor the ritual and the saints' works. All these people but especially the highland communities who experience much social stress project high hopes for a better existence into the saint. If we put aside constant gossip as a means of control, there is so far no moral critique of *khruba* wealth or its use among their followers in Buddhist Southeast Asia.

Khruba Keng's Entanglements with Centers of Political Power

The spectacular sculpture of Khruba Srivichai sits in the center of admiration of Khruba Ariyachart's monastery. The *khruba* clearly puts himself in line with the founding father and strives to imitate him. The *khruba* just sent out invitations for his birthday ceremony beginning on the eighth of January. In three days of rituals, Khruba Keng dramatically displays his status in Thai society and his wealth. For the ceremony, he has received generous donations, especially from a member of the royal family. Princess Aditayadornkitikhun, known as Princess Dita, daughter of Princess Churabhorn, was a close follower of Khruba Ariyachart whose way of preaching Buddhism in easy language pleased her. As usual for royal functions, the street is closed for the princess and the preaching hall with the big Buddha image reserved to her. Sacred water has been poured and the door is opened to let the light of wisdom enter the ordination hall. The princess has Khruba Keng just for herself. On the eighth, however, the sangha, other invitees, and the present crowd celebrate Khruba Keng's appointment to *jao khun*. For this ceremony, Ariyachart has invited the old and powerful Khruba Saengla from Tachilek, the most famous Khruba Boonchum from Muang Pong (Myanmar), but not Khruba Jao Theuang from Wat Bandensali Si Mueang Kaen, who has become his rival in the race for fame. The Thai sangha from Bangkok, Chiang Mai, Chiang Rai, and Mae Sai, members of parliament from the Thai military, business, and military elites, together with visitors from close by, are all invited to attend the ceremony.

After the procession, a leading publisher and close follower and supporter presents me with a book of Khruba Keng that he prepared for the occasion, including all photographs in bright colors. In it, the hagiography of Khruba Keng is presented. In the appendix, Khruba Keng gives precise figures about the impressive sums that he received for important Buddhist festivals from elite followers and invested into the building of religious temples, monastic structures, and the renovation of reliquaries, but also in schools, hospitals, police stations. The publisher and his family are among the most generous supporters of the *khruba*. Khuba Ariyachart is smart in manipulating the power structure of Northern Thailand to his advantage. Together, this social and cultural capital has reinforced his saintly reputation. For the publisher as well as for the monk, this is a win-win situation. The family of the publishing house is proud to present its friendship with and proximity to the rising star. His fast career in the Thai sangha raises his prestige to new heights and places him well in the patronage networks.

Entanglements of Charisma and Capital: A Discussion

Inspired by the Comaroff's notion of millennial capitalism (Comaroff and Comaroff, 2001), I explore the articulation of the saints' charisma with capital. This is a system both based on the charisma of the saint and contributing to it at the same time. The saint is the savior figure who provides people with social security, liberation from hardships, and the promise of a better life, comfort, and prosperity. For being able to operate as he wants, the saint is directly dependent on urban elites, providing them with his spiritual strength and divine presence. The saints are making use of the labor power of the impoverished highland communities or migrants for construction, the cleaning, and the preparation of the elaborate festivities.

What is taking place here is not a reciprocal gift exchange but the emergence of complex patronage networks, redistribution, and charismatic capitalist investments. In this system, the saint becomes the patron of a whole community, building extensive patronage networks, delivering services, and receiving free labor and other support. It is in the highly personalized birthday ceremonies that wealth is created and publicly displayed.

If tamed and domesticated in the right way, the Comaroffs explain, capitalism can have liberating, even salvific qualities (2001, 2). The charisma of the saint at least promises an exit from misery and hardship, if not in

FIGURE 11.1 Khruba Ariyachart, Chiang Rai, 2017 (Photo: Alexander Horstmann).

this life, then at least in the next. The reputation of a modern *khruba* is based on a sophisticated PR campaign in different social media channels that communicates the monk's ability to bring people closer to Buddhism, to heaven, or to nirvana. I hoped to show that the modern *khruba* claim strong bonds to the cultural heritage of Lanna Buddhism, which they however use for new inventions. The new temples have little similarity with the old ones, just keeping the old structure of *ubosoth*, *viharn*, and *chedi*, but adding important details and new elements, such as pictures of modern Khruba Jao Theaung (Figure 11.1) with old *khruba* Sriwichai as a pair on the interior walls of Jao Theaung's huge Wat (monastery).

By linking charisma to capitalism, I am concerned with a specific system of accumulation that connects to and articulates with the spiritual charisma and spiritual power and efficacy of the saint. Due to the specific credits that the saint develops through ascetic meditation, he provides a big opportunity for merit-making and receiving his spiritual energy in ritual. In line with other scholars on Buddhist and religious materiality, we can think about merit in terms of spiritual cash and charisma as the monk's social capital (Rambelli 2007, 263). The analysis of this interface and articulation of the noncapitalist sphere of Buddhism with millennial capitalism are helpful for a better understanding of the integration of Theravāda Buddhism in the growing occult economy (Jackson 1999).

The *khruba* play an important political role by regulating capitalism, using it for salvation, creation of wealth, and empire-building. The saint's success is showcased in the new material culture and monuments of Thai Buddhism Lanna style in the Mekong region, altering the landscape. Navigating the symbols of Buddhist millenarianism effectively, local and national elites provide legitimacy, wealth, and political influence for the saint.

Marketing reputation through documented performance is decisive for the successful imaging of the saint in a capitalist-consumerist-driven world. It is important to point out that the listed *khruba* do not constitute a homogenous group but diverge in personality traits. Thus, Khruba Ariyachart is interested in eloquent teaching, wisdom of the Buddhist scriptures, and spectacular architecture, Khruba Theaung is interested in luxurious design and association with the past of Northern Thailand (Lanna), while Khruba Boonchum is interested in meditation, educative preaching, monastic design, and Buddhist art and renovation of old Buddhist relics, with a special interest in the Himalayas and Tibetan Buddhism. What unites all *khruba* is their campaign of building a reputation that is based on their performance in the material world and their contribution to the greatness of religion, expressed in the material form of the monastery and displayed and reproduced in the social media. The *khruba* is an ascetic monk who adheres to the strict precepts but resides in a palace. The *khruba*'s individualized styles in presenting their special relationship to Theravāda Buddhism in a way reflect the increasing differentiation of society, appealing to different class spectrums who have little contact with each other, but all venerate the monks for their leadership in the religious realm that enhance Buddhism as well as their own position within the religious field.

NOTES

Introduction

1   In our preparatory workshop, Ariya Sasaki spoke about her own experience as a Jōdo shinshū priestess in Kyoto, and Harrison B. Carter presented a paper on a Shanghai nunnery.

Chapter One

1   I do not offer any more specific information about this temple to preclude identification of institutions and/or individuals. I use real institutional names when discussing publicly available information. All other names are fictitious.

2   Unlike the majority of temples in Japan run by a sole head priest supported by his or her family, the temple where Keiko's mother was buried was administered by multiple priests as well as lay staff.

3   The level of individual commitment to Buddhism and therefore the degree to which people have sustained contact with Buddhist priests and temples translates into ideas about the practicalities of priestly daily lives. In urban areas in particular, the lack of contact between the lay population and Buddhist priests has brought about a situation where priests and material items imbued with Buddhist meanings have turned into icons that exist on the periphery of popular imagination but do not attract sufficient reflection to be filled with stable meaning. It is therefore possible for the image of a Buddhist priest to be either idealized or vilified when the reality does not match the renouncement ideal. People who have more sustained contact with Buddhist priests and temples tend to problematize these extreme potentialities.

4   See Caple (this volume) for her discussion of the influence that the spreading "spirit of calculation" has on the diminishing respect for monks in Tibet.

5   The terms "laity" and "laypeople" in reference to Japan cover a range of statuses depending on the degree of individual commitment to Buddhism. Thus, there are people who may visit a Buddhist temple only on special occasions once or twice a year; those who actively engage in temple life and/ or attend dharma talks (*hōwa*), *zazen*, chanting sessions, or Buddhist bars; and those who choose to undergo a ceremony conferring a Buddhist name and thus mark their commitment to a particular denomination. There are also individuals who have undergone an initiation into Buddhist priesthood but who nevertheless live lives with little to no active engagement in formalized expressions of Buddhist identification. Regardless of this cursory classification,

however, Buddhism in Japan is a more or less prominent element of everyone's life by force of tradition. In this chapter, the terms "laypeople" and "laity" refer to anyone who has not undergone official initiation into priesthood, regardless of their individual commitment to Buddhism.

6   For a detailed account of how the *danka* system was established, see Hur (2007). Given the coercive nature of the original system, one could ask to what extent economic transfers within the *danka*-sangha relationship were ever based on the disinterested ideal that donations are expected to epitomize.

7   See Covell (2005), Nelson (2013), Reader (2011, 2012), Rowe (2011), Thomas (2016) for discussion of the challenges faced by contemporary temple Buddhism.

8   Today over two-thirds of Japanese live in cities with Greater Tokyo region alone being the home to nearly one-third of the population. When people do seek affiliation with a new temple this may not necessarily take the form of a bonding *danka* relationship (e.g., Nelson 2013; Rowe 2011).

9   For example, by 1995, 90 percent of the over 13,000 Sōtō Zen temples were dependent on funerary services while a survey of 349 temples from different sects published in 2003 by the Japan Buddhist Youth Association (*Zen Nihon Bukkyō Seinenkai*) showed that over 75 percent of income was generated from death-related services, including funerals, memorial services, and graves (Covell 2005, 144).

10   Rowe (2011) has shown that recent years have seen a development of new forms of burial and therefore new forms of affiliation with temples that (may) do away with the *danka* model and, more importantly, rely on itemized pricing and membership fees in an open way.

11   The expression "temple Buddhism" introduced by Covell (2005) is now commonly used in English-language studies to refer to "the Buddhism as lived by the members of those sects of Japanese Buddhism that were founded before the 1600s" (2005, 4, 199, note 4). The term differentiates these sects from the so-called new and new new religions in Japan that draw on Buddhist doctrine as well.

12   What is at stake is of course the recognition of not only the genuine religious motivation but also financial considerations as temples are eager to preclude formal recasting of the untaxable income from donations into taxable income from sales of services.

13   Compare this to the "outsourcing" of economic dealings to a layperson by Sri Lankan forest monks (Sirisena, this volume).

14   Since then the company changed its name to Yoriso. All data about the Priest Delivery service is based on the information provided on the company's website (https://corp.yoriso.com), accessed on several occasions between 2015 and 2018 and on their offer available on Amazon.

15   At the time of writing, 10,000 yen was equivalent to 95 US dollars.

16   While the possibility of purchasing religious services on Amazon, an epitome of contemporary consumption-made-easy, may be particularly arresting, it is not an isolated case of a commercial company mediating between religious specialists and lay adherents in Japan. Apart from the multitude of funeral houses, one of the best-known cases is that of Aeon, a retail giant, who launched its own funeral service in 2010. Perhaps a less widely known but possibly the earliest such initiative called *Obōsan dotto komu*, a company set

up by a Tendai priest offering a similar set of services to Minrevi, has been operating since 2004 (now also available on Amazon). What all these cases have in common are fixed prices covering all the expenses, including a sum that goes to the priest, and the fact that at one point or another they have all become a target of critique for turning religious rituals into a commercial product.

17 Placing one's ashes in a chamber means that the relatives are freed from an obligation (increasingly seen as a burden) to maintain the grave, such as by regular cleaning. It also frees the family from organizing and attending the regular commemorative ceremonies. Placement in chambers can include regular rituals by the temple covered by the initial fee or one paid over a pre-agreed period of time, without the need for the family to appear on these occasions (the so-called *eitai kuyō*, eternal memorial service, which however is not exclusive to *nōkotsudō*). See also Rowe (2011) for a more detailed discussion of eternal memorial graves (particularly pp. 56–65).

18 The suffix "-san" (meaning Mrs/Mr) is attached to some personal names as an expression of respect and reflects my own way of addressing people appearing in this chapter.

19 See Covell (2005, 140–56) for a comprehensive overview of the legal status of Buddhist temples and the taxation system.

20 In his monograph about new forms of burial and modes of association with Buddhist temples in Japan, Rowe (2011) shows that priests do successfully combine religious mission and expectations of the laity with profit-making. Their success can be measured equally by the number of new members choosing to affiliate with the temples Rowe introduces to his readers, as well as by the profitability of the ventures. Those two aspects do not contradict but reinforce each other. But even in Rowe's study, alongside the abbot successful in and comfortable with the amalgamation of profit-making and religious mission, we get to know a priest whose attitude is more ambivalent.

21 The popular Japanese term for priests who do not reside in temples and sustain themselves with officiating funerals and commemorative services (*manshon bōzu*) has derogative connotations. A thorough discussion of the reasons for this is beyond the scope of the chapter. Therefore, I avoid using the term in the main text.

22 Similarly, in Shangri-La the perception that monks are active agents of their own commercialization underlies the moral ambiguity about monks' engagement in profit-making activities (Klepeis, this volume).

23 In recent years, some Tokyo temples began opening cafes and offering activities such as concerts, which attract a wider range of people.

24 This individualization refers to the location of vested interests that the priests are seen to pursue rather than acknowledging their idiosyncratic characteristics (more on priests as individuals in the latter sense in Świtek 2018).

25 Motivations of those participating in the chanting event varied widely, from wanting to experience something extraordinary in the case of (sometimes foreign) tourists attracted by the sounds spilling out from the temple hall, to searching for a Buddhist practice one felt comfortable with, and to seeking a challenging ascetic practice to soothe one's need for something spiritual. Regardless of why individual people decided to join the event and therefore regardless of whether Uwamura-san's proposition had any merit, what

mattered in their discussion was the difference in logic between Uwamura-san and the abbot.

26 By officially stating that participants might nap but that they will not sleep (*kamin suru kamoshirenai kedo, suimin wa shinai*) during the event and thus suggesting that lodging rate did not apply, the abbot secured a discounted rental fee for the premises. For the same reason blankets rather than futons were provided, something that also meant lower cleaning costs.

27 What allowed him to stay aloof from financial concerns related to the event was a stable income from real estate built on the temple grounds. While not ostentatious in his spending or lavish in his lifestyle, the abbot had a financial margin that allowed him not to worry too much about having to rely on the temple's coffers. He could however impose a different pricing structure on the Unceasing Chant to bring more income. His decision not to pursue the idea of variously priced packages of activities marks the moment in which he refuses to take control over the financial flows generated by the event.

28 http://mirai-j.net.

29 Among his numerous media appearances, there is an article in the online version of Tōyō Keizai authored by Matsumoto Shōkei, the priest behind the Cram School, where he lays out his view of a *tariki*-guided business. While his emphasis differs from the bar owner's, he also points to something bigger than a singular business(wo)man as the active pillar of a company (Matsumoto 2013).

30 While not an official title, *tōmonsama* is a respectful term commonly used to refer to the head of the True Pure Land denomination by the sect's lay adherents as well as priests.

31 See Whitelaw (2018) for an analysis of the social significance of convenience stores in Japan.

32 *Tōmonsama* recognized, at the same time, that part of the problem lay with the temples themselves: people would opt for such services as Priest Delivery because it was only natural that they "don't choose temples with strange abbots" (*hen na jūshoku ga iru otera o erabanai*). What he was pointing to was not a quirkiness of sorts, but a particular attitude taken by abbots whose temples were in a relatively stable financial situation (*antei shite iru*) and who therefore did not (have to) actively engage in efforts to attract people to Buddhism as such. *Tōmonsama*'s reference was to the widespread perception of Buddhist priests as being concerned primarily with earning exuberant amounts of money from funerals, commemorating rituals, and the sale of graves, just to then spend the gains on excessively luxurious goods and controversial entertainment.

33 Compare this with Parry's analysis of the acceptability (and even laudability) of morally questionable merchant practices as long as they were followed by "zealous giving" (1989, 81).

Chapter Two

1 On the disenfranchisement of monks, see Larson (2016a). The *sangha-rāt* is the Thai spelling of a term perhaps more commonly known from Pāli, *sangha-rāja*. In places where I use terms that have Thai and Pāli equivalents, I will

use forms that are closer to Thai. Exceptions will include terms where the Pāli will be more familiar to readers of English, such as karma (Thai, *kam*) and dharma (Thai, *tham*), or to match terms used in this volume such as the term for meritorious giving, *dāna* (the Thai equivalent is *thān*).

2 Indeed, it may be that my status as a white foreigner was the only reason why he suggested a higher amount, knowing that he might be able to get away with something that he would never try with a Thai person.

3 *Somdet* is one of the highest titles for a monk in Thailand, reserved only for members of the Supreme Sangha Council. There are other monastic titles I will refer to throughout the chapter. *Luang pu* (venerable grandfather) and *Luang pho* (venerable father) are informal but common names for revered monks. *Phra* is the standard designation for a monk.

4 Most Thai monks are citizens, but their monastic status puts them in a distinct place as legal persons. For example, monks cannot vote, but they are also not required to pay taxes on their income. See Larsson (2016a) and Borchert (2016).

5 These are very broad generalizations and only partly explanatory of behavior. The appellations of "royalist" and "pro-democratic," while superficially true, can be misleading, as most in the royalist, yellow-shirt faction also favor democratic processes, and most in the red, pro-democracy camp also display great respect for the monarchy, at least of Rama IX. For a richer consideration of these issues, see the essays in Pavin (2020).

6 The abbot of Wat Dhammakāya has also been embroiled in financial improprieties over the years. On the issue of wealth, Wat Dhammakāya, and the mishandling of wealth, see Scott (2009).

7 It is worth stressing that much of this remains at the level of rumor. Most Thais that I have discussed this with assume that *Somdet* Chuang is part of a "pro-Dhammakāya" faction of the SSC, and they also assume that there are links between the Dhammakāya organization and Thaksin, but when I ask them about the evidence for it, their comments become very general. The claims in the previous paragraph are based on conversations with Bangkok Thais in 2014 and 2017. On the tax problems of Somdet Chuang, see King-oua and Aekarach (2016). On links between Thaksin and Dhammakāya, see Patcharawalai (2016) and Khemthong (2018).

8 Michaels and McDaniel (2020) make a related point. On the effect that "decline of the *sāsanā*" discourse has on the administration of the Thai sangha, see Kusa (2007).

9 She offered each monk 400 baht and paid for their transport from either Wat Dhammakāya or Wat Makkasan. When I witnessed this merit-making, the exchange rate was about 32 baht to the dollar. So, her weekly investment was about US$118–120. Over eighteen years, this has been more than US$100,000.

10 The requisites include an upper robe, a lower robe, an outer robe, an alms bowl, a razor, a needle and thread, a belt, and a water strainer.

11 I have been in a number of *wat* in Bangkok where one can see requests for attendance at a merit-making ceremony to benefit a rural temple. Often the abbot will have a relationship with this *wat*, perhaps because he founded it or because it is in his home region. The urban *wat* becomes the conduit for the spread of *dāna*.

12 An additional complicating variable is that Thai Buddhists practice temporary ordination. There are men who ordain for very short periods (a week or two)

to make merit for a recently deceased relative, most often a parent. It is also increasingly common for *wat* in Thailand to host ordination camps for boys in middle school during school holidays (Chladek 2018). For most of the last century, young men ordained in order to attend a monastic high school. These would normally remain in robes through high school but disrobe before going to college (McDaniel 2011). Increasingly, I have encountered men who ordain in their early thirties, having already worked for at least a decade. The majority of these men presume this to be a brief period as a respite from their work lives and then find they enjoy monastic life. Then there are those who ordain as young men and remain in robes throughout their lives. This affects how we understand the economic conditions of the sangha because men who ordain often maintain economic links to their lay life, such as bank accounts, because they presume they will only be monks for a short time. In my discussion, I am generally referring to long-term monastics.

13 The material from the next paragraphs comes from interviews with monks in Bangkok in 2017 and 2018.

14 None of the monks told me the value of their life insurance premiums, just the amount of the annual premium.

15 A monastic high school, *rongrian phra-pariyatti-tham*, is also a public school and receives public money through the Ministry of Education.

16 This claim is not clear in the ministerial regulations from the National Office of Buddhism which specify to whom *nittayaphat* may go but not their purpose (Khachaphan et al. 2011: 495–9).

17 See Bunnag (1973, 206–9) for a list of income and expenses of *wat* in Ayutthaya. While the amounts are dated, the types of expenditures and sources of income are still relevant. Bunnag elsewhere (1973, 197) notes that monks rarely are aware of the amount of *nittayaphat* a fellow monk receives; this ignorance is consistent with my experience.

18 When the arrests took place, two of the monks who were sought were out of the country. One was in Laos where he was captured and extradited back to Thailand; the other remains in Germany and has as of this writing resisted extradition back to Thailand.

19 Though perhaps not to the monks who were arrested. I have heard from sources I consider reliable that all of the monks were given a warning that the arrests were coming, but I cannot confirm this.

20 There is not a small amount of irony in the fact that the leader of the PDRC, Suthep Thaugsuban, has faced corruption charges throughout his career.

21 This is obviously too small a number to be a fully representative sample. However, I interviewed a diverse group of monks, including members of both the Mahānikāya and Dhammayut fraternities, an abbot, men who had been monks for several decades, young monks in their twenties, and a few non-Thai members of the sangha.

Chapter Three

1 For substantial contributions regarding Tibetan contexts, one can mention the studies (with varying textual vs. ethnographic emphases) by Mumford (1989) and Karmay (1998), for instance, as well as a number of papers on healing rituals in a recent volume (Ramble and Roesler 2015).

2   In Tibetan contexts, one can mention Ortner's (unfortunately not always very
     convincing) interpretive forays into the relations between Sherpa religion
     and society (Ortner 1978; for a critique of the chapter on exorcism, see,
     for example, Sihlé 2013a, 191–3). A study of the lay sponsorship of major
     collective rituals is to be found in Schrempf's unpublished doctoral dissertation
     (Schrempf 2001). For lower Mustang, substantial elements are present in
     Ramble's unpublished dissertation (1984)—here albeit with a primary focus
     again on collective rituals—and Sihlé (2001, 2013a). More recently, Caple has
     studied the ethical dimension of contemporary Amdo monastic economies
     more generally—the focus being here not on the actual ritual activity and the
     patronage interactions but on the ethical questionings (Caple 2019).

3   "Tibet" is understood here as the areas (within the boundaries of what is
     today the People's Republic of China) in which the native populations are
     predominantly of Tibetan culture. The areas under consideration in this
     chapter are primarily in Qinghai Province.

4   Thus, one finds the formulation *gedün (gyi)dé nyi* [dge 'dun gyi sde gnyis],
     literally the "twofold *sangha*" (see, for instance, the online dictionary entry
     http://rywiki.tsadra.org/index.php/pad_ma_'byung_gnas, accessed January 22,
     2016). The *sangha* (Skt. *saṃgha*) designates the Buddhist "community." This is
     understood most commonly, including in Tibet, as the monastic community (or
     one of its local groupings); another quite widespread meaning, in expressions
     such as the "fourfold *sangha*" (found in Tibetan and other languages), refers
     to male and female monastics and laypeople. The formulation quoted above is
     perhaps distinctly Tibetan.

5   In order to make the reading of Tibetan terms easier for non-Tibetanists,
     I provide phonetic transcriptions, according to the relatively standard
     "THL Simplified Phonetic Transcription of Standard Tibetan," proposed by
     Germano and Tournadre (2003). (For terms specific to the language of Amdo
     [A mdo], or northeast Tibet, I adapt the transcription slightly to the Amdo
     pronunciation, with the indication "Amdo: ....".) I add the transliteration
     in square brackets at the first occurrence of a term, following the version of
     the so-called Wylie system (with capitalization of root letters) used mainly in
     European academia (see Cantwell and Mayer 2002).

6   On the term "tantrist," see Stein (1987 [1962], 65), Karmay (1998, 9 and
     passim), Ramble (1984, 30), and Sihlé (2013a, 15–16). Tantric ritual practice,
     based on core texts called tantras, is at the heart of what is known in Western
     languages as tantric Buddhism—a major component of Buddhism in the
     Tibetan context, characterized by the centrality of ritual, ritual power, the
     use of mantras, initiatory practices, deity visualization, and the like. The
     only published book-length study of tantrists in Western languages to date is
     Sihlé (2013a), but the tantrists similarities with the Newar tantric Buddhist
     vajrācārya priests studied by Gellner (1992) and others. Beyond preliminary
     elements presented in Sihlé (2016), I will return in forthcoming work to the
     gender dimension.

7   The actual Amdo pronunciation is "Repkong," and for this key place name I
     prefer to keep that form. However, the most common Tibetan spelling seems
     to be [Reb gong], which is transcribed in the THL simplified phonetic system
     as "Repgong" (as in Caple, this volume).

8   The Bönpo tantrists of Repkong, who number themselves in the hundreds, have devised (at a more recent point, it would seem) a similar designation for themselves. (Repkong is one of only a few Tibetan areas with a sizeable Bönpo population.)

9   For one well-documented case, on the southwestern fringes of the Tibetan world, see Ramble (1984).

10 All names of living persons from Repkong given here are pseudonyms.

11 The term *zhapten* [zhabs brtan, lit. "(ritual for) firm feet"] is commonly used in Central Tibetan (see Cabezón 1996), but in Amdo it refers primarily to rituals carried out for the long life of religious masters.

12 See, for instance, Karmay (1996, 70).

13 A similar, nineteenth-century account can be found in the biography of the great Repkong saint Zhapkar Tsokdruk Rangdröl [Zhabs dkar tshogs drug rang grol] (1781–1851) (Ricard 1994, 526).

14 Most Repkong Bönpos are tantrists, but popular Buddhist discourse generally doesn't go into distinctions between these and the rarer monastic Bönpos.

15 A similar kind of discourse is also found in modernist, secularist state media, which often depicts the Tibetan tantrists (or "wizards") as charlatans and remnants of a past era. See, for instance, a 2002 article entitled "Science Conquers Sorcery in Rural Tibet" in *China Daily*, http://www.chinadaily.com. cn/en/doc/2002-03/20/content_111822.htm (accessed March 30, 2018).

Chapter Four

1   A *khamtsen* is a monastic subunit often compared to a college in the Oxbridge system; *khamsten* are more or less financially independent and have their own representatives in the monastery's management committee. Ganden Sumtsenling has a total of eight *khamtsen*, with sizes varying from as low as ten to a couple of hundreds of monks; assignment to a *khamtsen* is organized by one's home region.

2   For example, see Mette High (2013a, 2013b, 2017) on notions of polluted money and Buddhist self-transformation in the context of the Mongolian gold rush.

3   The Thangka Centre in Shangri-La, opened by the Gyalthang Association of Culture Preservation, provides young men and women from poor, rural households with stipends and a thorough training in the traditional Tibetan Buddhist art of *thangka* painting.

Chapter Five

1   The term *datsan* (plural *datsany*) is used in Buryatia to denote temple complexes and sometimes also single temples. I use the local term instead of calling them monasteries because this would imply residence within the monastic complex and observance of monastic vows, which does not apply in the Buryat case.

2   The Khambo Lama is deemed both the administrative and the spiritual leader of the central Buddhist organization in Buryatia called the Buddhist Traditional Sangha of Russia (hereafter, the Traditional Sangha). Most Buddhist temples in Buryatia are affiliated to this or other umbrella organizations. The Traditional Sangha derives from the centralized Soviet Buddhist administration and arguably from the pre-Revolution Buryat Buddhist hierarchy. For a more detailed discussion of Buryat Buddhist administration historically and now, see Bernstein (2013), Garri (2014a).

3   In Buryatia, all professional Buddhist specialists are referred to as "lamas."

4   There are, however, some debates about the issue as there are in Mongolia, see Abrahms-Kavunenko (2015, 333–6). Non-celibacy is partly a result of Soviet repressions of religion when lamas who were not executed or imprisoned during the Stalinist period were forced to lead a lay life. Yet even in pre-Soviet Buryatia part of the sangha was non-celibate. Today, as several lama informants estimated, there are only around ten celibate lamas in Buryatia. Non-celibacy among lamas in Russia in post-Soviet years has been openly criticized by the fourteenth Dalai Lama, the head of Gelug school, which is dominant in Buryat Buddhism.

5   These are clothes in a shade of red, often traditional Mongol- or Chinese-style. Many lamas in Buryatia wear such clothes instead of actual lama robes because the Dalai Lama criticized non-monastics wearing robes.

6   There is significant tension between Tibetan and some local lamas in Buryatia, related to debates on authenticity, purity, and autocephaly (see, for instance, Bernstein 2013; Garri 2014b).

7   http://gazeta-n1.ru/news/37962/?sphrase_id=117790 (accessed February 8, 2018).

8   In 2018, a lay donor bought the temple and now Budaev is continuing to repay the debt. When I last visited Ulan-Ude in October 2019, the temple was still closed.

9   Parry suggests that the very ideology of a "pure gift" is more likely to arise "in state societies with an advanced division of labor and a significant commercial sector" (1986, 467) and the presence of a world religion with the concept of salvation, as "pure gifts" there are opposed to other types of transactions where self-interest is involved and are interpreted as a way toward liberation.

10   https://vk.com/lamrimdatsan?z=video-107680664_171420662%2F306a487f9 9b78831a0%2Fpl_wall_-107680664 (accessed February 8, 2018).

11   The link between Buddhism, rural lifestyle, and Buryat identity is a tenacious one in Buryatia.

12   Queen (2002, 326) considers the global dimension of such organizations as one of the key aspects of Socially Engaged Buddhism today.

13   This does not seem to be very widespread but I met a number of lamas who held other jobs or had other income from business ventures, lecturing in secular institutions, working in kindergarten, and so on.

14   See Mills (this volume) for a discussion of "collective work" of the sangha and the laity in the context of Tibetan Buddhist ritual in the Western Himalayas.

15   Granted, the distance between the sangha and the laity might already be smaller in Buryat Buddhism than in many other Buddhist contexts due to its non-celibate and non-monastic lifestyles. However, the general distinction between sangha and laity still exists in Buryatia, as I demonstrated above.

Chapter Six

1 Fieldwork for this article was carried out in Ladakh between 1992–5 and 2011–12. The author owes much to the kindness and instruction of the monks of Lingshed Monastery, the hospitality and advice of the Shalatospa and Katar households of Lingshed and Leh, and the insight of Gelong Thubsten Palden of the J&K Cultural Academy, Leh.

2 Ladakhi is a dialect of Tibetan that shares the same written form as Central Tibetan, particularly for religious terms but not its pronunciation (Ladakhis tend to pronounce more of the written consonants than Central Tibetans). The following are the standard Wylie transcriptions for key Ladakhi terms (in alphabetical order) used in the text: *chinlabs* (sbyin rlabs); *chitun chi las* (spyi mthun phyi'i las); *choskyong* (chos skyong); Dorjé Jigjet (rdo rje 'jigs byed); Dorjé Khandro (rdo rje mkha' 'dro); *dos* (dos), Dosmoché (dos mo che), *drugchuma* (drug bcu ma), *dud* (bdud), *gut'uk* (dgu thug), *las* (las), *las gyu das* (las rgyu 'bras), *lhandré* (lha 'dre), *lud* (glud), *nyong-mongs* (nyon mongs), *rigs-ngan* (rigs ngan), Shinjé (gshin rje), *skangsol* (bskang gsol), *skangwa* (bskang ba), *sman* (sman), *smonlam* (smon lam), *sngowa* (sngo ba), *stongpanyid* (stong pa nyid), *tashispa* (bkra shis pa), *torlok* (gtor log), *torma* (gtor ma), *tsampa* (rtsam pa), *yang* (g.yang), *yugu* (g.yu gu), *zan ril* (zan ril), *zhindak* (sbyin bdag).

3 The Nyingma officiants come from Taktok Monastery, Ladakh, and Zanskar's only Nyingma Monastery, which holds a prominent place in the festival. Kagyu monks tend to hail from Hemis, Chemdre, and Lamayuru monasteries, and the Sakya from Mattho. Geluk school representatives come from a rota of Ladakh and Zanskar's many Geluk monasteries, usually from those belonging to Ngari Rinpoché's extensive monastic estates in the region, with a core sangha community from one Geluk monastery supported where necessary by monks from the same family of monasteries. This chapter largely centers on the ritual performance of Leh Dosmoché by a community of Geluk monks from Lingshed, a monastic community in the Trans-Sengge-la, on the border between the kingdoms of Ladakh and Zanskar, and my thanks go to them for their endless patience and kindness.

4 See also Mills (2001, 198–200).

5 "It is not individuals but groups or moral persons who carry on exchanges. The individuals of modern society are endowed with interests as against the world. The persons who enter into the exchanges which centrally concern Mauss do so as incumbents of status positions and do not act on their own behalf" (Parry 1986, 456).

6 Vasabandhu's *Abhidharmakoṣakārikā*, f. 134, b4.

Chapter Seven

1 See, for example, *Bangkok Post*, April 9, 2015 (https://www.bangkokpost.com/learning/advanced/523603/chequebook-buddhism-threat-to-buddhism-in-thailand, accessed March 13, 2018). According to this article, the National Institute of Development Administration estimated that in 2014 the country's

38,000-odd temples received between 100 and 120 billion baht in donations (3.07–3.62 billion US dollars), apart from state funding.

2   The one exception to this rule may be the heads of the local sangha (the monastic community composed of monks and novices), a handful of senior monks living in the central temples of Sipsong Panna, Wat Pajie, and Wat Long Moeng Lue, in Jinghong City, the capital of the prefecture. These are the only monasteries in the region not attached to any single village and where cash donations and other transactions are independently organized and managed by those monks themselves or by lay members of the local Buddhist Associations, with minimal supervision on the part of non-monastic groups.

3   For a brief introduction to (and a simultaneous criticism of) the concept of "moral economy," see Laidlaw (2014, 21–3). Here I will make use of the notion of "morality of exchange" as an explanatory device only in the broadest way. The aim of this chapter is not to discuss or clarify theoretical issues regarding the nature of exchanges taking place within Buddhist temples but to focus on the issue of financial management of a temple and more specifically on the position of monastics within the broader economic context of the village. For a discussion of categories and terminology related to exchanges in Buddhist contexts, see Sihlé (2017).

4   The local Tai term used to refer to the monastic community is *tupha*, literally, "monks [and] novices."

5   For an introduction to the identity politics behind the terms "Tai" and "Dai," see Hsieh (1995). For a historical perspective into the socioeconomic context of the Sipsong Panna, also under the People's Republic, see Liew-Herres et al. (2012). In this text I will use "Tai Lue," "Tai," and "Lue" indistinguishably to refer to the Tai-speaking populations of Sipsong Panna.

6   According to official statistics, Sipsong Panna's GDP was 27.23 billion yuan or renminbi (RMB) in 2013, accounting for approximately 2.3 percent of Yunnan Province's total. The agricultural sector accounted for 29.38 percent of the prefecture's GDP. As for the secondary sector, the second smallest contributor to the economy, mining, tea and sugar processing, and electricity (hydropower) are the major industries in the region. Tourism is the most important pillar of the service sector in Sipsong Panna, in turn the largest contributor to the economy. During 2013, a staggering 14.94 million tourists (mostly nationals) visited the prefecture, up 19.2 percent year on year, while tourism income totaled 17.17 billion yuan, representing a rise of 22.7 percent compared to the previous year. Since, as noted, Sipsong Panna borders Myanmar and Laos, foreign trade is important for the prefecture's economy. The total import and export value in 2013 amounted to US$2.94 billion. Major export goods are agriculture products and hardware, while import commodities include wood and ore. Myanmar is the most important trading partner of the Sipsong Panna Prefecture.

7   See Hansen (1999b). The Han are the largest *minzu* in the People's Republic of China, representing around 90 percent of the total population of the country.

8   For an overview of Buddhism in Sipsong Panna, see Kang (2009).

9   The community of monastics, known in Tai Lue as *tupha*.

10 See Hansen (1999a). On monastic education in Sipsong Panna, see Borchert (2017).

11 See Keyes (1986). On masculinity as a factor in the configuration of majority/minority identities in the People's Republic of China, see Hillman and Henfry (2006).

12 As I have argued elsewhere, these successful individuals become mediators between traditional, embedded agrarian economies and the transactional forms of exchange brought by capitalist development. By doing so, these Buddhist brokers place themselves in an ambiguous position vis-à-vis their communities (Casas 2016).

13 On the *to tham* or local script, and the contemporary politics of language and script use in the region, see Davis (2005).

14 The fact that less boys ordain does not mean that they take advantage of the educational opportunities available. Most of these teenagers will quit schooling as soon as they complete the nine years of compulsory education (six to fifteen years of age). Although somehow outdated, Hansen (1999a) is still a relevant source.

15 This is a pseudonym. As in several other Tai languages, the term "Ban" means "village" or "hamlet" in Tai Lue.

16 This process has affected Moeng Long as well as other lowland areas in Sipsong Panna. Several families in the village kept a small amount of paddy for household consumption. In 2015, villagers received an average of 3,500 yuan per *mu* of land—over US$500. The *mu* is a Chinese unit for an area equivalent to 666 2/3 square meters. In early 2018, the drop in the price of banana had provoked that some of the land had already reverted to other cash crops, such as watermelon or beans.

17 For a historical account of rubber cultivation in Sipsong Panna, see Shapiro (2001). According to a local former monk, some villagers may own up to 700 or 800 rubber trees. On contemporary rubber exploitation in Sipsong Panna, see Sturgeon (2012).

18 In 2012, where I collected most of the data used in this chapter, there were two monks and three novices living in the monastery. I have visited Ban Kao and its temple for different periods every year since 2004. In February 2018, two fully ordained monks and a single novice lived there.

19 Although not all households participate equally in temple activities or in the sustenance of the monastic community, in this chapter I will treat the village community as a homogeneous unit in this regard.

20 All this points to the nature of religious giving as an expression of status. On this issue, see especially Bowie (1998).

21 The *po chang*, usually a former monk, is the mediator between the monastic community and the laity in most temple and household rituals. On the figure of the lay specialist in Theravāda Buddhist societies, see Swearer (1976).

22 The *tan tham* may last for several days. According to the abbot of Wat Ban Kao, in 2017 the ritual was celebrated for seven days and seven nights—that is the amount of time it took for the monks and novices to read all books "purchased" by villagers.

23 On the increasing commitment of aging men and women toward temple activities among other Tai groups, see, for example, Tannenbaum (1995, 139–43) and Eberhardt (2018).

24   This "blessing" is an acknowledgment of the elders as followers of the basic five Buddhist precepts (Tai: *haksa sin ha*).

25   There is no time limit for this office, and *kamakan* members usually quit the position only when they feel they are too old to be concerned with temple affairs anymore. While officiating as *kamakan*, these men receive some money from the community for performing this task. According to the temple abbot, each of the two *kamakan* members received around 100 yuan (a little over 150 US dollars) per year. This annual salary is provided by villagers through a tax organized by the village head (Ch.: *cunzhang*; Tai: *chao ban*).

26   Cockfights are organized within temple grounds during religious events, such as the end of the Buddhist Lent retreat, known in Tai as *ok vassa*. Although money bets are placed during cockfights, and several other types of gambling and lottery may take place in the temple compound, I will not explore here this interesting aspect of Sipsong Panna temple life.

27   The negotiating power of a temple abbot in relation to the lay community may be considerably lesser if he belongs to a different settlement. This is the case with Bulang monks acting as abbots in Tai temples in some areas of Sipsong Panna. The Bulang or Blang (Ch.: *Bulangzu*) are a Mon-Khmer-speaking group inhabiting the hilly western areas of the region. Their children ordain as novices in Buddhist temples and learn to read the Tai script. Apart from their mother tongue, most of them speak Tai language.

28   A cohort of same-age boys ordaining together is a common phenomenon in Sipsong Panna monasticism. Their ordaining together usually marks the beginning of a lifelong friendship for the cohort (Tai: *poko*). For a discussion of the diverse motivations behind novice ordinations in Sri Lanka, see Samuels (2010).

29   While it is certainly problematic to talk of long-term goals or "monastic projects" when referring to boys of between ten and fourteen years of age, the final decision concerning ordination is in the hands of the boy himself. As a layperson, even a father cannot force nor oppose the desire of a boy to ordain.

30   See Sobo and Bell (2001, 22). For a discussion of "sacrifice" in monastic contexts, see Strenski (1983).

31   On the "ideology of merit" in Northeast Thailand, see Tambiah (1968).

32   On the importance of deportment in monastic contexts, see Samuels (2010).

33   The refusal of Tu Ho's father to allow him ordain as a novice may be understood as reflecting this uncertainty, at least in part. Furthermore, it is important to remember that in Sipsong Panna formal public education and temple education are for the most part formally separated. Apart from a handful of exceptions, and although this trend may be changing, a career in the temple means for the most part of men that they have rejected the educational system as an option of social advancement. See also note 14.

34   For instance, for some time the monk would leave the temple at night to help a friend hunt geckos, a prey used by locals in the production of "medicinal liquor" (Tai: *lao ya*). Geckos are very common in Sipsong Panna, but in 2012 the rumor was that high sums of money were paid for the largest specimens (which can weigh up to half a kilogram) by Han Chinese and Tai buyers from the other side of the border with Myanmar.

35   The term *pucha* actually emphasizes the aspect of "offering" to the temple, also in relation to the cash that is given to the abbot at the time these figurines are "purchased." See Sihlé (2017).

36 During my fieldwork in Ban Kao the process of household renovation was at full speed, and most of the old wooden buildings had already been replaced by new constructions or were in the process of being so. See Kang (2009, 36–7).

37 In spite of being part of the sangha already for around twenty years at the time.

38 The archway was built with money collected from villagers separately from temple money.

Chapter Eight

1   Unless specified, all non-English words appearing in this chapter are Pali.

2   Pārājikā 1 at Vin iii 21.

3   For a fascinating study on the transformations Buddhism has gone through in Sri Lanka in the latter half of the twentieth century, see Gombrich and Obeyesekere (1988).

4   SN 17.1 at SN ii 225.

5   AN 6.22 at AN iii 310.

6   MN 10 at MN i 55.

7   Meaning "Sri Kalyani" Group of Monasteries, thus named because its ordination lineage supposedly originates from the historical Kalyani region (contemporary Bago) in Myanmar.

8   There are a few monasteries for nuns managed by the *Saṃsthā* but not in forest settings.

9   Pācittiya 84 at Vin iv 161.

10 SN 3.24 at SN i 98.

11 Nissaggiya Pācittiya 18 at Vin iii 237.

12 Nissaggiya Pācittiya 18 at Vin iii 238.

13 AN 4.50 at AN ii 53.

14 Sattasatikakkhandhaka at Vin ii 294–308.

15 A popular traditional ceremony where Buddhist texts are chanted for "protection."

16 Shortened form of *kappiyakāraka,* a layperson acting as a monastic attendant.

17 Nissaggiya Pācittiya 30 at Vin iii 265.

18 Vin iii 219–23.

19 AN 1.87, 89 at AN i 16.

20 SN 17.1 at SN ii 225.

Chapter Nine

1   This project has received funding from the European Union's Horizon 2020 research and innovation program under the Marie Skłodowska-Curie grant agreement No. 747673. The financial support of the Leverhulme Trust for fieldwork conducted between 2012 and 2015 and the White Rose East Asia Centre (WREAC) for fieldwork that took place in 2008–9 is also gratefully acknowledged. I owe an enormous debt of gratitude to the monks and laypeople who have shared their knowledge, stories, and opinions with me but who must remain anonymous. Where cited in the text, personal names

have been changed. I would also like to thank Christoph Brumann, Saskia Abrahms-Kavunenko, Beata Świtek, and an anonymous reviewer for their comments on a previous version of this chapter. It has also benefited from insightful conversations with Hiroko Kawanami, Nicolas Sihlé, Bénédict Brac de la Perrière, Trine Brox, and Elizabeth Williams-Oerberg.

2   Tibetan terms are transcribed according to the "THL simplified phonetic transcription of standard Tibetan" (Germano and Tournadre 2003). Although not always reflecting the phonetics of oral Amdo Tibetan, it is the only relatively standard transcription system for Tibetan. I have privileged its legibility for a wider readership over the desirability of being faithful to local sounds. At the first occurrence of a term, I add the transliteration in square brackets, following the so-called Wylie system.

3   Schopen (2004, 56–81) examines and discusses the dating of two texts in the Mūlasarvāstivāda-vinaya that deal with rules for perpetual endowments, the principal of which monks are required to lend out at interest so that the capital can be maintained.

4   According to Tibetan geography, Amdo is one of Tibet's two eastern provinces, the other being Kham. Amdo is now incorporated into Qinghai, southwestern Gansu, and northwestern Sichuan provinces.

5   Also spelt Repkong (see Sihlé, this volume).

6   Monasteries in Amdo were disbanded in 1958, their monks and reincarnate lamas arrested, sent to labor camps, or returned to their villages. A few monks were able to return to the sites between 1962 and 1965, but the Cultural Revolution brought another wave of repression and destruction: all monasteries were closed and mostly destroyed, and private religious practice was forbidden. The Chinese Communist Party introduced more liberal religious policies in 1978, but it was not until 1980 that monasteries started to reopen. Even then, their revival was a gradual process (Caple 2019, 28–9).

7   In many cases the funds were established as central monastery funds for the annual round of dharma sessions and rituals, obviating the necessity of maintaining separate funds for specific festivals/rituals as was the case historically—and still is in Ladakh (see Mills, this volume). However, in some cases individuals or communities have established endowments (*chinjok* [spyi 'jog]) for specific events or days, or monasteries have established more than one fund. In all cases, the capital cannot be "moved" (*gül* [sgul]); it must be maintained through investment and the interest/profits used to fund the activity (or annual round of activities) for which the endowment/fund was established. Similarly, one-off donations given for a specific purpose, whether a monastic event or a project such as temple construction, must be used for that purpose. Other financial capital (*sokngül* [gsog dngul]) and wealth (*gyunor* [rgyu nor]) accumulated by the monastery (e.g., income from tourist ticket sales or from leasing land redistributed by the government) can be used as necessary.

8   Monastics in northeast Tibet and the Buryat lama both used the same trope of lay donations being a "burden." This might be a legacy of a shared socialist past and socialist critiques of religion in Tibet and Buryatia—and certainly echoes Chinese party-state discourse—but it should also be noted that criticism of monks as parasitic dates back to as early as the fifth century in China (Ornatowski 1996, 220).

9   Ideologically, there is no fixed price for household rituals, but there is an understanding that monks should be compensated appropriately (Caple 2015,

468). People are aware of the minimum and maximum amount appropriate to the service and monks involved—in 2014, a friend living in the city remarked that "150 to 200 *yuan* per monk is normal these days ... 300 is the highest." Although these remunerations mostly contribute to supporting the livelihood of individual monks, some of this wealth circulates back into the monastic community as gifts proper when monks and reincarnate lamas act as sponsors.

10   For further discussion on the different ways in which a communal tea can be funded and the distinction between gift and remuneration in the Geluk context, see Caple (2015, 463–4).

11   As a point of clarification, it should be noted that gifts proper can include intra-monastic as well as lay-monastic transfers. Although the flow of wealth from laity to monastics as gifts proper is asymmetrical and unidirectional (flowing upward to monks), it operates alongside a generalized ethic of redistribution mostly oriented toward the benefit of the sangha but increasingly these days also toward social welfare (see Caple 2020). Reincarnate lamas, whose estates are independent administrative and economic entities, can be particularly important patrons to the monasteries with which they are affiliated, but other monks can also act as sponsors, redistributing both gifts and remunerations for religious services. On the variety of flows in Buddhist economies, see Jonutytė (this volume).

12   The problem also extends beyond China. A *New York Times* report about fake Buddhist monks operating in New York, for example, cites similar cases in San Francisco, Canada, Australia, Hong Kong, Nepal, and India (Mele 2016).

13   On critiques of the economic-mindedness of Japanese Buddhist priests, see Świtek (this volume).

14   Charles Keyes (1992) points to a similar dynamic in northeast rural Thailand.

15   Stewards at two monasteries (one scholastic center, one village monastery) recounted a similar competitive dynamic among their predecessors responsible for collecting alms, causing anxiety among monks in line to take up this office, as well as increasing the burden on patron communities. This was one reason, they told me, why their monasteries had decided to stop this practice and to rely instead on profits generated from monastic capital if there were no sponsors forthcoming (Caple 2019, 62–3).

16   It is quite common to see prices for butter lamps displayed in the temples, particularly at larger monasteries. Some of my interlocutors were uneasy about this, feeling that the person making the offering should decide how much to give, but it does not seem to generate the same level of discomfort as the idea of fixing prices for ritual services. This is perhaps because butter has a clear economic value—it costs the monastery a certain amount to make these lamps.

17   See Craig (2011) for a discussion of the meanings of "safety," "quality," and "value"—and the question of who gets to define them—in relation to Tibetan medicine, its mass production, and its insertion into global governance regimes.

18   There appears to be historical precedent for laypeople viewing their business transactions with monasteries as a donation (Namri Dagyab, cited in Jansen 2018, 111).

19   Another aim of encouraging monks to use the monastery's businesses and services is to minimize the amount of time they spend in lay society.

20   A similar argument can be made for other modalities of monastic financing. For example, some of my interlocutors have objected to the notion that

fixed, obligatory contributions to monastic projects and events are a form of "tax" or obligation (*trel* [khral]), even if this is how we might define them "objectively" from a Testartian perspective (Sihlé 2015, 358)—and is how some of my other interlocutors view them (Caple 2017, 149–51). This modality of transfer can still be experienced as a volitional act that is expressive, performative, and generative of faith—and thus a gift proper (ibid.).

21   See also Paula Haas's (2016) discussion of trust as it is understood by Barga Mongols: to trust is to have good intentions and thoughts—it is to be trustworthy—and has the capacity to generate trustworthiness in others. It is therefore a moral action through which one acts upon oneself and the world.

Chapter Ten

1   Dharma centers are Buddhist centers that focus on lay education. My initial fieldwork for over a year from 2009 to 2010 was predominantly carried out at a center called Jampa Ling in the west of the city. This center, run under the auspices of Panchen Ötrul Rinpoche, ran regular dharma classes for laypeople on the weekend, was translating Buddhist texts from Tibetan into Mongolian, and conducted bimonthly *pūjās* (prayer ritual involving offerings) and other ritual activities. The center also had many charitable projects, including an NGO that marketed felt products made by single mothers. The people who attended regular classes and worked at the center were from a range of socioeconomic backgrounds, some having endured significant hardships in the previous decades, while others were relatively well-off middle-class people who traveled from the inner city to learn about Buddhism. I also spent time at the Foundation for the Mahayana Tradition's Dharma Centre Shredrup Ling, which had weekly meditation and dharma classes that were well attended by laypeople. This center, like Jampa Ling, is involved in charity. In this initial period of research I spoke to middle-class laypeople that I met in my daily life and attended ceremonies and other activities at local temples. In subsequent visits I carried out fieldwork again in Ulaanbaatar in 2013, for five months each in 2015 and 2016. I interviewed laypeople and monastics from local and transnational Buddhist organizations (although it should be noted that these are not exclusive categories), attended ritual activities, and visited pilgrimage sites.

2   A tourist camp made out of *ger*, round nomadic felt tents.

3   *Ariulakh* means "to purify." This kind of purification is used to speak about the processes of removing obstacles, such as bad karma or spiritual contamination (see Abrahms-Kavunenko 2019).

4   This practice is also carried out to greet the New Year at Tsagaan Sar in the countryside (Madison- Pískatá and Smith 2018).

5   These *bumba* are not the same as the ones used to attract wealth into the household (see Abrahms-Kavunenko 2020).

6   As Buddhist monastics do not tend to take extensive vows in Mongolia and often marry, living just like other householders, the laity and religious

specialists can be difficult to define. In this chapter, I am referring to the laity as those who do not carry out rituals, readings, or provide education for others.

7   Neighborhoods comprised of wooden fences enclosing one or more nomadic felt tents (*ger*). These areas also often contain an outdoor toilet and may also have a concrete building.

8   Lama Munkhbaatar told me that prior to 2007 Gandan paid a ten-percent tax on lay donations. He explained that Gandan still pays the government seven kinds of tax, including a land tax and a tax on the incomes of salaried lamas.

9   Thought to be the oldest surviving monastery in Mongolia, Erdene Zuu is located at the old site of Kharkhorum, the old capital of the Mongolian Empire. The temple was reopened in 1990 and is now an important temple in the sociopolitical landscape of Mongolia, see Jadamba 2018 regarding the enthronement of the Ninth Javzandamba.

10 Idealized Buddhist ruler who governs wisely and protects the dharma.

Chapter Eleven

1   The ethnographic research leading to this chapter was part of the project "Buddhism, Business, and Believers" directed by Trine Brox at the Center for Cross-Cultural and Regional Studies at the University of Copenhagen, Denmark. The research project was supported by the Danish Research Council for the Humanities. For conversations during conferences, summer schools and workshops, I would like to thank Trine Brox, Elizabeth Williams-Oerberg, Jane Caple, Dan Smyer Yü, Christoph Brumann, Roger Casas and Nicolas Sihlé. I also wish to express special thanks to my research assistant and potential future *khruba*, Nattapong Doungkaew, M.A.

BIBLIOGRAPHY

Abrahms-Kavunenko, Saskia. 2012. "Religious 'Revival' after Socialism? Eclecticism and Globalisation amongst Lay Buddhists in Ulaanbaatar." *Inner Asia* 14 (2): 279–97.

Abrahms-Kavunenko, Saskia. 2015a. "The Blossoming of Ignorance: Uncertainty, Power and Syncretism amongst Mongolian Buddhists." *Ethnos* 80 (3): 346–63.

Abrahms-Kavunenko, Saskia. 2015b. "Paying for Prayers: Perspectives on Giving in Postsocialist Ulaanbaatar." *Religion, State and Society* 43 (4): 327–41.

Abrahms-Kavunenko, Saskia. 2019. *Enlightenment and the Gasping City: Mongolian Buddhism at a Time of Environmental Disarray*. Ithaca: Cornell University Press.

Abrahms-Kavunenko, Saskia. 2020. "Tenuous Blessings: The Materiality of Doubt in a Mongolian Buddhist Wealth Calling Ceremony." *Journal of Material Culture* 25 (2): 153–66.

Adams, Vincanne. 1995. *Tigers of the Snow and Other Virtual Sherpas*. Princeton: Princeton University Press.

Ahmed, Sayeed. 2006. "Tibetan Folk Opera: Lhamo in Contemporary Cultural Politics." *Asian Theatre Journal* 23 (1): 149–78.

Ames, Michael M. 1966. "Ritual Prestations and the Structure of the Sinhalese Pantheon." In: *Anthropological Studies in Theravada Buddhism*, edited by Manning Nash et al., pp. 27–50. New Haven: Yale University Southeast Asia Studies.

Amogolonova, Darima D. 2014. "Buddhist Revival in the Context of Desecularization Processes in Russia (on Materials of Buryatia)." *Journal of Siberian Federal University: Humanities & Social Sciences* 7: 1165–76.

Amporn, Jirattikorn. 2016. "Buddhist Holy Man Khruba Bunchum: The Shift in a Millenarian Movement at the Thailand-Myanmar Border." *SOJOURN* 31 (2): 377–412.

Appadurai, Arjun. 1988. "Introduction: Commodities and the Politics of Value." In: *The Social Life of Things: Commodities in Cultural Perspective*, edited by Arjun Appadurai, pp. 3–63. Cambridge: Cambridge University Press.

Arai, Paula and Kane Robinson. 1999. *Women Living Zen: Japanese Sōtō Buddhist Nuns*. New York: Oxford University Press.

Ban de rgyal, sNgags 'chang. 2008. "Rang gi byung ba lhug par brjod pa slob ma'i dad gsos." In: *Rig 'dzin dgyes pa'i mchod sprin*, pp. 211–68. Reb gong sngags mang gi gdan sa Khung dgon mi 'gyur rdo rje gling: mTsho sngon zhing chen nang bstan rig gnas sgyu rtsal zhabs zhu lte gnas.

Bartholomeusz, Tessa J. 1994. *Women under the Bo Tree: Buddhist Nuns in Sri Lanka*. Cambridge: Cambridge University Press.

Bawden, Charles. 1968. *The Modern History of Mongolia*. London: Weidenfeld and Nicolson.

BBC News. 2014. "China: Temples to Get 'Authenticity Certificates.'" *BBC NEWS*, December 14. http://www.bbc.com/news/blogs-news-from-elsewhere-30344202 (accessed March 13, 2018).

Benavides, Gustavo. 2005. "Economy." In: *Critical Terms for the Study of Buddhism*, edited by Donald S. Lopez, pp. 77–102. Chicago: The University of Chicago Press.

Bernstein, Anya. 2013. *Religious Bodies Politic: Rituals of Sovereignty in Buryat Buddhism*. Chicago: The University of Chicago Press.

Bonilla, Lauren. 2016. "Internalizing External Debt." *UCL Emerging Subjects Blog*. http://blogs.ucl.ac.uk/mongolian-economy/2016/02/24/internalizing-external-debt (accessed July 1, 2018).

Borchert, Thomas. 2005. "Of Temples and Tourists: The Effects of the Tourist Political Economy on a Minority Buddhist Community in Southwest China." In: *State, Market and Religions in Chinese Societies*, edited by Fenggang Yang and Joseph B. Tamney, pp. 87–111. Leiden and Boston: Brill.

Borchert, Thomas. 2016. "On Being a Monk and Citizen in Thailand and China." In: *Buddhism and the Political Process*, edited by Hiroko Kawanami, pp. 11–30. Basingstoke: Palgrave Macmillan.

Borchert, Thomas. 2017. *Educating Monks: Minority Buddhism on China's Southwest Border*. Honolulu: University of Hawai'i Press.

Borchert, Thomas. 2020. "Bad Gifts, Community Standards and the Disciplining of Theravāda Monks." *Journal of Contemporary Religion* 35 (1): 53–70.

Borup, Jørn. 2008. *Japanese Rinzai Zen Buddhism: Myōshinji, a Living Religion. Studies in the History of Religions*. Numen Book Series. Leiden: Brill.

Bourdieu, Pierre. 1977. *Outline of a Theory of Practice*. Cambridge: Cambridge University Press.

Bourdieu, Pierre. 1998. *Practical Reason: On the Theory of Action*. Stanford, CA: Stanford University Press.

Bourdieu, Pierre. 2001 [1998]. *Practical Reason: On the Theory of Action*. Cambridge: Polity.

Bourdieu, Pierre and Loic J. D. Wacquant. 1992. *An Invitation to Reflexive Sociology*. Chicago, IL: The University of Chicago Press.

Bowie, Katherine. 1998. "The Alchemy of Charity: Of Class and Buddhism in Northern Thailand." *American Anthropologist* 100 (2): 469–81.

Bowie, Katherine 2014. "The Saint with Indra's Sword: Kruubaa Srivichai and Buddhist Millenarianism in Northern Thailand." *Comparative Studies in Society and History* 56 (3): 681–713.

Brumann, Christoph. 2000. "Materialistic Culture: The Uses of Money in Tokyo Gift Exchanges." In: *Consumption and Material Culture in Contemporary Japan*, edited by John Clammer and Michael Ashkenazi, pp. 224–48. London: Kegan Paul International.

Brumann, Christoph. 2009. "Outside the Glass Case: The Social Life of Urban Heritage in Kyoto." *American Ethnologist* 36 (2): 276–99.

Brumann, Christoph. 2012. *Tradition, Democracy and the Townscape of Kyoto: Claiming a Right to the Past*. London: Routledge.

Buffetrille, Katia. 2008. "Some Remarks on Mediums: The Case of the *lha pa* of the Musical Festival (*glu rol*) of Sog ru (A mdo)." *Mongolo-Tibetica Pragensia* 8: 13–66.

Bunnag, Jane. 1973. *Buddhist Monk, Buddhist Layman: A Study of Urban Monastic Organization in Central Thailand.* London: Cambridge University Press.

Busby, Cecilia. 1997. "Permeable and Partible Persons: A Comparative Analysis of Gender and Body in South India and Melanesia." *Journal of the Royal Anthropological Institute* 3 (2): 261–78.

Buyandelger, Manduhai. 2013. *Tragic Spirits: Shamanism, Memory, and Gender in Contemporary Mongolia.* Chicago: University of Chicago Press.

Cabezón, José I. 1996. "Firm Feet and Long Lives: The Zhabs brtan Literature of Tibetan Buddhism." In: *Tibetan Literature: Studies in Genre,* edited by José I. Cabezón and Roger R. Jackson, pp. 11–38. Ithaca, NY: Snow Lion.

Campergue, Cecille. 2015. "Gifts and the Selfless Work Ethic in Tibetan Buddhist Centres." *Religion Compass* 9 (11): 443–61.

Cantwell, Cathy and Robert Mayer. 2002. *Note on Transliteration: "Not Wylie" Conventions.* http://www.tbrc.org/ngb/csac/NGB/Doc/NoteTransliteration.xml. html (accessed April 18, 2014).

Caple, Jane. 2010. "Monastic Economic Reform at Rong-bo Monastery: Towards an Understanding of Contemporary Tibetan Monastic Revival and Development in A-mdo." *Buddhist Studies Review* 27 (2): 197–219.

Caple, Jane. 2015. "Faith, Generosity, Knowledge and the Buddhist Gift: Moral Discourses on Chinese Patronage in Tibetan Buddhist Monasteries." *Religion Compass* 9 (11): 462–82.

Caple, Jane. 2017. "The Ethics of Collective Sponsorship: Virtuous Action and Obligation in Contemporary Tibet." *Religion and Society* 8: 145–57.

Caple, Jane. 2019. *Morality and Monastic Revival in Post-Mao Tibet.* Honolulu: University of Hawai'i Press.

Caple, Jane. 2020. "The Lama's Shoes: Perspectives on Monastic Wealth and Virtue in Tibet." In: *Buddhism and Business: Merit, Material Wealth, and Morality in the Global Market,* edited by Trine Brox and Elizabeth Williams-Oerberg, pp. 22–39. Honolulu: University of Hawai'i Press.

Carey, Matthew. 2017. *Mistrust: An Ethnographic Theory.* Chicago: HAU Books.

Carrier, James. 2012. "Exchange." In: *The Routledge Encyclopedia of Social and Cultural Anthropology,* edited by Alan Barnard and Alan Spencer, pp. 271–5. London: Routledge.

Carrithers, Michael B. 1983. *The Forest Monks of Sri Lanka: An Anthropological and Historical Study.* Delhi: Oxford University Press.

Carrithers, Michael B. 1984. "The Domestication of the Sangha (correspondence)." *Man (N. S.)* 19 (2): 321–2.

Carstens, Charles. 2020. "Narrating Dāna: Studying Gifts through Narratives of a Theravāda Monk." *Journal of Contemporary Religion* 35 (1): 31–51.

Carter, Harrison. 2017. "A Shanghai Neighborhood Nunnery: Examining Connections between Organizational Structure and Production of Economic Flow to Temples on the City's Fringe." Paper presented at the workshop "Sangha Economies: Temple Organisation and Exchanges in Contemporary Buddhism Workshop," Max Planck Institute for Social Anthropology, Halle, September 22.

Casas, Roger. 2016. "The 'Khanan Dream': Engagements of Former Buddhist Monks with the Market Economy in Sipsong Panna, PR China." *The Asia Pacific Journal of Anthropology* 17 (2): 157–175.

Ch'en, Kenneth 1956. "The Economic Background of the Hui-ch'ang Suppression of Buddhism." *Harvard Journal of Asiatic Studies* 19 (1/2): 67–105.

Chladek, Michael Ross. 2017/2018. "Imagined Laity and the Performance of Monasticism in Northern Thailand." *Buddhism, Law and Society* 3 (1): 45–78.

Chuluundorj, Khashchuluun and Danzanbaljir Enkhjargal. 2014. "Financing Mongolia's Mineral Growth." *Inner Asia* 16 (2): 275–300.

Cohen, Paul T. 2000. "A Buddha Kingdom in the Golden Triangle: Buddhist Revivalism and the Charismatic Monk Khruba Bunchum. " *The Australian Journal of Anthropology* 11 (2): 141–54.

Cohen, Paul T. 2001. "Buddhism 'Unshackled': The Yuan 'Holy Man' Tradition and the Nation-State in the Thai World." *Journal of Southeast Asian Studies* 32 (2): 227–47.

Cohen, Paul T., ed. 2017. *Charismatic Monks of Lanna Buddhism*. Copenhagen: NIAS Press.

Cole, Jennifer. 2003. "Narratives and Moral Projects: Generational Memories of the Malagasy 1947 Rebellion." *Ethnos* 31 (1): 95–126.

Cole, R. Alan. 1998. *Mothers and Sons in Chinese Buddhism*. Stanford: Stanford University Press.

Comaroff, Jean and John L. Comaroff, eds. 2001. *Millennial Capitalism and the Culture of Neoliberalism*. Durham: Duke University Press.

Coningham, Robin A. 1995. "Monks, Caves and Kings: A Reassessment of the Nature of Early Buddhism in Sri Lanka." *World Archaeology* 27 (2): 222–42.

Cook, Joanna. 2008. "Alms, Money and Reciprocity: Buddhist Nuns as Mediators of Generalised Exchange in Thailand." *Anthropology in Action* 15 (3): 8–21.

Cook, Joanna. 2009. "Hagiographic Narrative and Monastic Practice: Buddhist Morality and Mastery amongst Thai Buddhist Nuns." *Journal of the Royal Anthropological Institute* 15 (2): 349–64.

Cook, Joanna. 2010. *Meditation in Modern Thai Buddhism: Renunciation and Change in Thai Monastic Life*. New York: Cambridge University Press.

Covell, Stephen G. 2005. *Japanese Temple Buddhism: Worldliness in a Religion of Renunciation*. Honolulu: University of Hawai'i Press.

Craig, Sienna R. 2011. "'Good' Manufacturing by Whose Standards? Remaking Concepts of Quality, Safety, and Value in the Production of Tibetan Medicines." *Anthropological Quarterly* 84 (2): 331–78.

Cwiertka, Katarzyna and Ewa Machotka, eds. 2018. *Consuming Life in Post-Bubble Japan: A Transdisciplinary Perspective*. Amsterdam: Amsterdam University Press.

Darlington, Susan M. 2003. "Buddhism and Development: The Ecology Monks of Thailand." In: *Action Dharma: New Studies in Engaged Buddhism*, edited by Christopher S. Queen, Charles S. Prebish and Damien Keown, pp. 96–109. London: RoutledgeCurzon.

Darlington, Susan M. 2012. *The Ordination of a Tree: The Thai Buddhist Environmental Movement*. Albany: State University of New York Press.

Davis, Sara L. M. 2005. *Song and Silence: Ethnic Revival on China's Southwest Borders*. New York: Columbia University Press.

Day, Sophie. 1989. "Embodying Spirits: Village Oracles and Possession Ritual in Ladakh, India." Unpublished PhD Thesis, London School of Economics.

DeLanda, Manuel. 2006. *A New Philosophy of Society: Assemblage Theory and Social Complexity*. London: Continuum.

Delaplace, Gregory. 2010. "Chinese Ghosts in Mongolia." *Inner Asia* 12 (1): 127–41.

Deleuze, Gilles and Felix Guattari. 1987. *A Thousand Plateaus: Capitalism and Schizophrenia*. Translated by Brian Massumi. London: The Athlone Press.

Denzin, Norman K. 2014. *Interpretive Autoethnography*. Thousand Oaks, CA: Sage.

Dumont, Louis. 1980 [1966]. *Homo Hierarchicus: The Caste System and Its Implications*. Chicago: University of Chicago Press.

Eberhardt, Nancy. 2018. "Caught in the Middle: The Changing Role of Buddhist Meditation for Older Shan Adults." *Contemporary Buddhism* 18 (2): 292–304.

Even, Marie-Dominique. 2011. "Ups and Downs of the Divine: Religion and Revolution in 20th Century Mongolia." In: *Proceedings of the Third International Symposium "The Book. Romania. Europa,"* edited by A. Berciu, R. Pop and J. Rotaru, pp. 627–44. Bucharest: Bibliothèque Métropolitaine de Bucarest.

Falk, Monica Lindberg. 2007. *Making Fields of Merit: Buddhist Female Ascetics and Gendered Orders in Thailand*. Copenhagen: NIAS Press.

Fedde, Corey. 2016. "Thailand's Buddhist 'Tiger Temple': Prison or Sanctuary." *Christian Science Monitor*, May 31. https://www.csmonitor.com/Environment/ 2016/0531/Thailand-s-Buddhist-Tiger-Temple-Prison-or-sanctuary (accessed December 28, 2018).

Fielder, Caroline. 2019. "Religiously Inspired Charitable Organizations (RICOs) and Their Quest for Religious Authority and Recognition in Contemporary China." *Asian Ethnology* 78 (1): 76–100.

Findly, Ellison. 2003. *Dāna: Giving and Getting in Pāli Buddhism*. Delhi: Motilal Banarsidass.

Fisher, Gareth. 2008. "The Spiritual Land Rush: Merit and Morality in the New Chinese Buddhist Temple Construction." *The Journal of Asian Studies* 67 (1): 143–70.

Florcruz, Michelle. 2013. "China's Fake Monks: Gangs of Men Use Buddhism to Cheat Tourists." *International Business Times*, February 18. http://www.ibtimes. com/chinas-fake-monks-gangs-men-use-buddhism-cheat-tourists-1091796 (accessed March 13, 2018).

Foster, Robert. 2002. "Bargains with Modernity in New Papua New Guinea and Elsewhere." *Anthropological Theory* 2 (2): 233–51.

Garri, Irina R. 2014a. "Buddizm v Buriatii v XX veke: rastsvet, upadok, vozrozhdenie." In: *Buddizm v Istorii i Kul'ture Buriat*, edited by I. Garri. Ulan-Ude: Buriad-Mongol Nom.

Garri, Irina R. 2014b. "Tibetskii Buddizm i Tibetskaya Obshchina v Religioznoi Kul'ture Buryat." *Etnograficheskoe Sibirevedenie* 6: 64–79.

Gekkan Jūshoku. 2016. "Shōgeki no saiban: Nōkotsudō ni naze kotei shisan zei o kakeru no ka to ji'in ga teiso ni itatta wake" (Shocking Trial: The Reason Why a Temple Brought a Lawsuit Questioning the Imposition of Property Tax on an Ossuary). *Gekkan Jūshoku*, January, pp. 32–9. Tokyo: Kōzansha.

Gellner, David N. 1992. *Monk, Householder, and Tantric Priest: Newar Buddhism and Its Hierarchy of Ritual*. Cambridge: Cambridge University Press.

Germano, David and Nicolas Tournadre. 2003. *THL Simplified Phonetic Transcription of Standard Tibetan*. The Tibetan & Himalayan Library. http:// www.thlib.org/reference/transliteration/#!essay=/thl/phonetics/ (accessed April 18, 2014).

Gernet, Jacques. 1995. *Buddhism in Chinese Society: An Economic History from the Fifth to the Tenth Centuries.* New York: Columbia University Press.

Goldstein, Melvyn and Paljor Tsarong. 1985. "Tibetan Buddhist Monasticism: Social, Psychological and Cultural Implications." *The Tibet Journal* 10 (1): 14–31.

Gombrich, Richard. 1971. *Precept and Practice: Traditional Buddhism in the Rural Highlands of Ceylon.* Oxford: Clarendon Press.

Gombrich, Richard. 2006. *Theravada Buddhism: A Social History from Ancient Benares to Modern Colombo* (2nd ed.) Oxford: Routledge.

Gombrich, Richard and Gananath Obeyesekere. 1988. *Buddhism Transformed: Religious Change in Sri Lanka.* Princeton: Princeton University Press.

Goodwin, Janet R. 1994. *Alms and Vagabonds: Buddhist Temples and Popular Patronage in Medieval Japan.* Honolulu: University of Hawai'i Press.

Graeber, David. 1996. "Beads and Money: Notes toward a Theory of Wealth and Power." *American Ethnologist* 23 (1) 4–24.

Gravers, Mikael. 2012. "Monks, Morality and Military: The Struggle for Moral Power in Burma—and Buddhism's Uneasy Relation with Lay Power." *Contemporary Buddhism* 13 (1): 1–33.

Gregory, Chris A. 1997. *Savage Money: The Politics and Anthropology of Commodity Exchange.* Amsterdam: Harwood.

Gutschow, Kim. 2004. *Being a Buddhist Nun: The Struggle for Enlightenment in the Himalayas.* Cambridge, MA: Harvard University Press.

Haas, Paul. 2016. "Trusting the Untrustworthy in Mongolia: A Mongolian Challenge to Western Notions of Trust." In: *Trusting and Its Tribulations: Interdisciplinary Engagements with Intimacy, Sociality and Trust,* edited by Vigdis Broch-Due and Margit Ystanes, pp. 84–104. New York: Berghahn.

Hansen, Mette Halskov. 1999a. *Lessons in Being Chinese: Minority Education and Ethnic Identity in Southwest China.* Seattle: University of Washington Press.

Hansen, Mette Halskov. 1999b. "The Call of Mao or Money? Han Chinese Settlers on China's South-Western Borders." *The China Quarterly* 158: 394–413.

Hart, Keith. 2007. "Money Is Always Personal and Impersonal." *Anthropology Today* 23 (5): 12–16.

Hasegawa, Kiyoshi. 2000. "Cultural Revival and Ethnicity: The Case of the Tai Lue in the Sipsong Panna, Yunnan Province." In: *Dynamics of Ethnic Cultures across National Boundaries in Southwestern China and Mainland Southeast Asia: Relations, Societies, and Languages,* edited by Yukio Hayashi and Guangyuan Yang. Chiang Mai: Lanna Cultural Center, Rajabhat Institute.

Hayami, Yoko. 2017. "Building Stupas and Constructing Charisma in the Myanmar—Thai Border Region." Paper presented at the International Conference of Thai Studies, Chiang Mai, Thailand, July 17.

Heim, Maria. 2004. *Theories of the Gift in South Asia.* New York: Routledge.

Hess, Sabine. 2006. "Strathern's Melanesian 'Dividual' and the Christian 'Individual': A Perspective from Vanua Lava, Vanuatu." *Oceania* 76 (3): 285–96.

High, Mette. 2013a. "Cosmologies of Freedom and Buddhist Self-Transformation in the Mongolian Gold Rush." *Journal of the Royal Anthropological Institute* 19 (4): 753–70.

High, Mette. 2013b. "Polluted Money, Polluted Wealth: Emergent Regimes of Value in the Mongolian Land Rush." *American Ethnologist* 40 (4): 676–88.

High, Mette. 2017. *Fear and Fortune: Spirit Worlds and Emerging Economies in the Mongolian Gold Rush.* Ithaca, NY: Cornell University Press.

High, Mette and Jonathan Schlesinger. 2010. "Rulers and Rascals: The Politics of
  Gold in Mongolian Qing History." *Central Asian Survey* 29 (3): 289–304.
Hillman, Ben. 2003. "Paradise under Construction: Minorities, Myths and
  Modernity in Northwest Yunnan." *Asian Ethnicity* 2 (4): 175–88.
Hillman, Ben and Lee-Anne Henfry. 2006. "Macho Minority: Masculinity and
  Ethnicity on the Edge of Tibet." *Modern China* 32 (2): 251–72.
Højer, Lars. 2009. "Absent Powers: Magic and Loss in Post-Socialist Mongolia."
  Journal of the Royal Anthropological Institute 15: 575–91.
Højer, Lars. 2012. "The Spirit of Business: Pawnshops in Ulaanbaatar." *Social
  Anthropology* 20 (1): 34–49.
Holmberg, David. 1989. *Order in Paradox*. Ithaca: Cornell University Press.
Holt, John C. 1981. *Discipline: The Canonical Buddhism of the Vinayapitaka*.
  Delhi: Motilal Banarsidass.
Hsieh, Shih-Chung. 1995. "On the Dynamics of Dai/Tai Lue Ethnicity. An
  Ethnohistorical Analysis." In: *Cultural Encounters on China's Ethnic Frontiers*,
  edited by Stevan Harrell, pp. 301–28. Seattle: University of Washington Press.
Humphrey, Caroline. 1992. "The Moral Authority of the Past in Post-Socialist
  Mongolia." *Religion, State and Society* 20 (3/4): 375–89.
Humphrey, Caroline. 1997. "Exemplars and Rules: Aspects of the Discourse of
  Moralities in Mongolia." In: *Ethnography of Moralities*, edited by Signe Howell,
  pp. 25–48. London: Routledge.
Humphrey, Caroline and Hürelbaatar Ujeed. 2013. *A Monastery in Time: The
  Making of Mongolian Buddhism*. Chicago: The University of Chicago Press.
Humphrey, Caroline and Ruth Mandel, eds. 2002. *Markets and Moralities:
  Ethnographies of Postsocialism*. Oxford: Berg Publishers.
Hur, Nam-lin. 2000. *Prayer and Play in Late Tokugawa Japan: Asakusa Sensōji and
  Edo Society*. Cambridge: Harvard University Asia Center.
Hur, Nam-lin. 2007. *Death and Social Order in Tokugawa Japan: Buddhism,
  Anti-Christianity, and the Danka System*. Cambridge: Harvard University Asia
  Center.
Jackson, Peter. 1999. "The Enchanting Spirit of Thai Capitalism: The Cult of
  Luang Phor Khoon and the Postmodernization of Thai Buddhism." *Southeast
  Asia Research* 7 (1): 5–60.
Jackson, Sarah. 2015. "Dusty Roads and Disconnections: Perceptions of Dust from
  Unpaved Mining Roads in Mongolia's South Gobi Province." *Geoform* 66:
  94–105.
Jadamba, Lkhagvademchig. 2018. "Double Headed Mongolian Buddhism." *The
  CESS Blog*. http://thecessblog.com/2018/02/28/double-headed-mongolian-
  buddhism-by-lhagvademchig-j-shastri-visiting-researcher-university-of-shiga-
  prefecture (accessed March 1, 2018).
Jadamba, Lkhagvademchig and Bernard Schittich. 2010. "Negotiating Self and
  Other: Transnational Cultural Flows and the Reinvention of Mongolian
  Buddhism." *Internationales Asienforum* 41 (1–2): 83–102.
Jansen, Berthe. 2015. "The Monastery Rules: Buddhist Monastic Organisation in
  Pre-Modern Tibet." Doctoral Thesis, University of Amsterdam.
Jansen, Berthe. 2018. *The Monastery Rules: Buddhist Monastic Organization in
  Pre-Modern Tibet*. Berkeley: University of California Press.
Jaquet, Carine and Matthew J. Walton. 2013. "Buddhism and Relief in Myanmar:
  Reflections on Relief as a Practice of Dāna." In: *Buddhism, International Relief*

Work, and Civil Society, edited by Hiroko Kawanami and Geoffrey Samuel, pp. 51–73. New York: Palgrave Macmillan.

Jinba, Tenzin. 2014. *In the Land of the Eastern Queendom: The Politics of Gender and Ethnicity on the Sino-Tibetan Border*. Seattle and London: University of Washington Press.

Jones, Alison D. 2011. "Contemporary Han Chinese Involvement in Tibetan Buddhism: A Case Study from Nanjing." *Social Compass* 58 (4): 540–53.

Jonutytė, Kristina. 2017. "Donations Inversed: Material Flows from the Sangha to the Laity in Post-Socialist Buryatia." Paper presented at the workshop "Sangha Economies: Temple Organisation and Exchanges in Contemporary Buddhism," Max Planck Institute for Social Anthropology, Halle, September 21.

Jonutytė, Kristina. 2020. "'Bez ovechei otary dostoinoi zhizni ne budet': Ustanovlenie granicy religii v kontekste social'no vovlechennogo buddizma v Buryatii ['There Will Not Be a Dignified Life without a Flock of Sheep': Negotiating Religion in the Context of Socially Engaged Buddhism in Buryatia]." *Gosudarstvo, Religiia, Tserkov' v Rossii i Za Rubezhom* 38 (1): 106–22.

Juo-Hsueh, Bhikkhuni. 2008. "Who Is Afraid of Gold and Silver? A Study of the Rule against Monetary Gifts in the Various Vinayas." In: *Papers of the 12th World Sanskrit Conference. Vol. 8: Buddhist Studies*, edited by Richard Gombrich and Cristina A. Scherrer-Schaub, pp. 35–96. Delhi, India: Motilal Banarsidass.

Kang, Nanshan. 2009. *Theravada Buddhism in Sipsong Panna: Past and Contemporary Trends*. RCSD Working Paper. Chiang Mai: Chiang Mai University.

Kaplonski, Christopher. 2004. *Truth, History and Politics in Mongolia: The Memory of Heroes*. London: RoutledgeCurzon.

Kaplonski, Christopher. 2012. "Resorting to Violence: Technologies of Exception, Contingent States and the Repression of Buddhist Lamas in 1930s Mongolia." *Ethnos* 77 (1): 72–92.

Kaplonski, Christopher. 2014. *The Lama Question: Violence, Sovereignty and Exception in Early Socialist Mongolia*. Honolulu: University of Hawai'i Press.

Karmay, Samten G. 1996. "The Cult of Mountain Deities and Its Political Significance." In: *Reflections of the Mountain: Essays on the History and Social Meaning of the Mountain Cult in Tibet and the Himalayas*, edited by Anne-Marie Blondeau and Ernst Steinkellner, pp. 59–75. Vienna: Verlag der Österreichischen Akademie der Wissenschaften.

Karmay, Samten G. 1998. *The Arrow and the Spindle: Studies in History, Myths, Rituals and Beliefs in Tibet*. Kathmandu: Mandala Book Point.

Kawanami, Hiroko. 1990. "The Religious Standing of Burmese Buddhist Nuns (*thilá-shin*): The Ten Precepts and Religious Respect Words." *Journal of the International Association of Buddhist Studies* 13 (1): 17–40.

Kawanami, Hiroko. 2013. "Implications of International Relief Work and Civil Society for Japanese Buddhists Affiliated with Traditional Denominations." In: *Buddhism, International Relief Work, and Civil Society*, edited by Hiroko Kawanami and Geoffrey Samuel, pp. 101–21. New York: Palgrave Macmillan.

Keane, Webb. 2008. "Market, Materiality and Moral Metalanguage." *Anthropological Theory* 8 (1): 27–42.

Keyes, Charles F. 1981. "Death of Two Buddhist Saints in Thailand." In: *Charisma and Sacred Biography: Journal of the American Academy of Religion*, edited by Michael A. Williams, pp. 149–80. Chico, CA: Scholars Press.

Keyes, Charles F. 1986. "Ambiguous Gender: Male Initiation in a Northern Thai Buddhist Thai Society." In: *Gender and Religion: On the Complexity of Symbols*, edited by Caroline Walker Bynum, Stevan Harrell and Paula Richman, pp. 66–96. Boston: Beacon Press.

Keyes, Charles. 1992. "Buddhist Practical Morality in a Changing Agrarian World: A Case from Northeastern Thailand." In: *Ethics, Wealth and Salvation: A Study in Buddhist Social Ethics*, edited by Russell F. Sizemore and Donald K. Swearer, pp. 170–89. Columbia: University of South Carolina Press.

Khachapan Jaroensri, Subin Bunmāyaem, Wiphāk Loumlek, Suriyā Sutatho and Songkhram Chayanan, eds. 2011. *Khumeu Phra Sangkhāthikān (Sangha Administrative Officer Handbook)*. Bangkok: National Office of Buddhism Publishers.

Khemthong Tonsakulrunruang. 2018. "Purging the Thai Sangha." *New Mandala*, May 28. www.newmandala.org/ncpos-purge-thai-sangha (accessed June 6, 2018).

Kieffer-Pülz, Petra. 2007. "Stretching the Vinaya Rules and Getting Away with It." *Journal of the Pali Text Society* 29: 1–49.

Kieschnick, John. 2003. *The Impact of Buddhism on Chinese Material Culture*. Princeton: Princeton University Press.

King, Matthew. 2016. "Buddhist Economics: Scales of Value in Global Exchange." In: *Oxford Handbooks Online*, edited by Oxford University Press. Oxford: Oxford University Press. https://www.oxfordhandbooks.com/view/10.1093/oxfordhb/9780199935420.001.0001/oxfordhb-9780199935420-e-64.

King, Sallie B. 2009. *Socially Engaged Buddhism*. Honolulu: University of Hawai'i Press.

King-oua Laohang. 2016. "Department of Special Investigations (DSI) Told to Speed Up Probe into Supreme Patriarch Nominee's Car." *Bangkok Post*, January 18. https://www.bangkokpost.com/news/general/830400/dsi-told-to-speed-up-probe-intosupreme-patriarch-nominee-car (accessed June 12, 2018).

King-oua Laohong and Aekarach Sattaburuth. 2016. "DSI to Quiz Somdet Chuang about Car Tax Scheme." *Bangkok Post*, March 10. https://www.bangkokpost.com/news/general/892024/dsi-to-quiz-somdet-chuang-about-cartax-scam (accessed April 4, 2018).

Kohn, Michael. 2006. *Lama of the Gobi: The Life and Times of Danzan Rabjaa Mongolia's Greatest Mystical Poet*. Ulaanbaatar: Maitri Books.

Kolas, Ashild. 2008. *Tourism and Tibetan Culture in Transition: A Place Called Shangrila*. London: Routledge.

Kusa, Julian. 2007. "Crisis Discourse, Response, and Structural Contradictions in Thai Buddhism, 1990–2003." Ph.D. dissertation, Australian National University.

Kwanchewan Buadaeng. 2017. "A Karen Charismatic Monk and Connectivity Across the Thai-Myanmar Borderland." In: *Charismatic Monks of Lanna*, edited by Paul T. Cohen, pp. 149–170. Copenhagen: NIAS Press.

Ladwig, Patrice. 2014. "Millennialism, Charisma and Utopia: Revolutionary Potentialities in Pre-Modern Lao and Thai Theravāda Buddhism." *Politics, Religion and Ideology* 15 (2): 308–29.

Laidlaw, James. 2000. "A Free Gift Makes No Friends." *Journal of the Royal Anthropological Institute* 6 (4): 617–34.

Laidlaw, James. 2014. *The Subject of Virtue: An Anthropology of Ethics and Freedom*. New York: Cambridge University Press.

Langelaar, Reinier. 2017. "Descent and Houses in Reb-gong. Group Formation and Rules of Recruitment among Eastern Tibetan Tsho-ba." In *Mapping Amdo: Dynamics of Change*, edited by Jarmila Ptáčková and Adrian Zenz, pp. 155–83. Prague: Oriental Institute CAS.

Larsson, Tomas. 2016a. "Buddha or the Ballot: The Buddhist Exception to Universal Suffrage in Contemporary Asia." In *Buddhism and the Political Process*, edited by Hiroko Kawanami, pp. 78–96. Basingstoke: Palgrave Macmillan.

Larsson, Tomas. 2016b. "Keeping Monks in Their Place?" *Asian Journal of Law and Society* 3: 17–28.

Liew-Herres, Foon Ming, Volker Grabowsky and Renoo Wichasin, eds. 2012. *Chronicle of Sipsong Panna: History and Society of a Tai Lü Kingdom, Twelfth to Twentieth Century*. Chiang Mai: Mekong Press.

Lindberg Falk, Monica. 2007. *Making Fields of Merit: Buddhist Female Ascetics and Gendered Orders in Thailand*. Copenhagen: NIAS.

Madison-Pískatá, Jessica and Marissa Smith. 2018. "White Tower, Yellow Dog: Kheviin Boov as the Centerpiece of Exchange and Transformation—Tsaagan Sar Index 2018." *UCL Emerging Subjects Blog*. https://blogs.ucl.ac.uk/mongolian-economy/2018/03/01/white-tower-yellow-dog-kheviin-boov-as-the-centerpiece-of-exchange-and-transformation-2018-tsagaan-sar-gift-index (accessed March 2, 2018).

Mahāchulālongkorn-Rājavidyālaya University. 2011. *Gān Pokkhrong Khana Song Thai (Thai Sangha Administration)*. Ayutthaya, Thailand: Mahāwithayālaya Mahāchulālongkorn-Rājawithayālaya.

Main, Jessica L. and Rongado Lai. 2013. "Introduction: Reformulating 'Socially Engaged Buddhism' as an Analytical Category." *The Eastern Buddhist* 44 (2): 1–34.

Majer, Zsuzsa. 2009. "Continuation or Disjuncture with the Past and the Tibetan Buddhist Tradition." *The Silk Road* 7 (Autumn): 52–63.

Makhachkeev, A. 2015. *Khamba Lama: Sed'khel Sanaany Bodomdzhonuud: Mysli Nayedine*. Ulan-Ude: Belig.

Makley, Charlene. 2007. *The Violence of Liberation: Gender and Tibetan Buddhist Revival in Post-Mao China*. Berkeley, Los Angeles and London: University of California Press.

Makley, Charlene. 2014. "The Amoral Other: State-Led Development and Mountain Deity Cults among Tibetans in Amdo Rebgong." In: *Mapping Shangrila: Contested Landscapes in the Sino-Tibetan Borderlands*, edited by Emily T. Yeh and Christopher R. Coggins, pp. 229–54. Seattle: University of Washington Press.

Makley, Charlene. 2018. *The Battle for Fortune: State-Led Development, Personhood and Power among Tibetans in China*. Ithaca: Cornell University Press.

Marriott, McKim. 1976. "Hindu Transactions: Diversity without Dualism." In: *Transaction and Meaning: Directions in the Anthropology of Exchange and*

Symbolic Behavior, edited by Bruce Kapferer, pp. 109–42. Philadelphia: Institute for the Study of Human Issues.

Marriott, McKim. 1990. *India through Hindu Categories*. New Delhi: Sage.

Matichon. 2018. "Duan!! Sān-ānātucarit May Hay Prakān Phra Thera 5 Rūp Khadī Ngenthown Wat Tong Seuk Khum Khao rian cam (Express!! Criminal Court arrests five senior monks—(essentially)—makes disrobe)." *Matichon Online*, May 24. https://www.matichon.co.th/news-monitor/news_969781 (accessed May 28, 2018).

Matsumoto, Shōkei. 2013. "'Bijinesu wa 'tariki hongan' de ikō!" (Let's Go with the "Original Vow of Tariki" in Business!). *Tōyō Keizai Online*, April 18. https://toyokeizai.net/articles/-/13685 (accessed August 17, 2016).

Maurer, Bill. 2006. "The Anthropology of Money." *Annual Review of Anthropology* 35, 15–36.

Mauss, Marcel. 1985. "A Category of the Human Mind: The Notion of Person; the Notion of Self." In: *The Category of the Person: Anthropology, Philosophy, History*, edited by Michael Carrithers, Steven Collins and Steven Lukes, pp. 1–25. Cambridge: Cambridge University Press.

Mauss, Marcel. 1990 [1922]. *The Gift: Forms and Functions of Exchange in Archaic Societies*. London: Routledge.

Mauss, Marcel. 2011 [1954]. *The Gift: Forms and Functions of Exchange in Archaic Societies*. Eastford: Martino Publishing.

Mauss, Marcel. 2016 [1925]. *The Gift: Expanded edition*. Chicago: HAU Books.

McDaniel, Justin Thomas. 2011. *Gathering Leaves and Lifting Words: Histories of Monastic Education in Laos and Northern Thailand*. Seattle: University of Washington Press.

Mele, Christopher. 2016. "The Fake Monks Are Back, Aggressively Begging." *New York Times*, July 1. https://www.nytimes.com/2016/07/02/nyregion/fake-monks-begging-buddhist.html (accessed March 13, 2018).

Meyer, Birgit. 1999. *Translating the Devil: Religion and Modernity among the Ewe in Ghana*. Edinburgh: Edinburgh University Press.

Meyer, Birgit. 2012. "Mediation and the Genesis of Presence: Toward a Material Approach to Religion." Inaugural lecture, October 19, University of Utrecht. https://www.uu.nl/sites/default/files/gw_meyer_birgit_oratie_definitief.pdf (accessed November 1, 2020).

Michaels, Sara E. and Justin Thomas McDaniel. 2020. "Money and Politics in Buddhist Sangha in Modern Thailand." In: *Routledge Handbook of Contemporary Buddhism*, edited by Pavin Chachavalpongpun, pp. 253–67. London: Routledge.

Michaud, Jean. 2010. "Editorial—Zomia and Beyond." *Journal of Global History* 5 (2): 187–214.

Miller, Robert J. 1961. "Buddhist Monastic Economy: The Jisa Mechanism." *Comparative Studies in Society and History* 3 (4): 427–38.

Mills, Martin A. 2000. "Vajra-Brother Vajra-Sister: Renunciation, Individualism and the Household in Tibetan Buddhist Monasticism." *Journal of the Royal Anthropological Institute* 6 (1): 17–34.

Mills, Martin A. 2001. *Identity, Ritual and State in Tibetan Buddhism: The Foundations of Authority in Gelukpa Monasticism*. Richmond: Curzon.

Mills, Martin A. 2009. "La double figure du moine: Monachisme et maisons." In: *Moines et moniales de par le monde: La vie monastique au miroir de la parenté*, edited by Adeline Herrou and Gisèle Krauskopff, pp. 161–71. Paris: Collection Religion et Sciences Humaines, Editions L'Harmattan.

Mills, Martin A. 2015. "The Perils of Exchange: Karma, Kingship and Templecraft in Tibet." *Cahiers d'Extreme Asie* 24: 189–209.

Moerman, Michael. 1966. "Ban Ping's Temple: The Center of a 'Loosely Structured' Society." In: *Anthropological Studies in Theravada Buddhism*, edited by Manning Nash et al., pp. 137–74. New Haven: Yale University Press.

Moses, Larry. 1977. *The Political Role of Mongolian Buddhism*. Indiana: Asia Studies Research Institute, Indiana University.

Mueggler, Eric. 1991. "Money, the Mountain, and State Power in a Naxi Village." *Modern China* 17 (2): 188–226.

Mumford, Stan R. 1989. *Himalayan Dialogue: Tibetan Lamas and Gurung Shamans in Nepal*. Madison: University of Wisconsin Press.

Nada Chansom. 2012. *Kanborihan Kanngeon Khong Wat Nai Prathet Thai*. Bangkok: Samnak Wichai Sathaban Bandit Patthana Borihansat.

Ñanamoli, Bhikkhu and Bhikkhu Bodhi. 1995. *The Middle Length Discourses of the Buddha*. Boston: Wisdom Publications.

National Institute of Population and Social Security Research (NIPSSR). 2017. Population Projections for Japan: 2016–2065 (with long-range Population Projections: 2066–2115). *Population Research Series* 336, July 31. Tokyo.

Nelson, John. 2013. *Experimental Buddhism. Innovation and Activism in Contemporary Japan. Topics in Contemporary Buddhism*. Honolulu: University of Hawai'i Press.

Nichols, Brian J. 2015. "Typologizing Religious Practice at Buddhist Monasteries in Contemporary China." *Foguang University Centre for Buddhist Studies* (佛光大學佛教研究中心) 2015 (4): 411–36.

Niwa, Nobuko. 2019. *Sōryo-rashisa to josei-rashisa no shūkyō shakaigaku: Nichiren josei sōryo no jirei kara* (*Buddhist Priesthood and Feminity: Experiences of Nichiren Buddhist Priestesses in Socio-Religious Perspective*). Kyoto: Kōyō Shobō.

Ohnuma, Raiko. 2005. "Gift." In: *Critical Terms for the Study of Buddhism*, edited by Donald S. Lopez, Jr., pp. 103–23. Chicago: Chicago University Press.

Ornatowski, Gregory K. 1996. "Continuity and Change in the Economic Ethics of Buddhism: Evidence from the History of Buddhism in India, China and Japan." *Journal of Buddhist Ethics* 3: 198–240.

Ortner, Sherry. 1978. *Sherpas through Their Rituals*. Cambridge: Cambridge University Press.

Osburg, John. 2013. *Anxious Wealth: Money and Morality among China's New Rich*. Stanford, CA: Stanford University Press.

Pabongka, Rinpoché. 1991. *Liberation in the Palm of Your Hand*. Boston: Wisdom Press.

Parry, Jonathan. 1986. "The Gift, the Indian Gift and the 'Indian Gift.'" *Man (N.S.)* 21 (3): 453–73.

Parry, Jonathan. 1989. "On the Moral Perils of Exchange." In: *Money and the Morality of Exchange*, edited by Jonathan Parry and Maurice Bloch, pp. 64–93. Cambridge: Cambridge University Press.

Parry, Jonathan and Maurice Bloch. 1989. "Introduction: Money and the Morality of Exchange." In: *Money and the Morality of Exchange*, edited by Jonathan Parry and Maurice Bloch, pp. 1–32. Cambridge: Cambridge University Press.

Pasuk Phongpaichit and Chris Baker, eds. 2016. *Unequal Thailand: Aspects of Income, Wealth and Power.* Singapore: National University of Singapore Press.

Patcharawalai Sanyanusin. 2016. "Damaging the Good Name of Buddhism.," *Bangkok Post*, January 26. https://www.bangkokpost.com/opinion/opinion/839216/damaging-the-goodname-of-buddhism (accessed May 8, 2018).

Patrul, Rinpoché. 1998. *Words of My Perfect Teacher.* London: Altamira Press.

Pattana Kitiarsa. 2012. *Mediums, Monks and Amulets: Thai Popular Buddhism Today.* Chiang Mai: Silkworm Books.

Pavin Chachavalpongun, ed. 2020. *Routledge Handook of Contemporary Thailand.* London: Routledge.

Pisith, Nasee. 2011. *Khruba Ariyachart Aryachitto, Divinity in Dharma.* Bangkok: Thamsataporn.

Pisith, Nasee. 2018. "Constructing the Charisma of *Khruba* (Venerable Monks) in Contemporary Thai Society." *Southeast Asian Studies* 7 (2): 199–236.

Poussin, Louis and La Vallee De. 1976. *The Buddhist Councils.* Calcutta: KP Bagchi.

Prost, Audrey. 2006. "The Problem with 'Rich Refugees': Sponsorship, Capital and the Informal Economy of Tibetan Refugees." *Modern Asian Studies* 40 (1): 233–53.

Pedersen, Morten, and Lars Højer. 2008. "Lost in Transition: Fuzzy Property and Leaky Selves in Ulaanbaatar." *Ethnos* 73 (1): 73–96.

Queen, Christopher S. 2002. "Engaged Buddhism: Agnosticism, Interdependence, Globalization." In: *Westward Dharma: Buddhism beyond Asia*, edited by Charles S. Prebish and Martin Baumann, pp. 324–47. Berkeley: University of California Press.

Quijada, Justine Buck. 2012. "Soviet Science and Post-Soviet Faith: Etigelov's Imperishable Body." *American Ethnologist* 39 (1): 138–54.

Raheja, Gloria Goodwin. 1988. *The Poison in the Gift.* Chicago: University of Chicago Press.

Rambelli, Fabio. 2007. *Buddhist Materiality: A Cultural History of Objects in Japanese Buddhism.* Stanford: Stanford University Press.

Ramble, Charles. 1984. "The Lamas of Lubra: Tibetan Bonpo Householder Priests in Western Nepal." D.Phil. dissertation, University of Oxford.

Ramble, Charles and Ulrike Roesler, eds. 2015. *Tibetan and Himalayan Healing: An Anthology for Anthony Aris.* Kathmandu: Vajra Books.

Reader, Ian. 2011. "Buddhism in Crisis? Institutional Decline in Modern Japan." *Buddhist Studies Review* 28 (2): 233–63.

Reader, Ian. 2012. "Secularisation, R.I.P.? Nonsense! The 'Rush Hour Away from the Gods' and the Decline of Religion in Contemporary Japan." *Journal of Religion in Japan* 1 (1): 7–36.

Reb gong pa mKhar rtse rgyal. 2009. *'Jig rten mchod bstod: mDo smad Reb gong gyi drug pa'i lha zla chen mo'i mchod pa dang 'brel ba'i dmangs srol rig gnas lo rgyus skor gyi zhib 'jug.* Beijing: China Tibetology Publishing House.

Reed-Danahay, Deborah. 2009. "Anthropologists, Education, and Autoethnography." *Reviews in Anthropology* 38 (1): 28–47.

Reynolds, Frank E. 1985. "Theravada Buddhism and Economic Order." *Crossroads: An Interdisciplinary Journal of Southeast Asian Studies* 2 (2): 61–82.

Ricard, Matthieu. 1994. *The Life of Shabkar: The Autobiography of a Tibetan Yogin*. New York: State University of New York Press.

Rowe, Mark. 2011. *Bonds of the Dead: Temples, Burial, and the Transformation of Contemporary Japanese Buddhism*. Chicago: University of Chicago Press.

Rowe, Mark. 2017. "Charting Known Territory: Female Buddhist Priests." *Japanese Journal of Religious Studies* 44 (1): 75–101.

Rozenberg, Guillaume. 2004. "How Giving Sanctifies. The Birthday of Thamanya Hsayadaw in Burma." *The Journal of the Royal Anthropological Institute* 10 (3): 495–515.

Rozenberg, Guillaume. 2010. *Renunciation and Power: The Quest for Sainthood in Contemporary Burma*. New Heaven: Yale University Press.

Ruegg, David S. 1991. "Mchod yon, yon mchod and mchod gnas/yon gnas: On the Historiography and Semantics of a Tibetan Religio-social and Religio-political Concept." In: *Tibetan History and Language: Studies Dedicated to Uray Geza on His Seventieth Birthday*, edited by Ernst Steinkellner, pp. 441–54. Vienna: Arbeitskreis für Tibetische und Buddhistische Studien, Universität Wien.

Sahlins, Marshall. 1972. *Stone Age Economics*. London: Tavistock.

Samuel, Geoffrey. 2013. "Afterword." In: *Buddhism, International Relief Work, and Civil Society*, edited by Hiroko Kawanami and Geoffrey Samuel, pp. 189–207. New York: Palgrave Macmillan.

Samuels, Jeffrey. 2007. "Monastic Patronage and Temple Building in Contemporary Sri Lanka: Caste, Ritual Performance, and Merit." *Modern Asian Studies* 41 (4): 769–95.

Samuels, Jeffrey. 2008. "Is Merit in the Milk Powder? Pursuing Puñña in Contemporary Sri Lanka." *Contemporary Buddhism* 9 (1): 123–47.

Samuels, Jeffrey. 2010. *Attracting the Heart: Social Relations and the Aesthetics of Emotion in Sri Lankan Monastic Culture*. Honolulu: University of Hawai'i Press.

Saxer, Martin. 2013. *Manufacturing Tibetan Medicine: The Creation of an Industry and the Moral Economy of Tibetanness*. Oxford: Berghahn.

Schonthal, Benjamin. 2016. "The Impossibility of a Buddhist State." *Asian Journal of Law and Society* 3 (1): 29–48.

Schopen, Gregory. 1997. *Bones, Stones, and Buddhist Monks: Collected Papers on the Archaeology, Epigraphy, and Texts of Monastic Buddhism in India*. Honolulu: University of Hawai'i Press.

Schopen, Gregory. 2004. *Buddhist Monks and Business Matters: Still More Papers on Monastic Buddhism in India*. Honolulu: University of Hawai'i Press.

Schrempf, Mona. 2001. "Ethnisch-religiöse Revitalisierung und rituelle Praxis einer osttibetischen Glaubensgemeinschaft im heutigen China: Am Beispiel ritueller Maskentanzaufführungen der Bönpo-Klosterföderation von Gamel Gingka in Amdo Sharkhog in der Zeit von 1947 bis 1996." Doctoral dissertation, Freie Universität Berlin.

Scott, James C. 2009. *The Art of Not Being Governed: An Anarchist History of Upland Southeast Asia*. New Haven: Yale University Press.

Scott, Rachelle M. 2009. *Nirvana for Sale? Buddhism, Wealth, and the Dhammakāya Temple in Contemporary Thailand*. Albany: SUNY Press.

Seneviratne, H. L. 1999. *The Work of Kings: The New Buddhism in Sri Lanka*. Chicago: University of Chicago Press.

Shapiro, Judith. 2001. *Mao's War against Nature: Politics and the Environment in Revolutionary China*. Cambridge: Cambridge University Press.

Shi, Yongxin. 2017. "China Clears Shaolin Temple's 'CEO Monk' of Corruption." *Financial Times*, February 17. https://www.ft.com/content/b2fe493c-ecee-11e6-930f-061b01e23655 (accessed March 13, 2018).

Sihlé, Nicolas. 2001. "Les tantristes tibétains (*ngakpa*), religieux dans le monde, religieux du rituel terrible: Étude de Ch'ongkor, communauté villageoise de tantristes du Baragaon (nord du Népal)." Doctoral dissertation, Paris-X-Nanterre University.

Sihlé, Nicolas. 2009. "The *ala* and *ngakpa* Priestly Traditions of Nyemo (Central Tibet): Hybridity and Hierarchy." In: *Buddhism beyond the Monastery: Tantric Practices and Their Performers in Tibet and the Himalayas*, edited by Sarah Jacoby and Antonio Terrone, pp. 145–62. Leiden: Brill.

Sihlé, Nicolas. 2013a. *Rituels bouddhiques de pouvoir et de violence: La figure du tantriste tibétain*. Turnhout: Brepols.

Sihlé, Nicolas. 2013b. "Money, Butter and Religion: Remarks on Participation in the Large-Scale Collective Rituals of the Rep kong (sic, for Repkong) Tantrists." In: *Monastic and Lay Traditions in North-Eastern Tibet*, edited by Yangdon Dhondup, Ulrich Pagel and Geoffrey Samuel, pp. 165–85. Leiden: Brill.

Sihlé, Nicolas. 2015. "Towards a Comparative Anthropology of the Buddhist Gift (and Other Transfers)." *Religion Compass* 9 (11): 352–85.

Sihlé, Nicolas. 2016. "The Emergence of a New Category of Tibetan Buddhist Religious Actors: *Ngakma* (Female Non-Monastic Tantric Practitioners) in Repkong." Paper presented at the international workshop "Buddhism, Humanities and Ethnographic Methods," University of Vermont, April 30.

Sihlé, Nicolas. 2017. "Towards a Comparative Anthropology of the Buddhist Gift (and Other Transfers)." *Religion Compass* 9 (11): 352–85.

Sihlé, Nicolas. 2018. "Why Hair Needs to Be Long: Religious Identity, Embodied Divinity and Power among the Repkong Tantrists (North-East Tibet)." *Ateliers d'anthropologie*, 45. https://journals.openedition.org/ateliers/10562 (accessed October 17, 2020).

Silber, Ilana F. 1981. "Dissent through Holiness: The Case of the Radical Renouncer in Theravada Buddhist Countries." *Numen* 28 (2): 164–93.

Silk, Jonathan A. 2008. *Managing Monks: Administrators and Administrative Roles in Indian Buddhist Monasticism*. New York: Oxford University Press.

Simmel, Georg. 1990 [1907]. *The Philosophy of Money*. Translated by Tom Bottomore and David Frisby. London: Routledge.

Smart, Alan. 1993. "Gifts, Bribes, and Guanxi: A Reconsideration of Bourdieu's Social Capital." *Cultural Anthropology* 8 (3): 388–408.

Smith, Marissa. 2018. "Making a Master: Monumental Construction on a Field of Pastoral Production." Paper presented at the Mongolian and Inner Asian Studies Unit, University of Cambridge, January 23.

Smyer Yü, Dan. 2012. *The Spread of Tibetan Buddhism in China: Charisma, Money, Enlightenment*. London: Routledge.

Sneath, David. 2002. "Mongolia in the 'Age of the Market': Pastoral Land-use and the Development Discourse." In: *Markets and Moralities: Ethnographies of Postsocialism*, edited by Ruth Mandel and Caroline Humphrey, pp. 191–210. Oxford: Berg.

Sneath, David. 2006. "Transacting and Enacting: Corruption, Obligation and the Use of Monies in Mongolia." *Ethnos* 71 (1): 89–112.

Snying bo rgyal, and R. Solomon Rino. 2008. "Deity Men: Reb gong Tibetan Trance Mediums in Transition." *Asian Highlands Perspectives* 3.

Sobo, Elisa J. and Sandra Bell. 2001. "Celibacy in Cross-Cultural Perspective: An Overview." In: *Celibacy, Culture, and Society: The Anthropology of Sexual Abstinence*, edited by Elisa J. Sobo and Sandra Bell, pp. 3–26. Madison: University of Wisconsin Press.

Sophorntavy Vorng. 2017. *A Meeting of Masks: Status, Power and Hierarchy in Bangkok*. Copenhagen: Nordic Institute of Asian Studies.

Spiro, Melford E. 1970. *Buddhism and Society: A Great Tradition and Its Burmese Vicissitudes*. New York: Harper & Row.

Spiro, Melford E. 1982. *Buddhism and Society: A Great Tradition and Its Burmese Vicissitudes* (2nd ed.) Berkeley: University of California Press.

Starling, Jessica. 2019. *Guardians of the Buddha's Home: Domestic Religion in Contemporary Jōdo Shinshū*. Honolulu: University of Hawai'i Press.

Stein, Rolf A. 1987. *La civilisation tibétaine* (2nd ed.) Paris: Le Sycomore/ L'Asiathèque.

Strathern, Marilyn. 1986. *The Gender of the Gift*. Cambridge: Cambridge University Press.

Strathern, Marilyn. 1992. "Parts and Wholes: Refiguring Relationships in a Postplural World." In: *Conceptualising Society*, edited by Adam Kuper, pp. 75–106. London: Routledge.

Strenski, Ivan. 1983. "On Generalized Exchange and the Domestication of the Sangha." *Man (N.S.)* 18 (3): 463–77.

Sturgeon, Janet C. 2012. "The Cultural Politics of Ethnic Identity in Xishuangbanna, China: Tea and Rubber as 'Cash Crops' and 'Commodities.'" *Journal of Current Chinese Affairs* 41 (4): 101–31.

Styllis, George. 2018. "Thai Crackdown Targets Buddhist Monks amid Accusations of Embezzlement and Fraud." *Washington Post*, June 24. https://www.washingtonpost.com/world/asia_pacific/thai-crackdown-targets-buddhist-monks-amid-accusations-of-embezzlement-and-fraud/2018/06/24/67847242-7000-11e8-bd50-b80389a4e569_story.html?utm_term=.50d90e9c89d1 (accessed March 8, 2018).

Suhartino, Muktita. 2018. "In Thailand, 'Obesity in Our Monks Is a Ticking Time Bomb.'" *New York Times*, August 12. https://www.nytimes.com/2018/08/12/world/asia/thailand-monks-obesity.html (accessed December 28, 2018).

Suraphot Taweesak. 2018. "Puttha Sāsanā Thī Thūk Patirūp Doey Fāy Yuom Rak-niyom (Buddhism Reformed by Conservatives)." *Prachatai*, June 2. https://prachatai.com/journal/2018/06/77246 (accessed June 9, 2018).

Svensson, Marina. 2010. "Tourist Itineraries, Spatial Management, and Hidden Temples: The Revival of Religious Sites in a Water Town." In: *Faiths on Display: Religion, Tourism, and the Chinese State*, edited by Tim Oakes and Donald S. Sutton, pp. 211–34. Lanham, MD: Rowman & Littlefield.

Swearer, Donald K. 1976. "The Role of the Layman Extraordinaire in Northern Thai Buddhism." *Journal of the Siam Society* 64 (1): 151–68.

Swearer, Donald K. 1995. *The Buddhist World of Southeast Asia*. Albany, NY: State University of New York Press.

Swearer, Donald. 2004. *Becoming the Buddha: The Ritual of Image Consecration in Thailand*. New Jersey: Princeton University Press.

Świtek, Beata. 2018. "Stuck in Religion: Buddhist Proselytising in Secular Japan." Paper presented at the 15th Biennial Conference of the European Association of Social Anthropologists. Stockholm, August 14.

Tambiah, Stanley J. 1968. "The Ideology of Merit and the Social Correlates of Buddhism in a Thai Village." In: *Dialectic in Practical Religion*, edited by Edmund R. Leach, pp. 41–121. Cambridge: Cambridge University Press.

Tambiah, Stanley J. 1980 [1970]. *Buddhism and the Spirit Cults in North-East Thailand*. Cambridge: Cambridge University Press.

Tambiah, Stanley J. 1984. *The Buddhist Saints of the Forest and the Cult of Amulets*. Cambridge: Cambridge University Press.

Tannenbaum, Nicola. 1995. *Who Can Compete against the World? Power-Protection and Buddhism in Shan Worldview*. Ann Arbor, MI: Association for Asian Studies.

Taylor, Jim. 1993. *Forest Monks and the Nation-State: An Anthropological and Historical Study in Northeastern Thailand*. Singapore: Institute of Southeast Asian Studies.

Tedesco, Frank 2003. "Social Engagement in South Korean Buddhism." In: *Action Dharma: New Studies in Engaged Buddhism*, edited by Christopher Queen, Charles Prebish and Damien Keown, pp. 152–80. London: RoutledgeCurzon.

Teleki, Krisztina. 2009. "Building on Ruins, Memories and Persistence: Revival and Survival of Buddhism in the Mongolian Countryside," *The Silk Road* 7 (Autumn): 64–73.

Testart, Alain. 2001. "Échange marchand, échange non marchand." *Revue française de sociologie* 42 (4): 719–48.

Testart, Alain. 2007. *Critique du don: Études sur la circulation non marchande*. Paris: Éditions Syllepse.

Testart, Alain. 2013. "What Is a Gift?" *HAU: Journal of Ethnographic Theory* 3 (1): 249–61.

Thai Rath. 2017. "Tamruat ca Padkwāt Wat (Police Will Sweep the Temples)." *Thai Rath*, December 6. https://www.thairath.co.th/content/1144435 (accessed June 10, 2018).

Thammapāla. 2018. "Rueang 'Ngen-thong' kap 'Thāng-uok' Khong Khana Song Thai (Wealth and the Exit of the Thai Sangha)." *Prachatai*, June 9. https://prachatai.com/journal/2018/06/77486 (accessed June 10, 2018).

Thanissaro, Bhikkhu. 2013. *The Buddhist Monastic Code I*. (3rd ed.) Valley Center, CA: Metta Forest Monastery.

Thomas, Jolyon Baraka. 2016. "The Buddhist Virtues of Raging Lust and Crass Materialism in Contemporary Japan." *Material Religion* 11 (4): 485–506.

Thrift, Edward. 2014. "'Pure Milk': Dairy Production and the Discourse of Purity in Mongolia." *Asian Ethnicity* 15 (4): 492–513.

Tiyavanich, Kamala. 1997. *Forest Recollections: Wandering Monks in Twentieth-Century Thailand*. Honolulu: University of Hawai'i Press.

Tsong-kha-pa. 2002. *The Great Treatise on the Stages of the Path to Enlightenment*. Volume II, edited by Joshua Cutler and Guy Newland. Translated by Lamrim Chenmo Translation Committee. Canada: Snow Lion.

Tsultemin, Uranchimeg. 2015. "The Power and Authority of Maitreya in Mongolia Examined through Mongolian Art." In: *Buddhism in Mongolian History,*

Culture and Society, edited by Vesna Wallace, pp. 137–59. Oxford: Oxford University Press.

Tucci, Giuseppe. 1971. *The Theory and Practice of the Mandala*. London: Rider Press.

Ukai, Hidenori. 2015. *Ji'in shōmetsu: Ushinawareru "chihō" to "shūkyō" (Temple Extinction: The Loss of "Localities" and "Religion")*. Tokyo: Nikkei BP.

Ukai, Hidenori. 2016. *Musō shakai: Samayou itai, kawaru bukkyō (Society without Funerals: Wandering Corpses, Changing Buddhism)*. Tokyo: Nikkei BP.

UNDP Mongolia. 2016. "About Mongolia." http://www.mn.undp.org/content/mongolia/en/home/countryinfo (accessed May 2, 2018).

Vanchikova, Tsymzhit P. 2014. "The Modern Religious Situation in Mongolia: Tradition and Innovation Processes." In: *Religion and Ethnicity in Mongolian Societies: Historical and Contemporary Perspectives*, edited by Karénina Kollmar-Paulenz, Seline Reinhardt and Tatiana D. Skrynnikova, pp. 167–76. Wiesbaden: Harrassowitz.

von Hinüber, Oskar. 1995. "Buddhist Law according to the Theravada-Vinaya: A Survey of Theory and Practice." *Journal of the International Association of Buddhist Studies* 18 (1): 7–45.

Wallace, Vesna. 2015. "Competing Religious Conversions and Re-Conversions in Contemporary Mongolia." In: *Conversion in Late Antiquity: Christianity, Islam, and Beyond*, edited by Arietta Papaconstantinou, with Neil McLynn and Daniel L. Schwartz, pp. 49–65. London: Routledge.

Walsh, Michael J. 2010. *Sacred Economies: Buddhist Monasticism and Territoriality in Medieval China*. New York: Columbia University Press.

Wang, Raymond Yu, Si Zhenzhong, Cho Nam Ng and Steffanie Scott. 2015. "The Transformation of Trust in China's Alternative Food Networks: Disruption, Reconstruction, and Development." *Ecology and Society* 20 (2): 19.

Wanner, Catherine. 2005. "Money, Morality and New Forms of Exchange in Postsocialist Ukraine." *Ethnos* 70 (4): 515–37.

Wassayos Inghamkham. 2018. "Senior Monks Defrocked after Raid." *Bangkok Post*, May 25. https://www.bangkokpost.com/news/general/1472209/senior-monks-defrocked-after-raids#cxrecs_s (accessed May 29, 2018).

Watts, Jonathan S. and Masazumi Shojun Okano. 2012. "Reconstructing Priestly Identity and Roles and the Development of Socially Engaged Buddhism in Contemporary Japan." In: *Handbook of Contemporary Japanese Religions*, edited by Inken Prohl and John K. Nelson, pp. 345–72. Leiden and Boston: Brill.

Weber, Max. 1958. *The Religion of India: The Sociology of Hinduism and Buddhism*. Glencoe, IL: Free Press.

Weber, Max. 1964. *The Theory of Social and Economic Organization*. New York: The Free Press.

Whitelaw, Gavin H. 2018. "Konbini-Nation: The Rise of the Convenience Store in Post-Industrial Japan." In: *Consuming Life in Post-Bubble Japan: A Transdisciplinary Perspective*, edited by Katarzyna Cwiertka and Ewa Machotka, pp. 69–88. Amsterdam: Amsterdam University Press.

Wijayaratna, Mohan. 1990. *Buddhist Monastic Life: According to the Texts of the Theravada Tradition*. Cambridge: Cambridge University Press.

Wood, Benjamin. 2013. "The Scrupulous Use of Gifts for the Saṅgha: Self-Ennoblement through the Ledger in Tibetan Autobiography." *Revue d'Etudes Tibétaines* 26: 35–55.

World Bank. 2015. *Land Administration and Management in Ulaanbaatar,*
    Mongolia. Washington, DC. https://www.worldbank.org/en/country/mongolia/
    publication/land-administration-and-management-in-ulaanbaatar-mongolia
    (accessed May 1, 2018).
Yan, Yunxiang. 2012. "Food Safety and Social Risk in Contemporary China." *The*
    Journal of Asian Studies 71 (3): 705–29.
Yeh, Emily. 2013. *Taming Tibet: Landscape Transformation and the Gift of*
    Chinese Development. Ithaca and London: Cornell University Press.
Yongxin, Shi. 2017. "China Clears Shaolin Temple's 'CEO Monk' of Corruption."
    Financial Times, February 17. https://www.ft.com/content/b2fe493c-ecee-11e6-
    930f-061b01e23655 (accessed March 13, 2018).
Zigon, Jarrett. 2008. *Morality: An Anthropological Perspective.* Oxford: Berg.

CONTRIBUTORS

Saskia Abrahms-Kavunenko is an anthropologist with interests in religion, postsocialism, economic anthropology, global warming and pollution, materiality, and psychological anthropology. She is currently a Marie Skłodowska-Curie Fellow within the Center for Contemporary Buddhist Studies at the University of Copenhagen. She is the author of *Enlightenment and the Gasping City: Mongolian Buddhism at a Time of Environmental Disarray* (2019).

Thomas Borchert is Professor of Religion at the University of Vermont. He is the author of *Educating Monks: Minority Buddhism on China Southwest Border* (2017) and the editor of *Theravada Buddhism in Colonial Contexts* (2018). His research focuses on monasticism in contemporary Asia, and he has published on Buddhism, politics, and nationalism, Buddhism and law in Thailand, monastic education, and monastics and secularism in Thailand and China.

Christoph Brumann is Head of Research Group at the Max Planck Institute of Social Anthropology, Halle, and Honorary Professor of Anthropology at the University of Halle-Wittenberg. He has published on urban anthropology, cultural heritage, international organizations, the concept of culture, utopian communes, and gift-giving, particularly in Kyoto and Japan. He is the author of *The Best We Share: Nation, Culture and World-Making in the UNESCO World Heritage Arena* (2021).

Jane Caple is an independent scholar with research interests in religion, economy, morality and emotion, and the anthropology of Buddhism. She has held a Marie Curie Fellowship at the Centre for Contemporary Buddhist Studies, University of Copenhagen (2017–19), and a Leverhulme Early Career Fellowship (2012–15) at the University of Manchester, as well as lectureships at the Universities of Manchester and Leeds, where she gained her PhD in 2011. She is the author of *Morality and Monastic Revival in Post-Mao Tibet* (2019).

Roger Casas is a researcher at the Institute for Social Anthropology, Austrian Academy of Sciences, Vienna. He obtained his PhD from the

Australian National University in 2015, with a dissertation on Buddhist monasticism and masculinity among the Tai Lue of Sipsong Panna (Yunnan, China), where he has lived and conducted research for long periods during the last fifteen years. At present, he is one of two principal investigators in the Austro-Japanese project "Religion, Economy and Gender in the Upper Mekong Region."

Alexander Horstmann is Adjunct Associate Professor of Asian Studies at Tallinn University, Estonia, and Research Associate at the Max Planck Institute for the Study of Religious Diversity, Göttingen, Germany. He is also a Visiting Professor in Peace Studies at the University Jaume I, Castellón, Spain, at the UNESCO Chair for Peace Philosophy. His research in the context of "Buddhism, Business and Believers" was generously supported by the Danish Research Council.

Kristina Jonutytė is Lecturer and Research Fellow at the Center for Social Anthropology, Vytautas Magnus University, and Lecturer at the Institute of Asian and Transcultural Studies at Vilnius University. Her research interests are in religion, economic and political anthropology, and postsocialism, with a regional emphasis on Buryatia and Russia.

Hannah Rosa Klepeis is a social anthropologist with interests in morality, economics, and the relationship between state policies and ethnic identity. She recently completed her doctoral studies at the Max Planck Institute for Social Anthropology, Halle, with a thesis concerning transformations in sangha-laity relations and Tibetan personhood under state-led development in the People's Republic of China.

Martin A. Mills is Senior Lecturer in Anthropology at the University of Aberdeen and Director of the Scottish Centre for Himalayan Research. Author of *Identity, Ritual and State in Tibetan Buddhism: The Foundations of Authority in Gelukpa Monasticism* (2003), his research interests lie in the constitutional history and organization of Buddhist monastic organizations and Himalayan states.

Prabhath Sirisena is a social anthropologist affiliated with the University of Colombo. Prior to his academic career he has been a fully ordained Buddhist monk in the Sri Lankan forest monastic tradition. His research interests are in early Buddhism and the anthropology of Buddhism.

Nicolas Sihlé is Director and a researcher at the Centre for Himalayan Studies (CNRS, Aubervilliers). His research focuses on Tibetan tantrists, resulting in the book *Rituels bouddhiques de pouvoir et de violence* (2013), and on the anthropology of Buddhism more generally. He has coedited a special issue on the Buddhist gift (*Religion Compass*, 2015) and a special section on the anthropology of Buddhism (*Religion & Society*, 2017).

Beata Świtek is Assistant Professor of Japanese Studies at the University of Copenhagen. After obtaining her PhD in social anthropology at the University College London, as Research Fellow at the Max Planck Institute for Social Anthropology, Halle, she conducted research among Buddhist temples in Japan. She is the author of *Reluctant Intimacies: Japanese Eldercare in Indonesian Hands* (2016).

INDEX